WARRIORS AND SCHOLARS

A MODERN WAR READER

Edited by

Peter B. Lane
Ronald E. Marcello

Foreword by

Alfred F. Hurley

University of North Texas Press
Denton, Texas

Printed in the United States of America.

10 9 8 7 6 5 4 3 2 1

Permissions:
University of North Texas Press
P.O. Box 311336
Denton, TX 76203-1336

The paper used in this book meets the minimum requirements of the American National Standard for Permanence of Paper for Printed Library Materials, z39.48.1984. Binding materials have been chosen for durability.

Library of Congress Cataloging-in-Publication Data

Warriors and scholars : a modern war reader / edited by Peter B. Lane, Ronald E. Marcello ; foreword by Alfred F. Hurley.
p. cm.
Includes bibliographical references and index.
ISBN-10 1-57441-197-7 (cloth : alk. paper)
ISBN-13 978-1-57441-197-3 (cloth : alk. paper)
1. Military art and science--United States--History--20th century. 2. Military art and science--United States--History--21st century. 3. United States--History, Military--20th century. 4. United States--History, Military--21st century. I. Lane, Peter B., 1939- II. Marcello, Ronald E.
U43.U4W37 2005
355'.00973--dc22

2005005321

Design by Angela Schmitt

This book was made possible by the generous funding of the Amon Carter Foundation.

CONTENTS

FOREWORD

This volume marks another step toward realizing the goal of the Department of History at the University of North Texas (UNT) to make military history one of its areas of excellence. As a result of vigorous recruiting, military historians in the department now number six. Wide-ranging course offerings attract large numbers of eager students majoring in history and other disciplines. The faculty's publications have begun to attract national notice, as has their sustained support of the World War II Oral History Project. That initiative has created one of the major collections of its kind in the United States. Finally, this book is a fresh reminder of the department's good fortune to work with the UNT Press, which emphasizes military history and is committed to maximizing publishing opportunities for writers in the field throughout the nation.

Readers will find herein a cross-section of papers from eight of twenty-two Annual Military History Seminars, dating back to 1983 and led by the undersigned. Since its inception, the series has concentrated on World War II and subsequent events, but in due course will cover earlier subjects. The seminar series responds to the interest in military history among a significant number of business and professional people in Texas, many having served in the military and nearly all being avid readers of the subject. Each seminar, a Saturday morning and an early afternoon experience, features a leading scholar, usually a military historian, and when time permits, a military veteran of the event, or events, under discussion. Each seminar almost always has promoted stimulating interaction during discussion periods following the presentations, which challenge the speakers and many members of the well-informed audience.

In the words of Dr. Donald Pickens, a member of the History Department: "This collection is valuable because it combines history as analysis—scholarly presentations—and history as narrative—the speeches of the military participants. Both are contributions to a full and balanced understanding of what happened: to understanding history, to weighing evidence, and to achieving some measured judgment."

In conclusion, the indispensable support for this publication and for the continuing seminar series must be acknowledged. Heartfelt thanks go to the Amon Carter Foundation of Fort Worth, Texas, for the grant that funded this volume. The keen interest of Carter Foundation board member Dr. Bobby Brown and the guidance of John Robinson, its Executive Director, helped mightily. As to the seminar series, the University of North Texas and a series of private donors have funded it. Those donors include Charles and Peggy Ladenberger and a long list of other generous fans of military history, usually regular attendees at every seminar. Several of those enthusiasts, such as Bob and Bette Sherman, Ross and Fran Vick, and Jerry Farrington, are contributing significantly to other, essential dimensions of the ongoing effort to build a military history program. Also of critical importance in developing and maintaining this series has been the unfailing counsel of my departmental colleagues, including the co-editors of this collection, Drs. Ronald Marcello and Peter Lane, as well as the advice of fellow military historians, including Dr. Calvin Christman of Cedar Valley Community College and Dr. Richard Kohn of the University of North Carolina at Chapel Hill, and fellow military veterans, Lieutenant General Charles Hamm, USAF (ret.) and Major General Alexander ("Bud") Bolling, USA (ret.). The smooth execution of the twenty-two seminars to date must be credited to Mrs. Kristen Staples, her successor, Ms Susie Autry, and the many other able staff members who make UNT such a special place.

Alfred F. Hurley
Professor of History
Chancellor/President Emeritus
Founding Director, Military History Seminar Series

Section I

WORLD WAR II—EUROPE

The first two sections of this work touch upon the war both in Europe and in the Pacific. For the European Theater, two papers address the war from very different perspectives: on the ground and in the air. The first analyzes the epic struggle that began with Operation Barbarossa, the Nazi attack on the Soviet Union, in June 1941. The second paper is the personal story of a surviving American airman from the "Bloody 100th" Bomb Group stationed in England, one of the initial units engaged in the aerial campaign against targets in Germany and Nazi-occupied countries. These two papers are very different yet are linked by the common word: sacrifice.

Any reader of military history is, indeed, fortunate to have a paper by the distinguished historian Col. David M. Glantz, who reviews the massive conflict in the East between Germany and its allies versus the Soviet Union that only ended with the Nazi surrender on May 8, 1945. His goal is to educate the reader as to the immensity of the struggle and then methodically address some of the myths, issues, and controversies that have emerged over the past sixty years regarding the Eastern Front.

On the ground, the Soviet armies, supported by the united Russian people, met and defeated the Nazi thrust at a tremendous cost in lives and material. The price in lives from all the participants makes this saga, perhaps, the costliest in all of military history. In his paper, Glantz asserts that the Soviet Union suffered over 35 million military and civilian casualties throughout World War II, an immense price to pay for a single nation. "The Great Patriotic War" has left an indelible mark on the Russian nation that colors its current and future policies.

The second author, Maj. John ("Lucky") Luckadoo, truly earned his nickname. This young airman was among the first to arrive in England with the B-17s to begin the strategic bombing of Germany and Nazi-occupied territory. The airpower visionaries were eager to put their ideas to the test of combat. So much had to be learned at such a great cost. The sacrifices of these pioneering aviators did not match the casualties on the ground in the Eastern Front, but their early losses of men and planes were also incredible, and chances for survival were not very high. The strategic bombing campaign represented the efforts by the United States and Great Britain to make airpower a new and decisive element of war. They were determined to relieve some of the pressure on the Soviets and take the war to the heart of the enemy twenty-four hours a day.

Major Luckadoo provides a personal view of the broad strategy of the campaign, and of special value is his perspective as a young airman thrust into a position of great responsibility with minimal training and preparation. These brave American aviators had to overcome the skills of veteran *Luftwaffe* pilots, adverse weather, heavy antiaircraft fire, and fatigue to deliver their bombs on target. He and others of his generation met the challenge. Luckadoo credits his survival to pure luck. Only four of the original forty members of his flying class who were assigned to the 100th Bomb Group completed a combat tour. His personal testimony and gracious sense of humor provide the reader a unique perspective on aerial combat in Europe in 1943. He surely earned his nickname.

THE SOVIET ADVANCE, JANUARY 1945

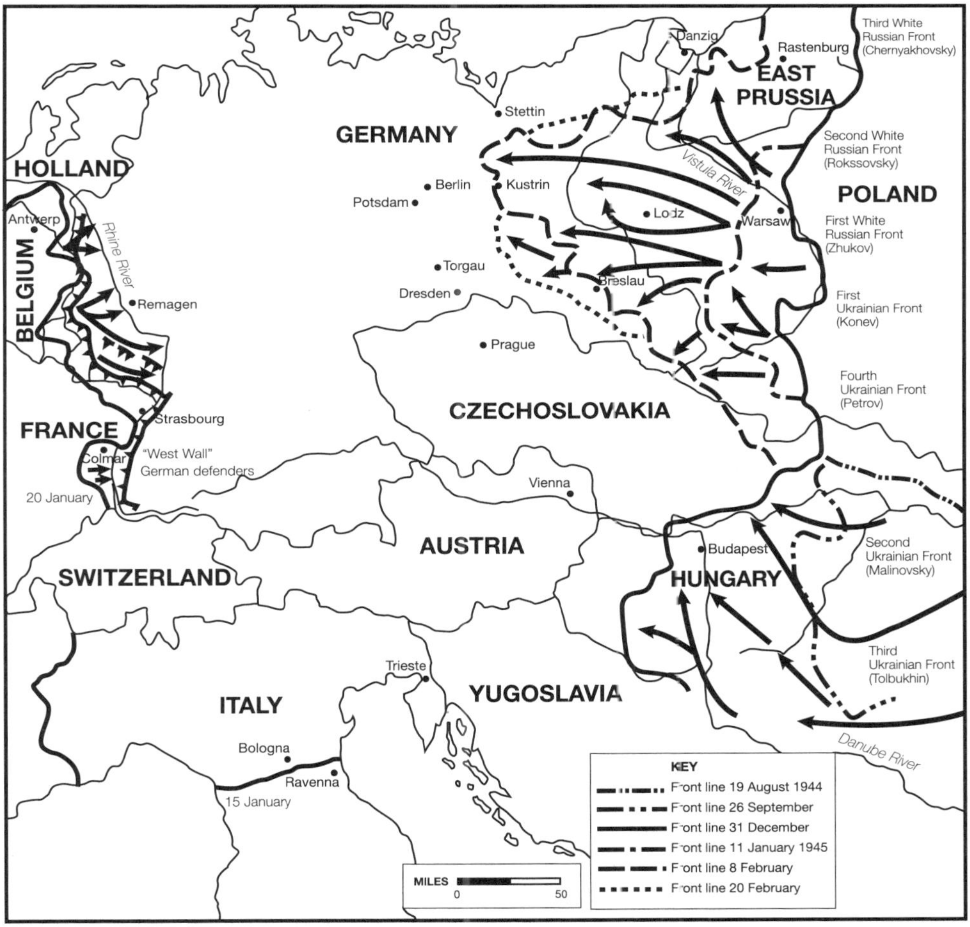

By the end of January 1945 the tip of the salient driven into eastern Germany was barely 50 miles from Berlin.

COLONEL DAVID M. GLANTZ, USA (RET.)

FACT AND FANCY: THE SOVIET GREAT PATRIOTIC WAR, 1941–1945

Col. David M. Glantz earned degrees in history from Virginia Military Institute (1963) and in modern European history from the University of North Carolina at Chapel Hill (1965). He is a graduate of the Defense Language Institute (1973), the U.S. Army Institute for Advanced Russian and Eastern European Studies (1975), the U.S. Army Command and General Staff College (1972), and the U.S. Army War College (1983). His over thirty years of military service included field artillery assignments with the 24th Infantry Division (Mechanized) in Europe and the II Field Force artillery in Vietnam and intelligence assignments with the Office of the Deputy Chief of Staff for Intelligence, U.S. Army Europe. During his last eight years of service, he founded and directed the U.S. Army's Foreign (Soviet) Military Studies Office, Combined Arms Command, Fort Leavenworth, Kansas.

Colonel Glantz founded and currently edits the *Journal of Slavic Military Studies* and is a member of the Academy of Natural Sciences of the Russian Federation. Among the numerous books he has authored on Soviet and Russian military affairs are: *Soviet Military Intelligence in War* (1990);

When Titans Clashed: How the Red Army Stopped Hitler (1996); *Stumbling Colossus: The Red Army on the Eve of World War* (1998); *Operation Mars: Marshal Zhukov's Greatest Defeat* (1999); *Kursk 1943: The End of Blitzkrieg* (1999); *Barbarossa: Hitler's Invasion of Russia* (2001); and *The Battle for Leningrad, 1941–1944* (2003). In addition, he has written numerous articles and chapters in journals and books published in Great Britain, Germany, and the Russian Federation.

I am going to address a massive topic, a topic that cannot be adequately addressed within the limited confines for this paper. My goal, however, is to give some sense of the immensity of what the Soviets called for fifty years, and what the Russians still call today, "The Great Patriotic War," a war that, I think, truly justified that. I am going to try to race through that war, identifying some of the salient features that have either been totally overlooked, forgotten, neglected, or, frankly, covered up, because something like 40 percent of that war and the military operations in that war have been consciously covered up for a variety of reasons. I call that section "Forgotten Battles." I am also going to look at a range of issues, debates, and controversies that have arisen from the war, understanding that the number of debates and controversies in so titanic a struggle probably number in the hundreds. I will identify and address in detail perhaps about ten or fifteen.[1]

Suddenly, and without warning, over 3 million Axis forces plunged across the Soviet state's border early in the morning of June 22, 1941, and began Hitler's infamous Operation Barbarossa. Spearheaded by four powerful panzer groups and protected by an impenetrable curtain of air support, the seemingly invincible *Wehrmacht* advanced

[1] Editor's note: Colonel Glantz presented this paper at the UNT Military History Seminar on September 15, 2001.

from the Soviet Union's western borders to the immediate outskirts of Leningrad, Moscow, and Rostov in the shockingly brief period of less than six months. Faced with this sudden, deep, and relentless German advance, the Red Army and the Soviet state were forced to fight desperately for their very survival. The ensuing struggle went on in a region of some 600,000 square miles and lasted for almost four years before the Red Army triumphantly erected the Soviet flag over the ruins of Hitler's Reich Chancellery in Berlin in late April 1945, just before the formal German surrender in May. The Soviet Union's Great Patriotic War was a war of unprecedented brutality. It was a veritable *Kulturkampf*, or "cultural struggle," a war to the death between two cultures. As many as 35 million Russian soldiers and civilians, almost 4 million German soldiers, and countless German civilians were casualties. The bulk of Central and Eastern Europe suffered unprecedented destruction.[2]

When this deadly conflict ended on May 8, 1945, the Soviet Union and its Red Army occupied and dominated much of Central and Eastern Europe. Within three years, an "Iron Curtain" that would divide the Continent for over forty years descended upon Europe. More importantly, the searing effect of this terrible war on the Soviet soul endured for generations through today, shaping the development of the postwar Soviet Union and ultimately, I believe, contributing to its demise in 1991. Despite its massive scale, cost, and global impact, it is indeed ironic that, for Westerners and Russians alike, much of the Soviet Union's Great Patriotic War remains obscure and imperfectly understood. Worse still, from our standpoint, this obscurity and misunderstanding have perverted history by masking the Red Army's and Soviet state's contributions to Allied victory.

[2] Editor's note: See David M. Glantz, *Barbarossa: Hitler's Invasion of Russia, 1941* (Stroud, UK: Tempus Publishing, Ltd., 1991).

Now, I would like to provide a sense of the immense scale, scope, and impact of the struggle. I will address those points directly. First, relating to scale, I shall address the immensity of the war on the Eastern Front. The combat front—that is, the front along which the forces struggled for almost four years—initially totaled 1,720 miles. These figures are "as the crow flies"; they do not allow for the bends and dips in the front that naturally occurred during the war. Compared to the United States, that scale matches the entire distance from northern Maine to southern Florida. The main Barbarossa front—that is, the front that most of the forces struggled across—extended some 820 miles, equivalent to the distance from New York City to northern Florida. At its maximum extent in 1942, the front extended 1,900 miles, equivalent to the distance from the Saint Lawrence River to southern Florida.

The depth of the German advance was also staggering in its proportions. Hitler's Barbarossa objectives extended over 1,000 miles, equivalent to the distance from the U.S. East Coast to Kansas City, Missouri. The *Wehrmacht*'s maximum advance in 1941 was 760 miles: from New York to Springfield, Illinois. And, if that was not bad enough for the Red Army, the following year the *Wehrmacht* advanced the equivalent of the distance from the U.S. East Coast to Topeka, Kansas. That, indeed, is an immense area.

As to the scope of this struggle, the numbers of Axis forces that engaged across the Eastern Front exceeded over 3 million—Germans, Italians, Romanians, and Hungarians. They faced some 2.5 million Soviet forces in the border military districts. Looking at the figures for the period from June 1941 through April 1945, the majority of German forces fought in the East rather than in the West. Eighty percent of the *Wehrmacht* fought in the East through 1942. After 1942, the figure declines to around 60 percent through 1945.

Also, consider the tremendous mobilization effort of the Red Army. Beginning with an army of 5.5 million men in 1941, expandable to 10 million, the Soviets lost in the first six months of the war almost the entire 5.5 million-man peacetime army, and yet they fought on. By the war's end, their superiority increased strategically from 2-to-1 to the level of roughly 3.5-to-1.

The human costs, too, are staggering. The official figure used by Russian authorities today is 29 million military casualties, of whom slightly more than 11.2 million were dead or missing and presumed dead. My sources in the archives of the Main Cadre Directorate of the General Staff state that the figure was probably closer to 35 million casualties and 14.7 million dead. That figure is almost beyond comprehension.

Nor was the damage limited to the Red Army itself. The casualties of the German *Wehrmacht* and *Luftwaffe*, while significantly lower than those of the Soviets, exceeded 11 million, with 3.9 million dead and over 3 million captured, many of whom never returned. Of the total *Wehrmacht* casualties of 13 million, 10 million, or 80 percent, were lost in the East. If one walks through any German cemetery today, one will see inscribed on numerous tombstones: "*Fallen nach Osten*" ("Fell in the East").

The damage extended well beyond Germany. To round out the losses, if one looks at the losses of the other Axis countries, one will see that Romania and Hungary suffered losses greater than the entire U.S. military death toll in the whole war. These are losses of staggering proportion. I will not attempt to discuss the amount of economic dislocation, which is equally staggering in its impact.

One must understand that the Soviet Army in the postwar years, and the Russian Army today—obviously with less tangible results—were wedded to the study of their military history to improve future combat performance. Thus, if one reads the formerly classified studies done by the Voroshilov General Staff Academy, and by the Frunze

Academy, one will find remarkably candid analyses of the Red Army's performance in the war. Many of these are available in the West today, and they give us a lot of the fresh source material.

To look at the whole war briefly, basically campaign by campaign, the Soviets have divided it into three major segments for educational and analytical purposes. The first period of war extends from June 22, 1941, to November 18, 1942, the day before the Stalingrad counteroffensive began. This was a period when, as the Soviets view it, the *Wehrmacht* held the strategic initiative in Russia, and the Red Army was on the defensive. The second period of war opened on November 19, 1942, when the 5th Soviet Tank Army began its counteroffensive against Romanian forces west of Stalingrad, ultimately helping to encircle the entire German 6th Army in the city. The fortunes of war sharply turned in the Soviets' favor. Over the ensuing year of 1943, the Red Army recorded victory after victory, and, we now know, defeat after defeat as well, though those have been neglected. That was a period of transition, a period when the initiative swung inexorably into Soviet hands. In the final period of war, from January 1, 1944, until May 9, 1945, it was clear to the Soviets themselves and to their Allies that there was no question of who held the strategic initiative. It was simply a question of time as to when victory would occur.

The Soviets also divided each of these periods of war into distinct campaigns. A campaign, by the Soviet military's definition, was a seasonal affair, a strategic effort planned by the General Staff of the *Stavka*, or High Command, as it is called, and by Stalin, who played an active role in all this activity, just as Hitler did on the German side. Looking at the war campaign by campaign, first from the conventional view—that is, the view that predominated in history until now—several issues have been forgotten, or, as I mentioned more candidly, neglected or covered up.

Most Americans know about the first major campaign of the war. This was not a Soviet Red Army campaign; it was a German campaign, a campaign initiated by Hitler's decision to launch Operation Barbarossa. On June 22, 1941, German Army Group North attacked from East Prussia, piercing and demolishing the Soviet defenses and advancing through the Baltic States toward Leningrad. This seemingly seamless advance carried German forces by September 8 to the southern shores of Lake Ladoga and brought the city of Leningrad under a total siege. In October the Germans attempted to envelop and destroy Leningrad from the east by linking up with Finnish forces. This was the famous Tikhvin Offensive, which failed, marking one of the first Soviet victories in the war.

The main attack of Operation Barbarossa, conducted by Army Group Center and two panzer groups, came out of eastern Poland. This attack smashed the Soviet Western *Front*—a *Front* is equivalent to a German army group—encircled three Soviet armies in the Minsk area, capturing roughly 600,000 Soviet troops, and drove onward toward Smolensk, precipitating major battles at Smolensk, on the road to Moscow. In the south, Army Group South and its single panzer group advanced toward Kiev. This was a more difficult advance since the preponderance of Soviet Red Army power was stationed in that region in accordance with their prewar defense plans.

In September 1941, realizing that the *Wehrmacht* faced heavy resistance on the road to Moscow and that Army Group South had achieved less in its march toward Kiev, Hitler issued his infamous order to General Heinz Guderian to turn his panzers southward to deal with the Soviet Southwestern *Front* defending Kiev.[3] After dealing with the Soviet Southwestern *Front,* the *Wehrmacht* encircled four Soviet armies in the Kiev region and another two to the south at

[3] Editor's note: At the time, General Heinz Guderian commanded Army Group Center's 2nd Panzer Group.

Uman', thereby liquidating another million Red Army soldiers. On October 1, 1941, Hitler began Operation Typhoon, the culminating stage of Operation Barbarossa, to seize Moscow. That effort came close to achieving its objective.

Some general remarks about this campaign are in order. On the surface, it was seamless. The German advance was inexorable along all three strategic axes, and Soviet resistance looked feeble at best. And yet, even in this initial period of war, as the Soviets call it, there are activities that have been concealed, including a series of planned Soviet counteroffensives in June, July, and August 1941 in the teeth of Operation Barbarossa. Contrary to popular belief, throughout the initial stages of Operation Barbarossa, *Stavka* did indeed order its armies to conduct what it hoped would be concerted counteroffensive action in June, immediately after the German advance: in July, along the Dnieper River; and, in August, in the Smolensk region, to the north and south. Some of these counteractions by the Red Army had success; most did not. One of the biggest gaps in the historical record relates to the fighting around Smolensk in August and September 1941, when Guderian was making his famous southward turn toward Kiev. Historians now know that while Guderian was marching south, Stalin was launching more than a million men in three *Fronts* in heavy attacks on German defenses at Smolensk, attacks masterminded by [General, later Marshal Georgi] Zhukov, which had devastating impacts on the Red Army in terms of casualties and losses. This largely explains why, beginning on October 1, the *Wehrmacht* enjoyed spectacular successes when it began its final assault on Moscow. The opposing Red Army simply had been decimated in fruitless offensives the month before.

Some of the more heated controversies associated with the war occurred during this initial period. There is the myth of Stalin's "preventative war." This is the Suvorov thesis, advanced by a

Russian émigré whose real name was Alexander Rezun, in his book, *Icebreaker,* several years ago.[4] Rezun used one document, a document signed by Zhukov on May 15, 1941, when he was serving as Chief of the General Staff. The document is a proposal that he submitted through Minister of Defense [Semyon] Timoshenko to Stalin. The document, which I have seen in the original, proposed that the Red Army launch a preemptive offensive against the Germans, who were obviously mobilizing in eastern Poland. The Suvorov thesis, obviously, is quite comforting for German historians today because it in some way obviates German blame for launching the war in the first place. It has been welcomed by two groups: a small group of German historians and a small group of Russian historians who are willing to blame Stalin for everything bad that has ever occurred in the world. Suvorov's thesis is indeed a myth. It is built on fragmentary evidence cut out of whole cloth. When it is examined against archival materials that outline the dilapidated state of the Red Army in 1941, it simply does not hold water.

Another controversy is the timing of Operation Barbarossa. Would Hitler have succeeded had he launched Barbarossa in May, rather than June? Would Barbarossa have succeeded had he launched it before dealing with Yugoslavia and Greece? This myth is also just that, in my opinion. Hitler's problems with Barbarossa and ultimately its goals rest more with his failure to understand the theater of operations into which he was committing the *Wehrmacht* than the actual timing of the attack itself.

Of Guderian's southward turn at Kiev, several historians recently have said that this, in fact, was the turning point of the war, and Hitler's decision to go after the Soviet forces at Kiev was a fatal flaw that delayed the attack on Moscow for one month. I think that

---

[4] Editor's note: See Viktor Suvorov, *Icebreaker: Who Started World War II?* tr. Thomas Beattie (New York: Viking, 1990).

if one examines the evidence now available, one will find that this, too, is false. In fact, Hitler's decision to turn south and the ensuing eradication of over a million men out of the Red Army paved the way for whatever success he achieved on the road to Moscow in October and November 1941. In the last analysis, he probably could not have achieved more.

The last "what-if" is what if Moscow fell. It did not, of course, and "what-ifs" are somewhat vacuous intellectual exercises. Had Moscow fallen in November or December 1941, it is now my opinion that Moscow could have turned into Stalingrad a year earlier.

The second campaign in the initial period of the war began with a Soviet counteroffensive. This began as counterattacks, which grew into counterstrokes, and finally into a massive counteroffensive in December 1941 at the gates of Moscow. By January and February 1942, those counterattacks, counterstrokes, and counteroffensives had grown into a full-fledged winter campaign. This campaign almost collapsed German Army Group Center and almost forced a German collapse on the entire Eastern Front because we also know that the Soviets attacked on other sectors of the front as well in the dead of winter and achieved considerable success. However, these were attacks by a Red Army that had not yet reformed itself. It was a Red Army that had not yet made up for the horrendous losses it had suffered during the previous six months. It was a Red Army that had no mechanized armor arm. It was a Red Army that counterattacked at Moscow with cavalry supported by airborne forces: fragile forces unable to sustain deep operations. Hence, by March 1942, Stalin's great winter campaign faltered, creating a front overlapping German and Soviet forces, both exhausted, extending all the way from Leningrad to the Black Sea.

There were also two, mostly neglected, operations during this period of the war that come to mind. First, a whole series of major Soviet attacks occurred on the flank of the Moscow counteroffensive.

None of those operations has been covered adequately by Soviet sources, and certainly not by German-based sources. Perhaps the most glaring of the forgotten battles was an operation that took place near Leningrad where Stalin tried to relieve the encircled city by marching on Leningrad from the southeast and committing an entire shock army to break through the German defenses and into the German rear. This was the famous 2nd Shock Army. Ultimately, the infamous General [Andrei] Vlasov took command of that army. He had been the deputy commander of the Volkov *Front* and replaced the army's commander when he became ill. Vlasov surrendered to the Germans in the summer of 1942 and eventually became the founder of the Russian Liberation Army, which served Hitler. That operation, until very recently, was part of the *tabula rasa* of operations on the Eastern Front. We are just now receiving adequate information about the fate of the 2nd Shock Army.

To consider the issue of historical debates, I have noted three that are most important, although there are many others. First, there is Hitler's stand-fast order. In reality, the orders that Hitler issued to the *Wehrmacht* outside of Moscow in late December 1941, in my opinion, saved the *Wehrmacht*, or at least Army Group Center, from total collapse and possibly a retreat replicating Napoleon's of 1812. Having said that, Hitler's success with issuing the stand-fast order in December 1941 conditioned him to act in a similar fashion in 1942, 1943, and 1944 with increasingly disastrous effect. I will track this issue of stand-fast orders and their utility as I go through the other campaigns. By the summer of 1944, it would cost Hitler the better part of a complete army group. This stand-fast order mutated into a *Festung* strategy, or a strategy requiring fortresses to be created and held by large *Wehrmacht* forces in the East.

A second controversy has been raised in Soviet historical circles for years. If one reads Zhukov's memoirs and the memoirs of others, one will find Stalin blamed for the Red Army's failures in 1941, 1942, and 1943. In the case of the Moscow counteroffensive, the blame is laid at Stalin's feet for trying to do too much too soon everywhere, rather than concentrating his forces in a given sector. Archival materials now indicate that Stalin alone was not to blame for this strategy. In fact, the strategy that the Red Army adopted in 1941 and adhered to through 1945 was always broad front. Many of these battles have been forgotten or covered up in order to keep the positive Soviet image intact. In fact, the Soviet army attacked on a broad front with Zhukov's approval, with [Chief of the General Staff Alexandr] Vasilevsky's approval, and with other *Stavka* planners' and *Front* commanders' approvals in this campaign and in subsequent campaigns.

Lastly, there is the issue of Moscow as a turning point. Oftentimes, the question is asked: "Where is the turning point of the war?" There was not a single turning point; there were several. I have identified three by the virtue of the characteristics of each. Moscow was indeed a turning point, because Moscow indicated that Hitler could not win the war on the terms he had laid out for Operation Barbarossa. That was the value of the Battle of Moscow. However, Hitler's failure to achieve his goals in Operation Barbarossa and Stalin's failures to achieve his goals in his counteroffensives at Moscow led to what occurred in the summer of 1942, the Summer–Fall Campaign of 1942. In this campaign, both sides planned to seize the strategic initiative: Hitler, obviously, because he was bothered by his failures with Barbarossa, and Stalin, obviously, because he was bothered by his failure to destroy at least a German army group in the Battle of Moscow. According to the plans of the two sides preceding the Summer-Fall Campaign, Hitler code-named his operation *Fall Blau*, or "Operation Blue." The *Wehrmacht* aimed at what Hitler considered the economic heartland of Russia, the eastern Donbas-Donets basin.

Ironically, during this campaign in the summer of 1942, Stalin also intended to take the offensive. His senior commanders—and this is perhaps correct—talked him out of it and said that the Red Army had to begin on the defensive and was not capable of conducting an offensive. But, having said that, Stalin persisted and did launch two major offensive operations into what he thought was the soft German underbelly. The Soviets assessed that Hitler was going after Moscow in 1942, and, of course, they were mistaken. The attacks occurred at Khar'kov and in the Crimea, and they were complete military fiascoes. They occurred in May 1942 and cost the Red Army somewhere in the neighborhood of 500,000 men. That, of course, was just prior to Hitler's launching of Operation Blue on June 28. When Blue was launched, with 500,000 men removed from the Soviet order of battle in the south, the *Wehrmacht* made rather rapid progress toward Stalingrad and into the Caucasus.[5]

The classic view has always been that the Red Army's stance during this period was one of utter passivity and getting out of the way while they raised forces for defense and counteroffensives somewhere down the line. That is patently false. In fact, Stalin, however mortified by Operation Blue beginning where he did not expect it to begin, reacted immediately. The Red Army responded violently when confronted with Operation Blue. The Soviet official history states that between July 5 and 7, 1942, the new Soviet 5th Tank Army launched heavy attacks on the Germans west of Voronezh. The attacks were futile and halted after two days of heavy combat. I have gone back and looked at that particular operation. It did not last from July 5 to 7; it lasted roughly from July 2 to 28. It resumed again in August and again in September. In the July operations, the Soviets did not have just the 5th Tank Army, a new army with 3 tank corps and 500 tanks; they also

[5] Editor's note: See David M. Glantz, *Kharkov 1942: Anatomy of a Military Disaster* (Rockville Center, NY: Sarpedon, 1998).

had 7 tank corps and 1,500 tanks that took part in that engagement. It failed, however, and its failure points out how dramatic the Soviet counteroffensive at Stalingrad was when it succeeded in November 1942. One of the debates associated with the Summer-Fall Campaign of 1942 regards the responsibility for the Red Army's May debacles at Khar'kov and the Crimea. This can be validly laid at the feet of Stalin trying to do too much too soon with too little, and also to the ineptitude of senior Soviet commanders, who with poor intelligence launched an offensive into the teeth of the German build-up for Operation Blue. It was suicide, basically.

Hitler's strategy for Operation Blue needs thorough reexamination. What Hitler did with Blue was a worse version of what he had done with Barbarossa. He assigned forces that were clearly inadequate to perform the missions he expected of them. In reality, he assigned one army group, Army Group South, which was supposed to cover one strategic axis, into an area that comprised three strategic axes. He finessed it by simply saying, "We will divide Army Group South into two army groups, A and B, and we will insert the Italian, Romanian, and Hungarian armies to fill the gaps." Of course, he paid the price for those mistakes at Stalingrad in November.

I use the Leningrad diversion because I just did a book on Leningrad, and it was educational because I had never studied that neglected theater of operations.[6] The Germans intended to take Leningrad in the summer of 1942. They moved [Field Marshal Erich] von Manstein's 11th Army out of the Crimea after it seized Sevastopol, and in doing so created a fatal flaw because that was the strategic reserve for Army Group South and its drive for Stalingrad. It was not there when it was needed. The 11th Army went north, and, in another almost forgotten battle, the Soviets actually preempted its assault on Leningrad by launching

[6] Editor's note: See David M. Glantz, *The Battle for Leningrad, 1941–1944* (Lawrence, KS: University Press of Kansas, 2002).

their own offensive at Siniavino, which tied up von Manstein's force, although the Red Army lost in its entirety the 2nd Shock Army in the offensive for the second time in 1942.

The Winter Campaign of November 1942 to April 1943 contains the second most important turning point of the war, the turning point that indicated that Germany would lose the war. The only question remaining was: how badly would she lose? This campaign began on November 19, 1942, with Operation Uranus, the Stalingrad counteroffensive. We now know that, in fact, *Stavka* ordered two major counteroffensives, Operation Uranus and Operation Mars. They covered up Mars because it failed. Zhukov commanded Mars, and Vasilevsky commanded Uranus. These men were the most prestigious figures in the Red Army's strategic circle. Mars was to cover the area west of Moscow, which was in the Soviets' view the main strategic axis. Uranus covered the Stalingrad region. Uranus succeeded, Mars failed; Uranus ended up in the history books, Mars did not. After the Soviets conducted their initial operation, incidentally, the success that they achieved surprised them. They encircled far more Germans than they expected. They then, characteristically, decided to exploit it and ordered one offensive after another throughout December 1942 and January 1943 until the offensive became, in essence, an entire winter campaign. It almost collapsed the German forces in south Russia. Now, that is the conventional view.

In addition to Operation Mars, the largest forgotten operation of the war is what I call the "Prelude to Kursk." Before I published my book on Operation Mars, when I was still in favor with the official Soviet historical circles, they came out in response to my little article on the "Prelude to Kursk" with a documents book that had all the documents I would ever have wished to see.[7] Several months later,

[7] Editor's note: See David M. Glantz, *Zhukov's Greatest Defeat: The Red Army's Epic Disaster in Operation Mars, 1942* (Lawrence, KS: University Press of Kansas, 1999).

my book on Mars was published, and the door slammed shut. I have seen no more documents after that. In any case, going back to this forgotten battle, this was a case where *Stavka* attempted to exploit the Stalingrad success. They committed a total of five *Fronts* in the Leningrad region. Zhukov masterminded this offensive and called it Operation Polar Star. It was designed to destroy Army Group North and relieve Leningrad. This operation had no code name, but it involved the western Briansk, Voronezh, and Central *Fronts*. [General Konstantin] Rokossovsky played the major role in it. The operation went almost to the Dnieper River before it stopped.

The legacy of that operation is the infamous Kursk bulge. In fact, conventional histories only talk about what happened in the south in this campaign and do not talk about what happened in the north, probably because the Soviets wanted to conceal the real strategic intent of the operation, which was the collapse of the entire German defense in the East in the winter of 1942–1943 and to drive the Germans back to the Dnieper River, an objective that they would not actually achieve until late 1943. The important thing about this operation is that people have praised von Manstein, who was appointed to command Army Group Don and then Army Group South, for his brilliant parrying of this blow in the Donbas region. They say that von Manstein's counterstroke was of immense proportion. In actuality, von Manstein's counterstroke not only prevented a collapse of the German army in south Russia, but it also contributed in a major way to the collapse and utter failure of Soviet offenses by drawing forces away from other regions at critical moments. In fact, one can argue that von Manstein saved the entire Eastern Front, and his counterstroke had the effect of a counteroffensive.

Stalin's strategic intention in November 1942 was to do far more than historians have accorded him with the willingness or desire to do. He aimed to collapse the entire German Eastern Front, and he did it initially with Operations Mars and Uranus. Stalin had planned follow-up operations, Jupiter and Saturn, but he only carried out one of those in abbreviated form. Of course, he pushed the German army to the limits of its endurance in the ensuing winter operations.[8] We have heard for many years about how Hitler condemned the 6th Army at Stalingrad to destruction by simply not permitting it to break out. The sad fact is that we now know that [General Friedrich] Paulus's 6th Army could not have broken out. He had insufficient forces to do so, and the Germans themselves at that time, and historians since, had no idea of the amount of force that the Soviets had placed in between Stalingrad and those relief attempts.

The Soviet winter offensive had strategic aims that far exceeded what historians up to now have accorded it. Von Manstein's February 1943 counterstroke had the effect of a major counteroffensive and was perhaps one of the most brilliant operations conducted in the war. It certainly had a momentous impact. Stalingrad was thus a turning point. It was a turning point because after November 19, 1942, the Russians were going to win the war in the East. The only question was to what degree or extent.

By the time of the Summer–Fall Campaign of 1943, the strategic initiative had shifted in the Red Army's favor across the entire front. In the two years before, the Red Army had never been able to stop the *Wehrmacht* at the tactical depth, the operational depth, or even the strategic depth. Was it now being called upon to do this in the summer of 1943? The answer is "no." Stalin adopted the proper strategy in the summer of 1943: initial defense of the salient at Kursk, which was the most obvious target, followed by a preplanned strategic counteroffensive across the entire front. The important feature here is that the Red Army planned its counteroffensive well before the

---

[8] Editor's note: Operation Little Saturn began on December 16, 1942, and prevented von Manstein's Army Group Don from reaching or relieving Stalingrad.

Germans launched their panzers against the Kursk bulge on July 5, 1943. The front began creeping substantially westward as these campaigns unfolded. What did occur at Kursk is that the Red Army performed the unprecedented feat of stopping the *Wehrmacht* before it reached significant operational depths. That had never been done before, and that is why it is something of an exercise in "Monday morning quarterbacking" to say, as von Manstein or other German generals did: "We should never have done that. It was foredoomed."[9] There was not a single German who expected that what occurred at Kursk would actually occur. And no sooner had the German attack been blunted at Kursk than counteroffensives rippled across the entire front in staggered sequence. Basically, every *Front*, from the Kalinin *Front* in the north all the way down to the south, was on the offensive. Of course, by virtue of those offensives, the Red Army drove the *Wehrmacht* back to the Dnieper River line, an objective it had set earlier in the year.

There are some major forgotten aspects of this campaign, the most important of which relates to the issue of broad front versus wide front. The classic interpretation is that, in this campaign, the goal was the Dnieper and the Ukraine, and that was all. In actuality, there were two major operations at the tail end of this campaign: a Byelorussian operation and a Ukrainian operation. The Byelorussian operation had some of the hardest fighting during 1943 but achieved some of the most meager results, and hence virtually all of its operations have been forgotten and covered up. The questions associated with this period of war—the wisdom, timing, and feasibility of Citadel—have variants.[10] Some have said that if Hitler had started Citadel in May, it would have been much easier to accomplish his goal. That is wrong.

[9] Editor's note: See Erich von Manstein, *Lost Victories*, tr. and ed. Anthony G. Powell (Chicago: Henry Regnery, 1958).

[10] Editor's note: *Unternehmen Zitadelle* (Operation Citadel) was the German codename for the Kursk offensive.

I have already addressed Stalin's broad-front strategy. The Battle of Kursk was a turning point because it became clear that a Soviet victory would be a total victory. That total victory would come sooner rather than later, and the Allies understood that, which is why the intelligence exchanges with the Russians began to erode.[11]

If one looks at the Winter Campaign of 1943–1944, one will find much of the same effect seen in the campaign that preceded it in the summer of 1943. It looked like the Soviet effort was in the south, in the Ukraine. The Red Army conducted a series of operations down there aimed at clearing the Ukraine, and at this point one begins to see the political content in Stalin's strategy in the war. That political content was a desire to reach the underbelly of Europe, but I would qualify that by saying that, while he was pounding into the Ukraine successfully, he was also ordering the Red Army to pound into Byelorussia, and that was less than successful. The Byelorussian operation, as mentioned earlier, was continuous from October 1943 to April 1944 and involved hundreds of attacks by tens of armies, most failing against the defenses of Army Group Center. Because they failed, they have been dropped from the histories; and because they failed, some have been able to assess their strategy as having been aimed at the Ukraine and nothing more.[12]

The Summer Campaign of 1944 was perhaps the most brilliant campaign from the standpoint of the Red Army because it was the campaign that destroyed the better part of three German army groups. A series of savage, strategic blows by multi-million-man forces,

---

[11] Editor's note: See David M. Glantz, *The Battle for Kursk, 1943: The End of Blitzkrieg* (Lawrence, KS: University Press of Kansas, 1999); David M. Glantz, *The Role of Intelligence in Soviet Military Strategy in World War II* (Novato, CA: Presidio Press, 1998).

[12] Editor's note: See David M. Glantz and Harold S. Orenstein, trs. and eds., *Belorussia, 1944: The Soviet General Staff Study* (London, UK: Frank Cass, 2001); and David M. Glantz and Harold S. Orenstein, trs. and eds., *The Battle for L'vov, July 1944: The German General Staff Study* (London, UK: Frank Cass, 2002).

successively but overlapping in time, began against Army Group Center in Byelorussia on June 23, 1944. It expanded to embrace central Poland and Army Group North Ukraine on July 13 and culminated in August with an attack on, and the virtual destruction of, Army Group South Ukraine and Romania. Certainly, this was the first case where Hitler's *Festung* strategy began to bear the worst of its fruit: the loss of whole armies in single operations. In the case of the Byelorussian operation, three full German armies disappeared from the order of battle. In the Iassy-Kishinev offensive in Romania, a German army disappeared from the order of battle; two Romanian armies disappeared from the Axis order of battle and, within two weeks, were in the Red Army's order of battle; a second German army limped out of Romania into Hungary in a sad, discombobulated fashion. The broad-front strategy prevailed, with maximum pressure at every point. The campaign concluded with vigorous operations into Romania and across the border into Hungary.

The Winter–Spring Campaign of 1944–1945 has generated considerable controversy, primarily because it was designed to take Berlin but did not. This campaign saw the Red Army smash German defenses and destroy German army groups in East Prussia and Poland and make major inroads into Hungary, to Budapest and beyond.

I will only raise one cardinal issue that has just now become clear regarding what should be the debate over the importance of this campaign. On February 2, 1945, after Soviet forces had cleared Poland and were on the Oder River, thirty-six miles from Berlin, and when Allied forces were located along the Rhine, 160 miles from Berlin, Stalin issued his attack orders. The 1st Ukrainian *Front* and the 1st Byelorussian *Front* were to seize Berlin by February 15. Abruptly, on February 10, six days after the operation's initial phase had begun, Stalin halted the advance on Berlin. For a variety of reasons, he ordered his forces to halt on the Berlin axis and instead clear the flanks. We now know—I might add that this decision took place at the precise time of the Yalta Conference, when Stalin, Roosevelt, and Churchill were meeting—with a fairly good degree of certainty that, in fact, Stalin made a strategic decision on or about February 8 to halt operations along the Berlin axis and to shift significant forces to the south. We now know that these forces were a whole new army, the 9th Guards Army, which had been a special, highly elite airborne army. He committed those forces in mid-March west of Budapest in a drive for Vienna. Vienna fell on April 13. Then, and only then, three days later, Stalin opened his assault on Berlin with Zhukov and [Marshal Ivan] Konev's *Fronts*.[13] That particular item is worthy of considerably more investigation. I think it has an immense message about the intention of the Soviet high command during this stage in the war.

This was Stalin's strategy, and to make that point in October 1944, he took many of his leading marshals—the ones about whose prestige he was worried—and put them in *Front* commands, and Stalin controlled the strategic planning out of Moscow. Zhukov followed his orders, and he did not do very well in Berlin. Stalin's strategy has been the subject of debate since the war's end. There was Konev, the 1st Ukrainian *Front* commander; [General Vasily] Chuikov's, 8th Guards Army; and Zhukov's 1st Byelorussian *Front* as well as others. Rokossovksy has now joined the debate, since his unexpurgated memoirs have just appeared. They were bitter over the decision not to go on to Berlin in February. To a man, they state, "We could have taken it," and they were right. They could have done so. None of the excuses for why Stalin should not have gone on hold any water at all. What they did was wait for three months, allowing the Germans to erect the best defenses they could possibly erect, and they paid for that

[13] Editor's note: In the Berlin operation, Zhukov commanded the 1st Byelorussian *Front*, while Marshal Ivan Konev led the 1st Ukrainian *Front*.

decision with 375,000 killed in the Berlin operation, which is about as many as we lost in the whole war.

There was a race to Berlin. The Berlin operation occurred in April and May 1945. That was followed by the Prague operation, which eradicated the last vestiges of the German army. In the race to Berlin, we now know that Zhukov, who received quite a bloody nose backing out of the Kustrin bridgehead on the direct route to Berlin, suffered immense losses. He performed as he had done on many other occasions. Konev operated much more successfully to the south, and Stalin allowed him to take part in reducing the city. We now know that Zhukov ordered his artillery to fire on Konev's forces as they came into Berlin. There was quite a bit of competition there. We do not know the full scope of that, but I have enough information now to know that there were some nasty acts committed by Zhukov to keep Konev out of the city.

What can we say, then, in conclusion? The Great Patriotic War cost the Soviet Union about 14.7 million military dead, half again as many men as the United States fielded in the entire war effort, and thirty times the 375,000 casualties the United States suffered in the war. The gruesome Soviet toll includes more than 35 million military and civilian casualties. An even more staggering casualty toll probably reaches about 20 million people. So, one ends up with an unimaginable figure of 35 million losses, and that may be conservative. What did all this achieve? The Red Army, in large measure, defeated the twentieth century's most formidable armed force, after what the Soviets themselves have described—or at least used to describe—as the effects of an atomic war, and they probably are not far from the truth. Hitler's "Thousand-Year Reich" perished in twelve years. That ended the Nazi domination of Europe, and the Red Army liberated about two-thirds of Europe. By the war's end, I think it is indisputable that the Red Army had emerged as the world's grandest killing machine.

Tragically, however, this killing machine proved as deadly for the Red Army's soldiers as it did for those serving in the *Wehrmacht*, and the Russians have not forgotten this. The Soviet Union emerged as one of the world's dominant superpowers and, of course, the dominant power in Eurasia. There is a saying that is ubiquitous in Soviet literature, and it says much about how the Soviet Union reacted after the war and how the Russian Federation reacts today: "No one will be forgotten, nothing will be forgotten." When a nation collectively utters that statement, it means 1941, and it means that it must maintain a military establishment foremost in the world, probably far more than the nation will ever need. And it means that the nation must conduct a foreign policy that addresses security matters. If one is a security expert, one must ask: "How much is enough? Where do you stop to be secure?" It is impossible to answer that question. In the last analysis, this fixation—the fixation symbolized by the saying, "No one will be forgotten, nothing will be forgotten"—bankrupted the Soviet Union. It bankrupted the Soviets economically; it bankrupted them technologically; it bankrupted them ideologically; and it also bankrupted their will because they could not sustain the effort any longer. That, in large measure, explains what occurred in 1991 when the Soviet system collapsed.

TARGETS FOR THE 8TH AIR FORCE, 1942-45

MAJOR JOHN LUCKADOO, USAAF (RET.)

LIFE IN THE BLOODY 100th

Born in 1922 in Chattanooga, Tennessee, John Luckadoo enlisted in the Aviation Cadet Program of the U.S. Army Air Forces in February 1942. Immediately after graduating as a multi-engine pilot in February 1943, he was assigned to the 100th Bomb Group (Heavy) flying B-17s. Luckadoo later flew overseas to England with his group to enter combat with the 8th Air Force.

Luckadoo's fate was to serve as a member of an air group that became known as "The Bloody 100th." Operating from an airfield near the English village of Thorpe Abbotts, the 100th flew a total of 306 combat missions between June 25, 1943, and April 20, 1945. During that time the 100th had lost 177 aircraft in combat and another 52 planes to operational accidents. The 100th was not the group with the highest losses in the 8th Air Force, but since its early losses often came in bunches, it soon acquired the reputation of a hard luck outfit along with the name "The Bloody 100th." It lost nine crews on the Regensburg-to-Africa shuttle in August 1943; seven over Bremen on October 8, 1943; twelve over Münster on October 10, 1943; fifteen over

Berlin on March 6, 1944, and another nine over the same target on May 24, 1944; and fourteen over Ruhland on September 11, 1944.

Luckadoo was one of the few original pilots of the 100th to survive twenty-five missions. His decorations, which were awarded to him by General Curtis LeMay, included the Distinguished Flying Cross and the Air Medal with three clusters. As a result of his combat experience, Luckadoo left England with the rank of captain and won promotion to the temporary rank of major in 1946. He resigned his Regular Air Force commission in 1948 and completed his college work at the University of Denver. He then had a civilian career in real estate management, development, construction, and financing throughout the Southwest.

I want to share with you briefly some of my experiences with the "infamous" 100th Bomb Group in England during World War II. It is personally gratifying that there seems to be a genuine resurgence of interest in first-person accounts of happenings in World War II, although, I suppose, that is not really too surprising since those of us who participated in the war are rapidly passing from the scene. To be exact, World War II veterans are currently dying at the rate of some 1,200 per day, so at this rate it will not be too many years hence that there will be scarcely anybody left who can give first-hand accounts to "tell it like it was." This is why so many of us look at the obituary page first to see if we have yet made it.[1]

To understand and appreciate some of my viewpoints, it is probably best that I first present a brief synopsis of my background to show where I am coming from. As a child of the Great Depression in the 1930s who grew up in the "Cradle of the Confederacy" in Chattanooga, Tennessee, I now realize after all these years that I actually had an

[1] Editor's note: Mr. Luckadoo presented this paper at the UNT Military History Seminar on September 30, 2000.

oddly warlike or military heritage. As a kid in elementary school on Missionary Ridge, I could actually gaze out of my classroom window into the memorial park across the street, which was replete with many huge, larger-than-life statues, cannons and stacked cannon balls, dozens of historical tablets, and even a four-story steel observation tower from the Civil War. I could virtually see the ghostly troops as they charged up the hill of that bloody battleground in 1863, rising up out of the mists that almost always hung over the ridge on most days. Little did I know then that my familiarity with that cloudy and foggy climate would so well acclimate me to the kind of weather I would encounter flying in England just a few years later.

About twelve miles from the city lay Fort Oglethorpe, Georgia, which was a regimental cavalry post where I spent several summers attending Civilian Military Training Camp as a teenager. As my father raised five-gaited Arabian show horses, our family was invited as "townies" to participate in many of the activities of that Army post, such as the horse shows, polo playing on Sunday afternoons, and the weekly fox hunts through the adjoining national park where the bloody Battle of Chickamauga was fought. It never ceased to amaze me, after joining the Air Corps more than eighty years after the Civil War, how we would spend such an inordinate amount of time in the barracks refighting and debating the so-called "War Between the States."

During my high school days, I was deeply involved in the ROTC unit at Chattanooga High School, and in my senior year I commanded one of the two battalions in the regiment. At that time I even entertained some possibility of applying for an appointment to West Point in anticipation of a professional military career. However, all of our lives here in America were instantly and drastically changed when, in my sophomore year at the University of Chattanooga, the Japanese suddenly and without warning attacked Pearl Harbor. Even at nineteen and twenty years of age, many of us then had already been convinced that with Hitler on a rampage through all of Europe, and with Great Britain next in line to experience the *blitzkrieg*, America would soon be unable to stay out of a world conflict and it would only be a matter of time before we would be inextricably drawn into a world war. The Japanese sneak attack on the United States on December 7, 1941, decided that question for us.

Consequently, it immediately became the nationally patriotic thing for all able-bodied young men to join one branch or the other of the military, as this country was galvanized into a prompt response to the humiliation we had received at the hands of the Japanese. In my case I enlisted in the Aviation Cadet Program in February 1942 and was accepted for flight training.

This mobilization of America's might and manpower was exactly what Prime Minister Winston Churchill and the British nation had been hoping for. And here, I think, is one of the most significant things about World War II that oftentimes tends to be overlooked: and that is that the enormous manufacturing capacity to produce war materiel plus the immediate mobilization of the nation's manpower bolstered the power of the Allies almost beyond measure. The will of the American people to shoulder the obligation of equipping ourselves as well as our Allies was overwhelmingly significant because this could all be done in relative safety from direct attack on our homeland, while the enemy had no such luxury. Thus, the awesome power of U.S. production rapidly ratcheted up to an incredible level, the likes of which the world had never before seen. This factor alone was eventually to deliver the death knell to the Axis powers.

Another very important factor in the mobilization of the country, which I believe also is seldom fully acknowledged, was the tremendous impact of American women on our work force. Never before had they been given the opportunity in this country to be fully integrated into the daunting task of producing every conceivable type of war materiel—guns, tanks, ships, airplanes, trucks, munitions, etc.—as well as immediately filling all types of administrative jobs in order to free up the male population for frontline duty. This was to mark the beginning of the true emancipation of women in America, and never again would they be content to be relegated to just the traditional role of "dishes and diapers."

For those of us who had had no previous military experience, a rather rude awakening came when we discovered that military service was not predicated on the democratic principle. One soon learned the true meaning of "Yours is not to question why; yours is but to do or die." For citizen soldiers this reality came as a rude and bitter lesson. From carefree college lads with little on our minds but hair, overnight we were to become serious and sober airplane drivers and killers engaged in a life-or-death struggle, and far from home to boot. Fate came to play a huge part in our lives, we soon discovered, and as ensuing engagements unfolded, we were sent hither, thither, and yon upon someone else's whim. One's destiny was completely in the hands of "Higher Authority," and we could only pray that our guardian angel was paying close attention.

To be suddenly confronted with the necessity of contemplating our morality (since we were to be trained as killers) as well as our mortality (since we were by the same token apt to be killed) was most disconcerting, to say the least. Some of my peers were quite resentful of their lives being disrupted by having to enter the service and fight a war; others were to view it as a rare opportunity to go places and do things they might never have otherwise been privileged to experience. I am happy to say that, although I was not overjoyed at the thought of being shot at, I was definitely of the latter persuasion.

I graduated from advanced flight training at Valdosta, Georgia, as a member of Class 43-B, which meant that we completed our training in February 1943. By Act of Congress, I was now "an officer and a gentleman" a little more than a month before my twenty-first birthday, upon receiving my commission and pilot's wings in the United States Army Air Forces.[2] Like most of my comrades in arms, I was faced with the sudden realization of terrific responsibility and mandatory maturity almost overnight.

Forty-three of my graduating classmates from flying school and I were promptly shipped to Kearney, Nebraska, to join a B-17 heavy bomber outfit, known as the 100th Bomb Group, as co-pilots. We soon learned that we were replacing the original co-pilots because the group had been refused certification for combat just as they were about to go overseas, causing the group commander to be replaced. This action occurred despite the overwhelming need at that time for heavy bombers in Europe to help stem the Nazi onslaught. It seems the group had been sadly lacking in "air discipline" and had not met the requirements of formation flying and all the other things one required to be considered "combat ready." The original co-pilots had accumulated more flying experience in the B-17 than most of the first pilots in some of the other groups that were then being sent overseas. So, they pulled all the original co-pilots out of the 100th Bomb Group and shoved forty-four from our class into the right-hand [co-pilot's] seats for all of the crews of that entire group.

We soon found that there were basically three types of fliers in the group: those who were cocky and self-assured and absolutely convinced they were invincible; those who were quite sure they would never survive any given mission; and then the third type, those who fell somewhere in between and were pretty much willing to take things as they came. Many seemed rather suddenly to become

[2] Editor's note: The U.S. Army Air Corps officially became the U.S. Army Air Forces on June 20, 1941.

seriously religious, and others were somewhat superstitious. Actually, most were probably both.

The consequence of these fledgling co-pilots being injected into the already established ten-man crews on a B-17 was hardly welcomed, and we soon found ourselves being treated like escapees from a leper colony. It also resulted in our eventually being shipped out for overseas duty with very little familiarity and flying time with the famous Flying Fortresses we were committed to fly to England. I think I had a grand total of only about eight hours flying time in the B-17 when we finally left the States some two months later and flew our new ships across the North Atlantic to Scotland, a flight of some fourteen hours with a good tailwind.

In my own case, my new crew resented me greatly because they were going to be deprived of the original co-pilot's presence, particularly in going into combat as a team. All through training, one of the greatest things that you learned was how to work with each other as members of a crew. You relied on each of your comrades, so if you did not have that homogeneity within the crew, and good morale and good discipline and commonality of purpose, you had lost a whole lot. That's how our journey across the Atlantic started.

From Bangor, Maine, we flew to Newfoundland, where we refueled and awaited favorable tailwinds before we could proceed to Scotland. While we were standing by, however, the first pilot of my crew managed to go across the base to where some British WAAFs [Women's Auxiliary Air Force] were billeted.[3] He managed to "make connections" there and contracted a social disease that put him in the hospital. As a consequence, the rest of the group took off as single planes and proceeded to England via Scotland while we remained an

---

[3] Editor's note: The Women's Auxiliary Air Force assisted the RAF primarily as ground controllers during World War II. They often handed the fliers their parachutes, drove them to their aircraft, manned radio towers, and talked crippled planes home over the radio.

extra ten days while he recuperated. When he was finally released, he was so weak that he could barely walk, and he literally had to be carried onto the plane. Thus, the crew now had to depend on my piloting ability to get us across the Atlantic, so this tended to take the edge off the resentment and the animosities that had existed up until this time. It did do some good toward kind of getting us all in the same canoe and paddling in the same direction. We landed at Prestwick, Scotland, without any difficulty, and from there we went to our base at Thorpe Abbotts in East Anglia, arriving there in June 1943.

Although still reeling from the Blitz during the Battle of Britain, the British warmly greeted us although there seemed to be a critical difference of opinion between the Bomber Command of the Royal Air Force [RAF] and the U. S. 8th Air Force as to exactly how we were to be best used. The RAF tried daylight formation bombing and had been devastated by both the *Luftwaffe* and the deadly German antiaircraft battery defenses, so the British were firmly convinced that "daylight high-altitude precision bombing" was nothing short of suicidal, particularly as long as the German fighters maintained air superiority over continental Europe. During the period 1943–44, for every 100 aircrew members sent on missions by the RAF Bomber Command, 51 were killed, 9 crashed, 12 survived as prisoners of war, and one was shot down and evaded capture—a total of 73 losses per 100 crewmembers.

On the other hand, the 8th Air Force was just as firmly attached to the idea that with our heavily-defended B-17s and B-24s, together with the Norden bombsight (our reputed "secret weapon"), in daylight high-altitude formations we could demolish German manufacturing, shipping, rail yards, power stations, and other primary strategic targets, and ultimately even break the civilian will to make war. All of this was to be done in broad daylight from approximately 30,000 feet above the ground. But in the end, we were to suffer losses equal to or greater than the RAF's 73 percent.

Another problem that we did not entirely anticipate from our stateside training was the effects of the northern European weather on our operations. Most of our crews had trained in Texas, New Mexico, or Arizona, so nothing—absolutely nothing—would have prepared us adequately for the weather conditions we were required to contend with when we got to England, even though they were not the worst at that time of the year. We would encounter the worst English weather in the fall and winter months.

The whole process of taking off and forming up could also be extremely hazardous. When you are going down the runway with an aircraft that has a full load of gasoline, a bomb bay full of bombs, and you have got all that ammunition aboard, you are hard-pressed to know how long it is going to take to get your airplane off the ground. It has to get up to flying speed before you can pull it off. Also, most of the time in England, you are going to be pulling up directly into an overcast, so you will be climbing and using instruments on a prescribed course through this "pea soup." You may climb up 8,000 or 10,000 feet before you finally break out, and you hope you will not run into anyone in the interim. It is certainly a complicated process, and it is time-consuming because when you get to this point in the mission, you have already been airborne for some time. As you break out of the overcast, you then must get your bearings, immediately recognize where your rendezvous point is, and go to form up first with other members of your squadron, and then your group. Your group then forms up with whatever other groups are going with your division or your wing formation. Then you start out on your track and proceed to the target while hoping that visibility over the target will be sufficient for you to identify the initial point, the aiming point, and the target area so you can put the bombs where you intend to drop them.

There are other factors that affect bombing accuracy. Flying tight formations is extremely difficult because you have to contend with air currents, and you have to be concerned about prop wash from the exhaust of the plane that you are following. We flew what was called the "box" formation, which consisted of three squadrons flying at slightly different altitudes. The theory was that the "box" enabled the planes in the squadrons to offer mutual assistance because of the tremendous firepower that many B-17s could bring to bear on German fighters. Of course, when you got into enemy territory, you were subjected to attacks by enemy fighters, and they would come from any direction. You had to ignore them as a pilot, however, and concentrate on the plane next to you that you were guiding on, assuming that it had not been shot down. Finally, bear in mind that we were flying under these conditions for maybe eight hours, although the longest mission I flew was fourteen hours. To maintain formation you really had to force this huge airplane around by sheer muscle. All these factors made a successful mission extremely difficult.

Although the British welcomed us cordially enough upon our arrival, they soon came to view us with some disdain. It is not difficult to see how young men in their early twenties, facing death on a daily basis in the skies over Europe, would tend to be somewhat boisterous in their behavior and attempt to wring every last drop of pleasure out of each moment they had to live. These attitudes did not particularly endear us to the British, as they are traditionally much more reserved than we Yanks. In fact, they even went so far as to say that there were only three things about us that they objected to: we were overpaid, oversexed, and over there!

Someone else soon greeted us by radio after our arrival: "Axis Sally."[4] She welcomed the 100th's entry into the European Theater

[4] Editor's note: "Axis Sally" was the nickname of Mildred E. Gellers, an American-born Germanophile who made propaganda broadcasts for the Nazi regime during World War II.

of Operations (ETO) by telling us what a huge mistake we had made in leaving the U.S., and she proceeded to identify our commanding officers by name and hometown and other personal information such as their wives' names, the schools they had attended, etc. All of her broadcasts were intended to flabbergast us and make us think the Germans knew even more about us than we did about ourselves. It was a known fact that when shot down and taken prisoner, we were required by the Geneva Convention to give only name, rank, and serial number. But the Germans never asked for this information, for they quoted these statistics even before questioning started. They also could even cite our individual positions in the formation, targets assigned for that mission, and how many planes had been shot out of the formation. We soon developed a very healthy respect for German intelligence.

The range of the RAF fighter escorts was only about 390 to 400 miles, so we soon accepted the fact that we would be totally on our own soon after crossing the enemy coast. Enemy fighters in relays challenged our formations as we proceeded to the target, and evasive action was nearly impossible while maintaining close formation, which meant that flak from antiaircraft batteries was also a constant threat. The B-17 Flying Fortress was a formidable war machine, but certainly not invincible nor invulnerable to enemy fire. In all, of the 12,731 B-17s built, 4,750 were lost in combat. And while 50 percent more B-24s were built (18,482), the B-17 was still acknowledged as the leading heavy bomber of the U.S. Army Air Forces in the European Theater.

The worst of all, of course, were the German fighters, which had developed a very effective technique of attacking us head-on, straight and level. This enabled the attackers to present us with a smaller target, but it gave them a broader spectrum of the entire, spread-out formation for them to hit. They would then fishtail and try to spray us with rockets as well as incendiary bullets. The tenacity with which they exhibited their intent to divert us or to throw us off the mark was so impressive that you could not help but admire the guts of somebody who would make a frontal attack while we were on the bomb run. They were experts—veterans—at that point, so they were very good. We gained a healthy respect for them very quickly because it was clear that they knew what they were doing as they capitalized on our vulnerability to head-on attacks. Their foremost objective was to try to knock out or sufficiently damage a plane on the periphery of the formation and force it to leave the formation. Then they would pick on it at their leisure.

Flak was almost as hazardous as the fighters. The Germans were getting very, very accurate in fusing their antiaircraft shells so as to explode at the proper altitude. What they would do is lead our airplanes and fire in front of us and, also, because we were staggered at various heights, they attempted to spray our box with explosive shells. Once the shells exploded in black puffs, shrapnel spread in every direction.

When you saw these flak bursts for the first time, you would think, "Well, that's rather interesting. What on earth was that?" And then it dawns on you that these are 88-millimeter shells that are bursting; and you are seeing them, and you may be seeing the last one that you will ever see because it could not only knock out your airplane, but it could go through the plane and catch you. When that shrapnel penetrated the fuselage, it tended to ricochet and go in all directions. It goes through, and you can hear the "PING," and then you can hear all these pieces of shrapnel rattling around. It is like being a target in a shooting gallery.[5]

[5] Editor's note: By the end of 1943 there were over 55,000 light and heavy German antiaircraft guns to combat the Anglo-American air offensive. Seventy-five percent of those weapons were the famous 88-millimeter guns. Most were organized into heavy batteries and concentrated around the most important industrial targets.

Still other dangers awaited us when we finally entered the bombing run. Opening our bomb bay doors created a drag and slowed us down. A B-17 flying at 28,000 feet while fully loaded is literally hanging on its propellers. The air is so thin that the plane is barely able to maintain flight. Therefore, its maneuverability and its speed are reduced almost to slow motion, so you are pretty much a sitting duck.

When our RAF escorts reached the limit of their range, they would return to base, refuel, and try to rendezvous with us as we headed back to England. As soon as the escort fighters left us, the *Luftwaffe* immediately went to work on the fringes of our formations by concentrating on any planes that had experienced mechanical difficulties or had been partially disabled by flak or fighters. A straggler separated from the formation was rather easy pickings.

Our losses began to drop when the 9th Air Force gradually introduced the P-47s [Republic Thunderbolt fighters] and later the P-51s [North American Mustang fighters] as escorts. Then later the development of drop tanks greatly increased their range beyond that of the RAF escorts.

However, due to extremely heavy losses from the very beginning, myth and mystery quickly began to surround the 100th, which then became dubbed "The Bloody 100th." It was something of an unwritten creed of aerial combat (a sort of "gentleman's agreement" among combatants) that if a severely damaged plane was forced out of the formation, it could send a surrender signal by lowering its landing gear. The enemy fighters would then cease firing and escort it to the nearest airfield to land. Some wags soon began to wonder what would happen if the surrender signal were made, and when the fighters left the plane alone, thinking it would land somewhere immediately, the crippled plane then pulled up its gear and scooted for home or maybe even shot down the escort fighters.

Such an occurrence, to my knowledge, has never been documented in fact in our group but, in all probability, was simply cocktail conversation among crewmembers while living it up in some pub. It was also probably natural that, combined with the notorious hard luck of the 100th, people assumed that if such a thing did happen, it would most likely happen with us. Thus, the legend and questionable reputation of "The Bloody 100th" became commonplace.[6]

Certainly, just as many acts of sheer heroism and miraculous escapes occurred in the 100th as in any other group in the ETO, but the spotlight was on the group with the Square D on the tail of its aircraft. Its questionable reputation spread throughout the entire theater and even back to the States like wildfire. In actual fact, the 100th's losses were not the greatest among all the heavy bomber groups throughout the war, but this certainly was the case during the early days of aerial combat in 1943. At that time, the average life of a crew in the "Bloody 100th" was eleven missions, while a completed combat tour was set at twenty-five missions. Of the 388 B-17s assigned to the group during the war, 229 (59 percent) were lost, scrapped, or salvaged (that's 59 percent). This wartime record ranked second only to the 96th Bomb Group, which lost a total of 238 ships.

While the 8th Air Force strove mightily to prove the validity of daylight, high-altitude, precision, formation bombing, we did sustain

---

[6] Editor's note: The legend arose that a plane that had fallen out of formation was about to be attacked by several ME-109s. The plane's pilot allegedly told the co-pilot to drop the landing gear as a sign of surrender. Upon seeing this, three ME-109s slowed their attack and started to escort the bomber to a German airfield. Two ME-109s flew formation with one fighter on each wing, while the third came up just under the tail. After surveying their plight, the pilot ordered the tail gunner and the waist gunners, on his signal, to aim for the cockpits of the fighters and shoot them down. The two fighter pilots flying formation were killed, but the third fighter pilot on the tail escaped since the ball turret could not be maneuvered as quickly as the hand-held waist guns. Then, according to the legend, the word spread throughout the *Luftwaffe* to concentrate especially on attacking planes with the distinctive tail markings of the 100th Bomb Group. This never happened.

disastrous losses. Ultimately, it proved to be a valid strategy given an overwhelmingly large bomber force operating in an eventual environment of absolute air superiority and with fighter escort. Our contention that, with the secret Norden bombsight, we could drop a bomb into a pickle barrel from 30,000 feet was pure fiction and fantasy. Bomb results assessments revealed that we scarcely got 25 percent of our bombs within five miles of the target throughout the war. And the British did no better with their nighttime bombing. Even with round-the-clock bombing of the same target by the RAF at night and the 8th Air Force in daylight, it rarely was rendered more than 30 percent damaged.[7]

[7] Editor's note: From the middle of 1943, the defeat of the German air force became the central Anglo-American objective. Once the Allies had produced ever-increasing numbers of long-range fighters, German airpower could be neutralized permanently. The result was not a single victory, but rather a slow erosion of the enemy's fighting capability.

Aerial bombing affected the German economy both directly and indirectly. Directly, bombing physically reduced the quantity of weapons and equipment produced by German factories; indirectly, the bombing forced the diversion of resources to cope with bombing, resources that German industry could have turned into military hardware. In the last two years of the war, German industrialists had to battle against the endless inconveniences produced by bombing, the interruption of work, the loss of supplies and raw materials, and low morale among the workforce. When Albert Speer and his colleagues met in Berlin to analyze what bombing had done to production schedules for 1944, they found that Germany had produced 35 percent fewer tanks than planned, 31 percent fewer aircraft, and 42 percent fewer trucks and other vehicles as a result of the bombing.

Denying these huge resources to German forces in 1944 greatly weakened their response to bombing and invasion, and facilitated the advancement of Allied armies. The bombing offensive forced the German economy to switch very large resources away from equipment for the fighting fronts, using them instead to combat the bombing threat. By 1944, one-third of all German artillery production consisted of antiaircraft guns; the antiaircraft effort absorbed 20 percent of all ammunition produced. The bombing also depleted Germany's scarce manpower: by 1944, approximately two million Germans were engaged in antiaircraft defense, in repairing damaged factories, and in cleaning up the general destruction. See Richard Overy, *Why the Allies Won* (New York: W.W. Norton, 1995).

I do not wish to horrify people with tales of what it was like to participate in a bombing raid, because there is no way to address adequately the terror and indescribable panic of being attacked by enemy fighters, struggling to stay in formation, dodging the flak, and all the while trying to retain your sanity. Suffice it to say that it was sheer hell. Not knowing when the next burst of gunfire or flak will have your name on it is bad enough, but seeing your comrades go down in flames and realizing that you are still unscathed did not allow you to even rationalize, until you were back at your base. Even with temperatures in the minus 50- to 60-degree Fahrenheit range, you would find yourself perspiring profusely. Many times while under attack, I would find myself thinking: "How in the hell did you ever let yourself get in this predicament?" It was not even uncommon for some fliers to turn white-headed during a particularly stressful mission. This horrendous experience across twenty-five missions turned my hair white at the age of twenty-two. I was not unlike similar victims in my group, who would return from a mission with a patch of gray hair on part of their head. My hair turned completely white, which is pretty indicative, I think, of how frightening that sort of experience is.

In retrospect, one or more missions stand out as being particularly nightmarish. Mine was on my twenty-second mission on October 8, 1943, over Bremen, Germany. Most of the members of the crew I had gone over with had completed their tour and had been rotated back to the States. Since there were not many people on the base (because of our loss ratio) who had flown as many missions as I, that day I was flying with a newly arrived replacement crew on their first baptism of fire. We were leading the last element in the low squadron of the low group in the formation, otherwise known as "Purple Heart Corner."

The city of Bremen was heavily defended and had been bombed repeatedly by the RAF at night and the 8th Air Force by day, but it was still a high-priority target that had sustained relatively little damage.

On that particular raid, we mounted a force of over 600 bombers, and it took over an hour-and-a-half for the entire formation to pass over the target. The flak was so heavy that day that we could almost walk on it, and the *Luftwaffe* was for the very first time actually flying through their own flak to attack us. (Incidentally, the *Official Statistical Summary* of the 8th, 9th, and 15th Air Forces Operations, published in 1945, states, "Of the known causes of American aircraft losses over Europe, 70 percent of the fighters and 55 percent of the bombers were downed by flak.")

Just as we reached the initial point (IP) to turn onto our bomb run, I noticed out of the corner of my eye two German fighters that were definitely targeting our squadron. They were barreling in and heading straight for us from about the eleven o'clock level position. They never deviated. Our gunners were desperately firing at them and may have even killed the pilot of the lead ship, as he did not veer the slightest bit but flew directly into the aircraft in front of me, knocking it out of the formation in a mid-air collision in which both planes exploded. His wingman actually scraped across my top turret as he went by. Almost simultaneously, the group leader and the other squadron leader were shot out of the formation, and of the initial eighteen aircraft in the 100th Bomb Group only six were still flying. Just the same, we bombed the target, rallied the remaining forces, and headed for home.

My ship had lost an engine, and we were slowed down considerably but managed to tack onto a formation of B-17s that was coming along behind us in the bomber stream. The nose of my aircraft—the Plexiglas—had been penetrated, and very cold air came rushing through. The temperature at that altitude was anywhere from minus fifty degrees to minus sixty degrees Fahrenheit, and my feet became frostbitten. Both were on the rudder pedals, and even with the fleece-lined boots, my feet froze. I was actually using the rudder pedals with my heels since my toes were frozen.

But I got all six remaining planes back to the base. My plane was the last to land. Since I was unable to walk, they carried me from the plane and hospitalized me. I was, in fact, unable to walk for ten days while they had my feet packed in ice. After ten days of hospitalization, I was able to walk with a cane. I hobbled around, but it was very painful.

The mission was the beginning of the "Black Week" for the 100th and contributed mightily to its reputation as "The Bloody 100th." The next day, October 9, we bombed Marienberg and lost nearly half the formation. The following day, October 10, the group went to Münster, and the 100th lost twelve aircraft with only one crew returning to base.

I know that in the ensuing years many people have asked me how I felt about killing women and children with the bombs that I was responsible for dropping, and I have to tell you that I did not think about it. That was war, and it was inconsequential, really, what my conscience dictated. I had no control over what targets were selected, and I had only limited control over where the bombs struck. I was striving for survival, and so were the other members of the crew; so if we were successful in living through it while performing our mission, that is what we were there for, and that is what we did. Therefore, so far as my conscience is concerned, I must truthfully admit that it was not really much on my mind, if at all.

To have flown and completed a combat tour with "The Bloody 100th" and to come out unscathed was, in the final analysis, just pure luck. Why one's friends and comrades are lost and you are spared is always a mystery and source of wonderment. My only physical injury was frostbitten feet. We were not heroes. I think it is a grave mistake to say that we were heroes. We were survivors. It was the luck-of-the-draw that we survived. It was not because of sheer skill. It was just that we were lucky enough to have survived that horrible experience.

I do not deny that it was a scary time. I was scared spitless the whole time I was flying in combat, but I did it.

Others were not so fortunate. In fact, of the forty members of my class from flying school who went to the 100th, only four completed a combat tour. As one of those four, I have quite naturally been known as "Lucky" ever since. Given the miraculous nature of my experience, I truly think I should be called "Extra Lucky."

Section II
WORLD WAR II—PACIFIC

The Japanese attack at Pearl Harbor marked the entry of the United States into World War II. A determined president and a newly united nation pledged to pursue the war in the Pacific until the final capitulation of the Japanese enemy. This section presents three papers that cover the gamut of warfare experiences from the young Marine radio operator participating in a series of bloody landings on Pacific islands to the B-29 navigator who participated in the strategic bombing campaign against the Japanese homeland to a historian who analyzes the decision to drop the atomic bomb on Japan.

Roy Appleton was a carefree college student at the University of Texas when the war began. He and a high school buddy decided to enlist in the Marine Corps after viewing the film, *Wake Island*. Thus began a long journey that took him to basic training, the Aleutian Islands, Tarawa, Saipan, Tinian, and Iwo Jima. His story is a personal one that includes the noise, emotions, and even the odors of combat. Appleton's story typifies that of thousands of young men who served in all theaters and forged a tradition of service to the nation.

David Braden also left the academic life of a college student to join the U. S. Army Air Forces Reserve. He was soon activated and trained as a navigator with a B-29 crew in the Pacific. Braden was assigned to a bomb group on the island of Saipan, recently liberated by the Marines mentioned in the paragraph above. Lieutenant Braden came to respect the vastness and dangers of flight over the Pacific. His crew ditched in heavy seas once and also made four emergency landings on Iwo Jima. His service as an airman is further testimony to the linkage between the Marines, who captured Iwo Jima, and the airmen, who were saved by the emergency landing facilities there.

These fields were won at a great price in Marine blood. Lieutenant Braden finally received his "welcome home" parade at a ceremony sponsored by the Admiral Nimitz Museum in Fredericksburg, Texas, in 1995, a touching end to a poignant story of gallantry and sacrifice.

Finally, Dr. Robert Divine from the University of Texas analyzes the decisions that surrounded the use of the atomic bomb on Hiroshima and Nagasaki in August 1945. Few political-military decisions in history have been discussed as much as President Harry Truman's decision to employ this revolutionary weapon. Divine meticulously examines the factors that went into Truman's decision. U.S. leaders were driven by the primary goal of ending the conflict as soon as possible with the least loss of American life. Divine concludes that Truman acted properly in employing the bomb, which swiftly brought World War II to an end. His paper emphasizes the critical interaction of political, diplomatic, and military factors used to achieve final victory over Japan. The bombing of Hiroshima and Nagasaki gave mankind a vivid look at the horrendous destruction of nuclear war, and, as Professor Divine notes, "Their suffering helped to keep the Cold War cold." This introduction to the nuclear age changed warfare forever.

AMERICAN ADVANCE ACROSS THE PACIFIC, 1942-45

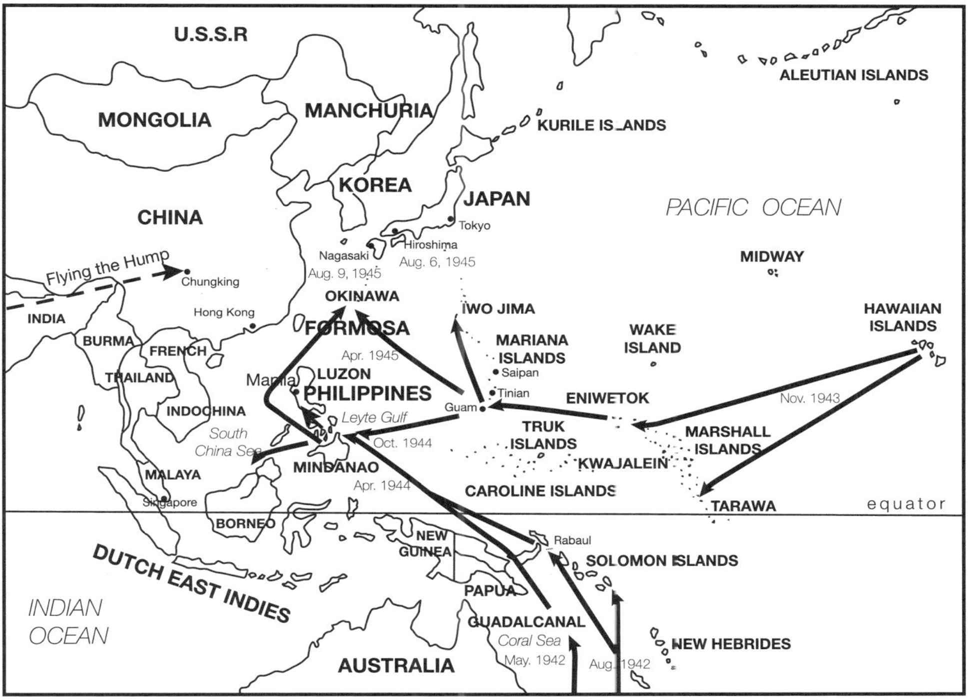

CORPORAL ROY APPLETON, JR. (USMCR)

AN ENLISTED MARINE'S PERSPECTIVE ON THE PACIFIC WAR

Roy Appleton, Jr., was a seventeen-year-old freshman at the University of Texas when he decided to enlist in the Marine Corps in October 1942. After completion of Marine boot camp at San Diego Recruit Depot, he was assigned to Headquarters Company, Signal Battalion, 5th Amphibious Corps, and put into a new outfit, JASCO (Joint Assault Communications Company). He subsequently participated in or observed five Marine landings.

After a brief stint at Kiska, Aleutian Islands, he was sent to New Zealand to join the 3rd Battalion, 8th Marines, 2nd Marine Division, which was making preparations for the upcoming invasion of Tarawa, Gilbert Islands, in November 1943. He still served with Signal Battalion, 5th Amphibious Corps, and subsequently participated in the invasion of Iwo Jima in February 1945. This account thus deals with his direct combat experiences in both of those operations as well as his observations of the abortive landing at Kiska and the fighting for Saipan and Tinian in the Mariana Islands.

After his discharge in November 1945, Appleton resumed his education at the North Texas State College (now the

University of North Texas) in Denton. Upon graduating, he found employment with the local newspaper, the *Denton Record-Chronicle*, starting out in classified advertising sales. He advanced through the newspaper's ranks, becoming head of advertising in 1951, general manager in 1958, vice-president in 1960, and president in 1988. He retired as president in 1991.

Over the years, Appleton has been heavily involved in civic affairs. He served as president of the Denton Chamber of Commerce, which gave him the Otis Fowler Award, its highest civic honor. In 1989 he was honored as a distinguished alumnus by the University of North Texas.

In September 1942, my best friend from high school and I enrolled at the University of Texas as music majors. In October of the same year, after we had seen the movie *Wake Island*, we decided to join the Marines. I was seventeen; he was eighteen.[1]

Following boot camp in San Diego, my friend was assigned to the Marine base band, while I was sent to radio operators school. Upon graduation, I was assigned to Headquarters Company, Signal Battalion, 5th Amphibious Corps, and put in a new outfit called JASCO [Joint Assault Communications Company]. This assignment opened the door to an exciting adventure for a Texas teenager anxious to see the world.

In June 1943, fifteen of us from JASCO were sent by train to Nanimo, British Columbia, on Vancouver Island. There we were sent to units of the Canadian Army, and in my case I was attached to the Winnipeg Grenadiers. Working in three-man teams (a naval officer and two radiomen), we were to land with the assault waves on Kiska Island [Aleutians, Alaska], set up observation posts, and direct naval shelling in support of the ground troops.

[1] Editor's note: Mr. Appleton presented this paper to the UNT Military History Seminar on September 10, 1994.

The Japanese had evacuated Kiska in a dense fog, and the island had been secured without a fight, except for one. The first night ashore, before anyone knew the Japanese were gone, and in the heavy fog that was common on the island, we battled the U.S. Army troops, who had landed on the other side. There were casualties on both sides, but we were never told how many.

The Canadian units we joined were part of the Canadian Home Guard. By Canadian law, the Home Guard could not be sent overseas. The Canadian government said Kiska was *not* overseas, but the Home Guard thought otherwise. These troops also thought that the U.S. had created the problem by urging Canadian participation in the landing; and since we were Americans, they focused their anger on the fifteen of us. As a result, during our stay in Nanimo, we were issued side arms for our protection and required to stay out of the camp from before reveille until taps each day. The Canadians were restricted to camp around-the-clock. We thought this was a great joke until we stopped at Adak Island [Aleutians] for maneuvers on the way to Kiska and found ourselves spotting for the Canadian artillery. We kept waiting for a short round. Fortunately, none came.

On the ship returning to San Diego, we were directed to proceed to New Zealand by the fastest available transportation to join the 2nd Marine Division. The fastest available transportation turned out to be a carrier and three destroyers headed for Wellington, New Zealand. That trip showed me just how big the Pacific Ocean is and how much water there is between the Aleutians and New Zealand. On arrival at the 2nd Marine Division base in New Zealand, we were split among the various units. I was assigned to the 3rd Battalion, 8th Marines.

We sailed from Wellington with the 2nd Division. After a stop for maneuvers at Efate, New Hebrides, we received orders to head for an island named Betio, which is part of the Tarawa Atoll.[2] Briefings emphasized that the heaviest shelling and bombing attacks in history would take place before we arrived and that it was very likely that there would be few, if any, of the 5,000 Imperial Japanese Marines left by the time we landed.[3]

---

[2] Editor's note: Betio was less than three miles long, no broader than 800 yards at its widest point, and contained no natural elevation higher than ten feet above sea level. According to Marine observers, every place on the island could be covered by direct rifle and machine gun fire. Concrete and steel tetrahedrons, minefields, and long strings of double-apron barbed wire protected the beach approaches. The Japanese also built a barrier wall of logs and coral around much of the island. Tank traps protected heavily fortified command bunkers and firing positions inland from the beach. Pillboxes, nearly 500 of them, were everywhere, and most were fully covered by logs, steel plates, and sand. The Japanese on Betio were equipped with 8-inch, turret-mounted naval rifles (the so-called "Singapore guns" because they had allegedly been salvaged after the fall of that island and emplaced on Betio), as well as a large number of heavy-caliber coast defense, anti-boat, and field artillery guns and howitzers. Complementing the defensive weaponry were dual-purpose 13-millimeter heavy machine guns, light tanks (mounting 37-millimeter guns), 50-millimeter "knee" mortars, and an abundance of 7.7-milimeter light machine guns.

[3] Editor's note: The term "Imperial Marines" is not quite accurate as a description for these naval personnel, who were actually ground soldiers. The correct name for these troops was Japanese Special Naval Landing Forces (SNLF). Despite their relatively small numbers, they comprised a significant augmentation of the Japanese combat capabilities on land. After August 1942, the SNLF were almost exclusively involved in defensive fighting, holding various island outposts against the growing U.S. offensive.

Perhaps the most famous defensive stand by the SNLF came at Tarawa Atoll in November 1943. Here there were no Japanese army troops, only the 1,497 men of the 7th Sasebo SNLF, and a little more than 1,100 members of the 3rd Special Base Unit (formerly the 6th Yokosuka SNLF). With more than 100 machine guns pointed at the Marine landing beaches and fifty artillery pieces of various sizes supporting them, the SNLF withstood a ferocious bombardment and still emerged to inflict one of the worst bloodbaths in U.S. Marine Corps history. The SNLF was organized to conduct an overall decisive defense at the beach. More than 3,000 Marines became casualties before the vicious fighting was over. The SNLF earned grudging respect from the Marines for their esprit, discipline, marksmanship, proficiency with heavy weapons, small-unit leadership, bravery, and stoic willingness to die to the last man.

Later, it occurred to me that in all briefings before battles, the troops we would be fighting were described either as Marines, Imperial Marines, or Japan's "best fighters." I suppose this was to help our egos. There was even some speculation as to whether Tarawa would still be afloat by D-Day. It was and the Japanese were still there.

For my indoctrination into combat, I could not have had better teachers than the men who comprised the 2nd Marine Division in 1943. They were hardened veterans of the fighting at Guadalcanal and Tulagi and had been overseas for more than a year. Many had malaria, and most had developed a fatalism that made them appear fearless. Perhaps, most importantly, they had developed great confidence in themselves, in their outfit, and in the Corps. They were disdainful of the Army, the Navy, the Japanese, and just about everyone else. Many of them did not expect to get home alive.[4]

They took great pride in a story, which I now believe was untrue, that early in the war while making an inspection trip to the South Pacific front for her husband, First Lady Eleanor Roosevelt had said that after visiting the Marines on Guadalcanal she believed that when the war was over all Marines should be sent to an island off the mainland, where they could be re-civilized before they were discharged.

I will turn once more to the fighting on Tarawa, which I would describe as "bedlam." The dictionary defines bedlam as a "place of noise and confusion." If you add the words "with a terrible odor," you have a perfect description of the place.

Luckily, the coxswain of the boat I was in managed to get us to the end of a smoldering coconut log pier that extended 500 yards from

[4] Editor's note: The commander of the 2nd Marine Division was Major General Julian Smith. His utmost concern when he assumed command on May 1, 1943, was the physical condition of his troops. The division had redeployed to New Zealand from Guadalcanal with nearly 13,000 cases of malaria. Half the division would have to be replaced for the Tarawa campaign.

shore and just beyond the reef. We crawled from the boat to the cross braces, in the water, under the end of the pier. Firing from all types of weapons seemed to come from every direction. The water all around was peppered as though it was raining. Shells from our cruisers and destroyers were passing overhead toward the Japanese emplacements, and Navy planes were bombing and strafing Japanese machine gun nests in an old burned-out hulk of a Japanese freighter a few hundred yards to our right.[5]

Eventually, our team made it to the beach, where the confusion was even greater. Units were separated, officers were dead or missing, equipment and weapons had been lost in the surf. We spent the first night in a hole at the base of a three-foot-high coconut seawall, about twelve or fifteen feet from the water's edge. That was our beachhead perimeter.[6] Fortunately for us, the Japanese did not counterattack during the first night. If they had, the outcome would have been in question.

Next morning, we went over the wall and moved about forty or fifty yards inland. All around us things began to get better organized. Our job on Tarawa was to direct close air support: strafing and low-level bombing. The naval fliers did a remarkable job, especially considering the close quarters and the troop congestion. Betio was less than 300 acres in size, yet there were 5,000 Japanese and Koreans and nearly 17,000 Marines fighting on it.

After seventy-six hours, the battle was over. Only seventeen wounded Japanese and 129 Korean laborers of the 5,000-man garrison survived. The Marines had 990 killed and 2,296 wounded.

---

[5] Editor's note: Located in the sector that the Marine command designated as Red Beach No. 2 was a pier 1,000 yards long that jutted due north over a fringing reef into deep lagoon waters. It was an attractive logistics target for the Marines. In addition, many of the landing troops sought refuge under the pier to escape the withering Japanese fire.

[6] Editor's note: Constructed of vertical coconut logs driven into the ground, sandbags, coral blocks, and concrete, and laced with rifle pits, the seawall was approximately three to four feet high and was located almost on the water's edge.

The smell I referred to earlier came from the growing number of bodies, bloating on the ground and in the water, under the equatorial sun. By the end of the first day, the odor was bad; by the third day, it was overpowering and unforgettable. To this day, when I see a picture of Tarawa, I smell it. It was not until the final hours of battle, when the few remaining Japanese had been pushed to the east end of the island, that a bulldozer could dig trenches to begin taking care of the dead.

Another sight and sound of combat that I first experienced on Tarawa, and have never forgotten, was the nightly sound of flares as they rose, like roman candle balls, and then made their distinctive "plop" noise as the small parachute opened and began the slow descent to the ground, casting a blue-gray light that always reminded me of the artificial moonlight towers that the city of Austin had installed.

On the way back from Tarawa to Hawaii, I heard another sound for the first time that has also remained with me. It was the sound of the canvas-wrapped bodies of the wounded Marines who had died on board hitting the water as they were buried at sea.

Saipan and Tinian [both in the Mariana Islands] were entirely different experiences for me. I was assigned to the command ship *Rocky Mount*. Our job was to handle radio circuits between the V Amphibious Corps Headquarters aboard ship and the troop commanders ashore. It was nice to participate in a landing operation and still have hot meals, hot showers, and a good bunk. But, I will admit, I suffered from guilt as I sent and received messages to and from the guys ashore. Two or three times, I managed to hitch a ride ashore with some of the small boats running back and forth between the ship and the beach just to see how the guys were doing.

It was during this operation, from aboard the *Rocky Mount*, that Maj. Gen. Holland Smith, the V Amphibious Corps commander, relieved Maj. Gen. Ralph Smith of his command of the U.S. Army's

27th Infantry Division. This was done because the 27th was not moving fast enough up the center of the island, thus exposing the flanks of the 2nd and 4th Marine Divisions on either side of the 27th. After the war I learned that this action caused trouble for Holland Smith back in the States. But it made him even more of a hero with the Marines on Saipan. Among the troops he was known as "Howling Mad" Smith, and there were many stories about him. One said that he had come up through the ranks and had taken thirteen years to make private first class. I do not believe that one is true.[7]

Saipan was declared secure on July 9, 1944. It had taken twenty-four days. The casualties included 30,000 Japanese dead, 2,382 Marines dead and 8,769 Marines wounded, 1,059 Army dead and 2,696 Army wounded.

Tinian was declared secure on August 1, 1944. It had taken eight days. The casualties included 4,500 Japanese dead, 416 Marines dead and 1,735 wounded.

With Tinian secured, our group transferred to another ship and went to Guam [also in the Marianas] to set up a radio station in preparation for a move of V Amphibious Corps Headquarters from Pearl Harbor to Guam. We arrived at Agana about August 10, the date the island was declared secure. Sniper fire was still very heavy. In fact, mopping-up operations on Guam continued well into 1945.

The natives welcomed us with open arms and big smiles. It was the closest thing that we experienced to what the GIs in Europe must

---

[7] Editor's note: Born in 1882, Holland M. Smith graduated from Alabama Polytechnic Institute in 1901 and earned his bachelor's of law degree from the University of Alabama in 1903. After practicing law in Montgomery for two years he left the practice in 1905 to enlist in the USMC and receive a direct commission as a second lieutenant. During his forty-six-year career in the Marine Corps, his service included sea duty, expeditionary service from the Philippines to Haiti, and combat in World War I. He is sometimes called "the father of modern U.S. amphibious warfare" and was one of the top commanders in the Pacific during World War II.

have seen when they liberated a city. We were invited to several parties in homes near where we began radio operations. After a few weeks, we were suddenly ordered back to Pearl Harbor, and the V Amphibious Corps move was cancelled.

Something should be said about life aboard ship. Troopships moved very slowly—the Liberty ships usually moved at about six to eight knots—and considering the great distances traveled, the troops could be aboard for two or three weeks at a time. Actually, most troops spent much more time aboard ship, going and coming, than they did ashore during the battles. Conditions were usually crowded. Bunks consisted of canvas stretched on steel pipe frames. They were usually stacked four or five high, with two to three feet of space between a Marine and the guy sleeping above him. They were located in the hold of the ship. Outside air was blown in from vents on deck, and there were usually a few electric fans inside trying to stir the air. It was always hot and stuffy. Showers were saltwater. Chow was usually served in mess halls, where you stood and ate off waist-high tables. Dungarees were washed, when possible, by tying them to long ropes and letting them drag off the fantail of the ship.

Because of the need for total blackout at night, most troops spent the day on the deck and the nights in the hold. Boredom was a problem. When and where possible, duties were assigned such as radio watch, gun watch in the antiaircraft turrets, chipping paint, or painting the bulkheads. Of course, there were always the never-ending, round-the-clock card games: pinochle, bridge, and poker. Some Marines read, some cleaned and re-cleaned their weapons, and many slept.

For the Iwo Jima operation, I was going ashore again. After a brief stop at Saipan, we joined the largest number of ships off the coast of Iwo that I had ever seen. In pre-landing briefings, we were told again about the number of tons of shells and bombs that were going to be used to soften up the Japanese before we landed. This time I do not think anyone was much impressed. D-Day was February 19, 1945, and within minutes of the first wave approaching the beach, it became clear that the bombing and shelling had not helped much here, either.

The enemy was not my biggest worry as I awaited orders to go ashore. I had been assigned to drive a four-wheel-drive truck with a radio station in the back. The truck was pulling a trailer with a gasoline generator mounted on it. I was to get it ashore, find a spot in the narrow neck of the island between Mount Suribachi and Airfield No. 1, and get it in operation.[8] To get to that area, I needed to drive the truck off the boat ramp, then up a high and steep embankment of deep, loose sand. Reports were saying the troops were having difficulty getting up the embankment on foot. Still, my biggest problem was that I didn't know how to drive the truck. Back home I had never had the opportunity to learn to drive. In Hawaii, by watching others, and by trial and error, I had managed to drive a Jeep a few times, but this was different. The problem kept my mind off the fighting.

It was the fourth day before enough of a beachhead had been established to begin landing some of the heavier equipment. Finally, my time came. In the ship's hold, I had gotten some tutoring in how to shift the gears and how to double-clutch. When the ramp of the LCT dropped, I could see that someone had placed steel mesh plates on the sand. I hit the gas, and with a lot of pushing and shoving and the grinding of a few gears, we made it. I found a low spot among some piles of rubble that would give some protection, and I got the radio going.

I don't know if the Japanese were homing in on our transmitter or not, but the next few days were among the most frightening I had

[8] Editor's note: American objectives on Iwo Jima included the seizure of three Japanese airfields, designated as Airfield No.1, Airfield No. 2, and Airfield No. 3. These airfields were to be repaired and refurbished as quickly as possible by the Seabees so that they could be used as safe havens for fighters and bombers damaged during the bombing raids over Japan proper.

experienced. During that time, we were subjected to heavy shelling by artillery and heavy mortars on a regular basis. Tarawa and Guam had shown me that you can adjust to being shot at, but I had a difficult time adjusting to sustained shelling when I did not know where or when the next one was going to land. To me it was more frightening at night when you were trying to sleep, and a couple of times, with shells hitting within a few feet in all directions, I was introduced to bouts of uncontrollable shakes.

During this time, I was assigned a Navajo code talker. The Navajo have no written language, and we were told that few, if any, outside the tribe could speak it. With a talker on each end of the circuit, you could give the Navajo with you a message, and he would talk to the Navajo on the other end in the tribal language and give you an answer in English.[9] Later, when the occupation of Japan began, we occupied the radio station at the Japanese Naval Academy in Sasebo. The Japanese staff was very curious about the new code we had started using near the end of the war. They said it totally confused them. I did

[9] Editor's note: The Navajo code talkers took part in every assault the U.S. Marines conducted in the Pacific from 1942-1945. They transmitted messages by telephone and radio in their native language: a code that the Japanese never broke. In May 1942, the first twenty-nine Navajo recruits attended boot camp, and then at Camp Pendleton this first group created the Navajo code. They developed a dictionary and numerous words for military terms. The dictionary and all code words had to be memorized during training. Once a Navajo code talker had completed his training, he was sent to a Marine unit deployed in the Pacific Theater. The code talkers' primary job was to talk, transmitting information on tactics and troop movements, orders, and other vital battlefield communications over telephones and radios. They also acted as messengers and performed general Marine duties.

At Iwo Jima, Major Howard Connor, 5th Marine Division signal officer, declared, "Were it not for the Navajos, the Marines would never have taken Iwo Jima." Connor had six Navajo code talkers working around-the-clock during the first two days of the battle. Those six received or sent over 800 messages, all without error.

As of 1945, about 540 Navajos served as Marines. The Japanese, who were skilled code breakers, remained baffled by the Navajo language.

not learn until recently that the young Navajos had volunteered, as a group, to help with the war effort. I believe they should have received more recognition for their help.

Near the end of February, as the enemy was pushed back from Airfield No. 1, I was given a new assignment. It was to take a smaller radio in a Jeep to whatever line unit I was directed to each day, so that Corps could have direct communications with field commanders as they prepared for pushes along the line.

On March 8, I finally got to the 24th Marines [4th Marine Division], my high school buddy's outfit. I arrived about five in the afternoon and learned that he had been killed that morning just before noon. As a musician, he was serving as a Jeep ambulance driver and had been hit by a mortar.

I have other lingering memories of Iwo Jima. First, I remember the prevailing smell of sulphur. It was years before I learned that much of Japan's sulphur was mined on the island.[10] In fortifying the island for the war, they had made use of many of the mineshafts and tunnels, some as deep as seven stories. It was a mystery at the time, but easy to see now why it was seldom, if ever, that any Japanese activity was seen above ground. It also explains why the island had to be taken a

[10] Editor's note: Iwo Jima means "Sulphur Island" in Japanese. As the island was described by one Imperial Army staff officer, the place was "an island of sulphur, no water, no sparrow, no swallow." Less poetic American officers saw Iwo's resemblance to a pork chop, with the 556-foot dormant volcano Mount Suribachi dominating the narrow southern end, overlooking the only potential landing beaches. It was an ugly, barren, foul-smelling chunk of volcanic rock barely ten square miles in size. Wreathed in volcanic steam, the twisted landscape appeared ungodly, almost moon-like. More than one surviving Marine compared the island to something out of Dante's *Inferno*. With steep cliffs and canyons to the north, which were dotted with caves, it was a defender's dream. Iwo's volcanic sand mixed readily with concrete for installations, and the soft rock lent itself to rapid digging. Masked gun positions provided interlocking fields of fire, miles of tunnels linked key defensive positions, and every cave featured multiple outlets and ventilation tubes.

few yards at a time by flamethrowers, satchel charges, grenades, and bulldozers sealing up caves and tunnels.

The second memory is the sight of the first crippled B-29 side-slipping in for an emergency landing on Airfield No. 1 while the fighting was still going on. I happened to have my radio set up alongside the runway, and I saw the plane landing and watched as the crew jumped from the plane, fell on their stomachs, and kissed the ground.[11]

A third memory is the moonscape appearance of the island's surface. The sand was black, and there were no buildings or vegetation standing. What, if anything, that had been there had been burned or blown away. It was a totally desolate, gloomy landscape of rocks, ravines, rubble, sand, and crevices.

Iwo Jima was declared secure on March 25, 1945. On March 26, the Japanese made their final desperate *banzai* charge on a bivouac area near Airfield No. 1.[12] The operation had taken thirty-five days. The casualties included 22,000 Japanese dead, 5,527 Marines dead, and 23,697 Marines wounded.

On V-J Day, with the PA systems throughout the ship broadcasting the celebrating going on in New York and other cities stateside, we were pulling out of Wailuku, Maui, Hawaii, headed toward Japan for

---

[11] Editor's note: As mentioned previously, crippled B-29s flew in from Honshu. The capture of Iwo Jima served to increase the operating range, payload, and survival rate of the bombers and their crews.

[12] Editor's note: During the night of March 25 (D + 34), a force of 300 Japanese took all night to move into position around the island's vulnerable rear base area, the tents occupied by the newly arrived Army pilots of the VII Fighter Command, adjacent to Airfield No. 1. The Japanese achieved total surprise, falling on the sleeping pilots out of the darkness with swords, grenades, and automatic weapons. The fighting was as vicious and bloody as any that occurred in Iwo Jima's many arenas. The surviving pilots and members of the 5th Pioneer Battalion improvised a skirmish line and launched a counterattack. Seabees and elements of the redeploying 28th Marines joined the fray. Sunrise revealed an awful carnage: 300 dead Japanese, more than 100 slain pilots, Seabees, and pioneers, and another 200 Americans wounded.

occupation duty. After sailing down the long, narrow harbor to the docks at Sasebo, and seeing the fortifications that had been built and were still being built, I was thankful that the war had ended.

Since joining the Marines, I had never had a furlough, never been home, and, other than a couple weekend passes, had had no time off. When orders came to leave for Japan, especially since Japan had surrendered, I was discouraged and talked to my company commander about it. He told me that the quickest way home would be through Japan, and he was right. A few weeks after arrival at Sasebo, the point system for discharge was announced, and I had more than enough points to be among the first out.

There were eleven of the original JASCO group with me on the way home, and throughout the long trip to San Diego, we spent hours planning a pre-discharge party. It was to be held at a well-known San Diego nightclub, and it was going to be the party to end all parties. Ironically, when the day came and we arrived at the entrance to the club, the Shore Patrol checked our IDs and would not let me in. I was not twenty-one. I spent the evening at the movies.

On November 9, 1945, I received my discharge: thirty-seven months and four days from the day I enlisted. As I walked out of the gates at the San Diego Marine Base, I put my hand over my heart and thanked God for bringing me home safely. I made a promise in return that as long as I lived, I would never again sleep on the ground or spend a night in any place where there was not a flush commode. To date, I have not broken that promise.

1ST LIEUTENANT DAVID R. BRADEN (USAAC)

B-29 OPERATIONS AGAINST JAPAN: A SURVIVOR'S STORY

Born in Dallas, Texas, in 1924, David Braden was a freshman aeronautical engineering major at North Texas Agricultural College when the Japanese attacked Pearl Harbor. Shortly thereafter, he enlisted in the U.S. Army Air Forces Reserve, a program that allowed him to stay in school until called to active duty. His call came in February 1943. Much to his disappointment, he was designated for navigator training rather than pilot training due to vision problems. Nevertheless, he quickly adapted, finishing in the top 10 percent of his class and then going forward to qualify as a radar bombardier.

On January 28, 1945, Braden's B-29 landed on Saipan, Mariana Islands, with the first replacement crew for the 870th Bomb Squadron, 497th Bomb Group, 73rd Bomb Wing, 20th Air Force. During his thirty-five missions, Braden participated in the incendiary raids on Japanese cities in March 1945. As a result of damage caused by enemy fire, his planes made one crash landing at sea and four emergency landings on Iwo Jima.

After the war, Braden graduated from the University of Texas with a degree in architecture. He eventually formed his own firm in Dallas and established a national practice. After forty-two years, he retired from his firm in 1991 and began a term as chairman of the board of the Dallas-Fort Worth International Airport.

I graduated from advanced aerial navigation school in June 1944 at Selman Field in Monroe, Louisiana. I was nineteen years old and a brand-new second lieutenant in the U.S. Army Air Forces. My first act, due to that "substantial" increase in pay and responsibility, was to subscribe to *Time* magazine so that I could be better informed about the events of the war. In 1994, I realized that I had been a *Time* subscriber for fifty years and was still not really informed about the events of my war years and, sadly enough, was still receiving the magazine with a mailing label addressed to "2nd Lieutenant David R. Braden." This had become embarrassing, because everyone who saw this commented: "Fifty years, and this guy was never promoted!"[1]

One night at a cocktail party, I met a young lady who worked for *Time* in New York City. I said, "Look, I would like a promotion. After fifty years, I should at least be a colonel by now, like all those people in the Confederate Air Force." We laughed, and I forgot all about it. But a month later, I looked at my label—just by accident—and my *Time* was now addressed to "General David R. Braden." I tell you this in order that you may have more respect for the depth of this presentation. After all, the insights of a general do offer more than those of a teenaged lieutenant.

On graduation, I received orders to report to Boca Raton, Florida, to a radar bombing school. There I learned that I had been handpicked for assignment to the combat crew of a B-29, an airplane I had never seen. The only thing I knew about the B-29 bomber was that, like my

[1] Editor's note: Mr. Braden presented this paper at the UNT Military History Seminar on October 7, 1995.

radar training, it was top-secret. In eighteen months, I had never seen one at any airfield where I had a training assignment. I only knew that it was special.

On completion of my radar schooling, I was given the Army Air Forces occupational designation, called "MOS," of navigator-radar bombardier-gunner and was assigned to the flight crew of Lt. Norman Westervelt's plane. I was sent to Clovis, New Mexico, for combat crew training prior to overseas assignment.

There I learned that the B-29 was indeed a special plane, and the men who flew them were special, too. Our head men [first pilots] were called airplane commanders, and they were all extremely experienced multi-engine aircraft instructors or veterans of European combat on their second tour of duty. The usual co-pilot was called the pilot. The navigators, bombardiers, flight engineers, and pilots were all commissioned officers. The flight engineers had in-depth training about the operation and maintenance of this high-performance aircraft. All other members of the crew were staff sergeants. There were four gunners, a radio operator, and a radar operator. They had all graduated in the top 10 percent of their training classes. Eleven in all made up the crew.

Among the many things that made the B-29 significant was its size. The largest bomber of World War II, it was surpassed at that time only by Howard Hughes's *Spruce Goose*, which never really flew. The design for this plane began in 1940, and in May 1941, the U.S. Army Air Corps ordered 250, at a cost of $630,000 per plane. It was not designed specifically for atomic missions, but rather for load and distance. It was powered by four piston engines—Wright R-3350 Cyclones—and was ninety-nine feet long and had a wingspan of 141 feet. It also had a tricycle landing gear. Its top speed was about 350 miles per hour at 25,000 feet, and its cruising speed was 220 to 250 miles per hour. It could fly as high as 35,000 feet, and it could carry ten tons of bombs in its two bomb bays—five times the bomb load of the B-17—and 7,000 rounds of .50-caliber ammunition for a distance of 3,200 miles, along with its crew of eleven. It had a remote-controlled, four-turret gun system of ten .50-caliber machine guns, and there were two more machine guns and one 20-millimeter cannon in the tail. This defensive armament was operated by computer-controlled electronic sights, which could be operated simultaneously by a single central fire control gunner or transferred to gunners in other locations by him. The cabins fore and aft were pressurized and connected by a tunnel tube across the top of the bomb bays, which had fast-action hydraulic doors that would open or close in seven-tenths of a second.

We were definitely in a class by ourselves. This was so much so that to protect the secrets of our weaponry, we were required to wear side arms on our training flights in the U.S. in order to mount a twenty-four-hour guard for the plane in case of an emergency landing, which could only be made at designated airfields.

Production of the B-29 had begun in earnest in January 1944, and in April the first wing was formed. The 58th Bomb Wing moved to a base in India in June 1944, the same month I was commissioned, and flew its shakedown mission to bomb the railway shops at Bangkok, Thailand.

In the meantime, the Marines had invaded and secured Saipan, Tinian, and Guam [Marianas Islands] by August 1944. From the Marianas, the 20th Air Force could attack the Japanese home islands with its B-29s. The 73rd Bomb Wing, then training at bases in Kansas, was poised to be the first unit based in the Marianas. Personnel from the 73rd began their move to Isley Field on Saipan in July 1944. Two 9,000-foot runways were under construction, and living conditions were very rough.

The 58th Bomb Wing, still based in India, was flying gasoline and bombs over "The Hump" [Himalaya Mountains] to forward bases in Chengtu, China, to support the bombing of the Japanese home islands. The runways for this base were hand-built by 20,000 Chinese coolies. The use of B-29s as tankers to fly fuel over "The Hump" was a logistical nightmare. It took two gallons of aviation fuel to deliver one gallon. Against a headwind, it sometimes took twelve gallons to deliver one. Added to the fact that little of a true strategic value had been accomplished, it is easy to see why this entire operation was abandoned as ineffective and too expensive. In January 1945, the 58th Bomb Wing packed up lock, stock, and barrel and moved to Tinian after only seven missions to Japan.

Meanwhile, on Saipan, the 73rd flew its first mission on November 24, 1944. General [Emmett] "Rosie" O'Donnell and Major [Robert] "Memphis Belle" Morgan led eighty-eight planes on this mission. Only twenty-four of the eighty-eight B-29s reached the primary target and bombed from 24,000 feet. Fifty-nine enemy fighters attacked. Two enemy aircraft were destroyed, and one B-29 was lost. The results were poor, a preview of things to come on high-altitude raids. Nobody knew about the jet stream, which could reach 200 miles an hour and sometimes more. The standard approach to the target was from downwind, so with the airplane going approximately 500 to 600 miles an hour, the Norden bombsight could not keep up with the airspeed. Even if the crews had good visual bombing conditions, they could not hit specific targets. It was frustrating to go through all that and not to be able to hit the target. This was typical of all high-altitude missions.

In Clovis, New Mexico, our crew finished combat crew training, and in December 1944 we picked up a brand-new B-29 at Kearney, Nebraska: *The Padded Cell.* In January 1945 we flew it to Saipan, where we were assigned to the 73rd Bomb Wing of the 20th Air Force. A wing comprised four bomb groups. The 73rd Bomb Wing consisted of the 497th, the 498th, the 499th, and the 500th bomb groups. A group had three squadrons of thirty planes. There were ten planes and 110 fliers in a squadron. In total, a wing had 120 planes.

The 73rd was the only bomb wing based on Saipan. We were the first replacement crew sent to our squadron, the 870th. When we arrived late in the day, we were assigned to a Quonset hut and, literally, to the cots of men who had been lost the previous day in a raid on Tokyo. The 497th Bomb Group had lost five aircraft, including three from our squadron. Almost one-third of this squadron, which had trained and flown together for months, had been wiped out in a single mission. A pall hung over all the personnel, especially in our Quonset hut. But then, as is the case with soldiers, we accepted our fate, and our crew—the new guys—were accepted and welcomed as members of the team.

Our first mission, in early February 1945, was a taste of things to come. We flew straight off the runway, carrying as little fuel and as many bombs as possible. We flew in loose formation all the way to Japan at an altitude of about 1,500 feet above the sea. It was terribly difficult for the pilots to fly in formation that long because it was all manual flying. They did not even use their airplanes' automatic pilots. About 100 to 150 miles off the coast, we tightened formation at an assembly point and climbed to an altitude of 25,000 feet. We had about twelve fighter attacks on that first mission. In addition, cloud cover obscured the target, so we had to bomb by radar, which was not very accurate. As a result of the fighters and cloud cover, we missed the target. Once we dropped the bombs, with the jet stream behind us, we headed toward the coast, then south for Saipan as individual planes with every crew for itself. On this first mission, we lost one plane and five of its airmen when it attempted to ditch.

On this very first mission, I learned that the B-29 had a number of enemies. First, there was flak, which was not as accurate as German flak. Second, there were fighters, which were very aggressive. They could fly from 350 to 380 miles per hour, had a ceiling of 38,000 feet, and climbed at 3,900 feet per minute. Third, there was fuel, or the lack thereof. Fourth, there were the plane's four Wright Cyclone engines. We had a lot of trouble with them through overheating. Flying on three engines was not unusual in flying a B-29. Finally, the last enemy was the Pacific Ocean. We had to fly 3,000 miles over open water using dead reckoning and celestial navigation all the way to Japan and all the way back to Saipan, part of it by night and part of it by day. We had no radio aids. As a result, we lost five times the number of planes to crashes in the sea than to enemy aircraft.

One of the most dangerous times for the crew was takeoff. We were surrounded by 7,000 gallons of high-octane aviation fuel, 10 tons of bombs, and 7,000 rounds of ammunition, weighing much more than the gross weight at which the B-29 was designed to fly. The airplane commander and pilot stood on the brakes, revved the engines as high as they could, and then released the brakes to roll down the full length of the 9,000-foot runway. We rolled through the "Valley of Death," the point where, if you lost an engine, you were going too fast to stop and too slow to lift off. At the end of the runway on Saipan was a 250-foot cliff overlooking the Pacific. Just before the end of the runway, the airplane commander would lift the nose, pull up the gear, and fly straight off the end. At the cliff's edge, we would dive for the ocean to gain airspeed to fly, and it was just like going down on a fast elevator. Your stomach would churn. The ocean was so close to the plane that we would kick up prop wash on the water. Nevertheless, that would give us enough airspeed momentum to wobble up into the air for a thirteen- to fifteen-hour flight. Let me tell you, it was an exhilarating experience!

These high altitude mission tactics were exhausting for the pilots and the rest of the crews. We were in manual flight formation for about seven of the thirteen hours in the air. Fuel conservation was a nightmare for the flight engineer. The navigators had to depend on celestial bodies for guidance. You could compare our navigation to that used by Christopher Columbus, except we were on a 300-mile-per-hour airship.

On the second mission to Tokyo, we had the same weather and the same results. The third mission was again to Tokyo. We kept going back, not because we liked it, but because we kept missing it!

On our third mission, we were hit by Japanese flak. When leaving the Japanese mainland, we would close the camera hatch located in the rear of the plane that was used to determine the results of the bomb run. When our radarman closed it, he saw gasoline streaming all along the bottom of the aircraft and blowing up into the hatch. We had been hit in a wing tank and were rapidly losing gasoline. Airplane Commander Norman Westervelt still had full control of the plane because the engines had not been hit. Immediately, however, we knew that we were in trouble and that we might not be able to make it back to Saipan. The Marines had not yet secured Iwo Jima, so we were unable to land there. As the navigator, I constantly upgraded our position, while the radio operator alerted other planes in the squadron to fly "buddy." Other crewmembers stripped the plane to lighten the weight and lengthen our mileage. We threw everything out, including the Norden bombsight. I still remember Gordon Nedderson, our bombardier, literally wrenching the Norden bombsight off the floor and throwing it out. The radio operator and I worked in tandem because we had to know where we were if we were ever going to be found. To find a life raft in the Pacific Ocean is not a simple matter, so I was trying to establish either a fix or a dead reckoning position every thirty or thirty-five minutes. Meanwhile, the flight engineer was constantly trying to determine how much fuel we had left as he transferred gasoline from one tank to another.

We almost made it home, but we made a mistake by not allowing for the fuel necessary to make a successful crash landing at sea. Late in the afternoon, we were about 220 miles north of Saipan, near Anatahan Island [Northern Mariana Islands], when the engines began to sputter. All four engines were completely out of gas, and we were forced to make a dead-stick landing in a very rough sea. When the intelligence officers later debriefed us, they said we had made the perfect preamble to ditching. Westervelt flew into the wind and across the ocean swells, which were very rough. He then dragged the tail in the water and was able to pull the plane over the first swell. These swells were about fifteen feet high.

Then all four engines died, leaving us with no power to pull up the nose. We hit a giant wave head-on at about 100 miles per hour. The Plexiglas "greenhouse" shattered with an impact similar to hitting a brick wall at that speed. When that happened, Westervelt had either already unbuckled his safety belt in anticipation of evacuating the plane, or the belt snapped. In any case, the impact of the wave on the "greenhouse" nose just pulverized it. He went right through the wreckage and was beheaded. The bombardier, Gordon Nedderson, was immediately killed upon impact. We later surmised that his skull was crushed. He did not get out of the plane, so we never saw him again. The central fire controlman, Bob Curtis, was sitting on the floor with his back broken. Nevertheless, he managed to crawl out and lay spread-eagled and screaming on top of the plane. The co-pilot, John Betia, had a chunk of flesh about as big as a fist torn from his right calf. The rest of us were cut, bruised, and shaking from shock. I personally had some cuts from ripped metal on the plane as I attempted to get outside.

After crawling out of the plane, the survivors lashed together two life rafts and then determined who was aboard. We saw Westervelt floating, without any head, out in front of the aircraft. We attempted to get back to the aircraft to look for Nedderson, but the ocean was so rough we could not maneuver the rafts. Curtis was in great pain, but we could not administer morphine because somebody had stolen it from the first aid kits on each raft. Fortunately for us, a "buddy" plane had spotted us and dropped a "Gibson girl" [a portable emergency radio] and identified our location.

There we were, in life rafts, when, right at twilight, we heard the engines of a Navy PBY "Dumbo," an air-sea rescue plane. In eighteen months, its crew had never found a soul. They were ready to rotate and needed an accomplishment, so down they came, in a very rough sea, to get us. God bless them! We got Curtis into the plane, and eight more of us climbed aboard to fill the plane. Because of his broken back, Curtis was screaming from the pain, but we managed to tranquillize him after we got him in there. I was assigned to sit on the floor between the pilot and co-pilot.

So far, my day had gone like this. I had been up all night and all day; I had been shot at and hit; I had flown 3,000 miles; I had crashed in the Pacific; I had seen two of my best friends killed; all nine of the rest of us were wounded, some more severely than others; and I had been floating in a life raft for about three hours. It was the loneliest place in the world! I was cold, wet, hungry, bleeding, seasick, and in a mild state of shock. Now I was sitting on the floor of this Navy "tin can," which I could not decide was a boat or a plane. But I was doing pretty well until I looked up, and suddenly I was terrified. The airplane had windshield wipers on it, and they were going! I had flown in all kinds of planes, and this was the first one that ever flew so slowly that it had windshield wipers! I thought we were going to crack up while trying to get off the water. We were just bouncing all over, and from where I was sitting, I really felt a rougher impact in taking off in that PBY than in going down in our B-29.

At the hospital on Saipan, they bound up our wounds and gave us cigarettes, steak, and eggs. There were two things that the armed forces of those days believed would help you in tough circumstances: nicotine and cholesterol. The prevailing theory, I think, is that if something failed to kill you today, we will get you later in life.

I then joined the crew of Captain James Buckheit. Joining me was Flight Engineer Lowell Sharrett, Radar Operator Warren Huntington, and Waist Gunner Lloyd Kelley. I was pleased to join their crew, and I went on to fly thirty-two missions with them. We all knew one another in Buckheit's crew because we had been living together in the same Quonset hut. Buckheit's crew had ditched two nights earlier, and their navigator had been severely wounded. They had also lost their flight engineer, radar operator, and a third crewmember.

I had a lot of respect for James Buckheit. He was a totally different kind of man from "Wes," but what impressed us the most is that when they had ditched, some of Buckheit's men had not made it to the life rafts. They were floating around in the dark of night in "Mae West" vests, were not strong swimmers, they were scared, and they were hurt. Buckheit was a strong swimmer, so he jumped out of the life raft and swam into the darkness and pulled the two men in. He received a Soldier's Medal for that. Buckheit was a great leader, and we really felt good about being on his crew.

We flew in plane *A-32*. The plane had been stripped of excess weight, so we nicknamed it *Stripped for Action.* Its nose art was a naked gal lying on an Army cot. These planes belonged to us, and we did just about anything we wanted with them. We were the ones who flew it, and it was like our second home, considering the length of the missions. So, it was really our plane, and we were proud of it. Our ground crew babied the plane and us crew members like mother hens.

Since I was the plane's navigator, one of the things I had already learned was that to sit on the navigator's seat was equivalent to sitting on a typist's chair. Sitting for twelve to fifteen hours in an environment with a high amount of tension got to be pretty damned old and very uncomfortable. Added to that were the two big, heavy parachute straps running under your legs. So, one night—to show you that it was our airplane—I went over to the Air Transport Command strip. I had already borrowed a Jeep, some wrenches, and some pliers, and I went right into a C-47 and took the pilot's comparatively luxurious seat out of it. I asked the ground crew to install it in our plane for me. Then I got a piece of quarter-inch steel plate someplace and had it welded to the bottom of my new chair. Thereafter, I flew in complete comfort.

Squadron morale was low. We had had ineffective results, high losses, and there was no assigned tour of duty. We were still flying high-altitude daylight missions, but no longer flew in formation the full distance to Japan. We flew to Sofu Gan, a point off the coast, to circle for assembly, and then we would fly to the target in formation. With the jet stream behind us, target accuracy was still impossible.

Then good things began to happen with the arrival of a new general: "Old Iron Pants," Curtis LeMay. He had already shown in England that he was a superb tactician and a warrior. LeMay gave us a thirty-five-mission tour, which lifted our spirits. He then told us that our next mission was an incendiary night raid on Tokyo at 5,000 feet, and we would carry no defensive armament, except in the tail. There would be no jet stream at low altitude. All the crews were sure that their tour was going to be less than thirty-five missions—and maybe only one more. We really thought that we had been designated as America's first *kamikazes*.

The first incendiary raid to Tokyo occurred on March 9, 1945, followed rapidly by others, primarily to Nagoya, Osaka, Kobe, and some smaller Japanese industrial cities. On March 9, the center of Tokyo burned to the ground. Approximately 16.5 square miles of the city burned. There were 84,000 to 100,000 dead and one million left homeless. No single act of war, before or since, has ever caused as great a toll on life and property as this one raid. This included the use of the atomic bomb on Hiroshima.

On April 7, we flew another high-altitude mission. It was the first time we had P-51 fighter escorts. There were 107 B-29s. On this mission 101 Japanese fighters were shot down, 80 by B-29s. Our *A-32* shot down two before the gun cables were severed by gunfire, leaving us defenseless except for the P-51s and B-29 wingmen. The Japanese had a good way of scaring you when they got down to the end of their gasoline. They would drop their landing gear, which meant they were going to ram us and die for their emperor! It made us wonder what kind of folks these Japanese were; this was a culture that Americans did not understand.

Nevertheless, we were able to land on Iwo Jima with one engine out. There were 184 holes in the plane, including a thirty-inch hole in the vertical stabilizer. We spent two nights on Iwo Jima. It was the first of four times Iwo Jima saved my life.

Several other wonderful things happened to make my task a bit easier. One was that we got two LORAN [Long Range Aid to Navigation] stations. To a navigator that was like God had smiled on you, because in a matter of seconds you could find out exactly where you were on the face of the Earth. It took **all** the stress off you. Before the coming of the LORAN stations, I would **never** stop working for fifteen hours, since I would try to get a fix on where we were every thirty minutes. I was the guy who had to stay awake all the time—work all the time—because, if we ever had a problem, and I did not know where we were, we were just out of luck and lost at sea. So, LORAN stations were just a tremendous relief for me. Celestial navigation became a thing of the past.

Another thing that made navigation easier was our radar, which gave us a high level of confidence. The radar enabled us to identify by fixes off the chain of Bonin Islands and Iwo Jima.

On May 8, there were more incendiary raids. The B-29s were over Tokyo for fifty minutes. In June, we dropped leaflets on fifty-eight smaller cities with populations of 100,000 to 200,000. We had air superiority, and the Japanese were hoarding fighters to carry out *kamikaze* attacks against our forces before the expected invasion of the home islands. We were sent to bomb airfields on Kyushu in support of the Okinawa invasion, which began on April 1, 1945. By the end of August, 50 percent of Tokyo was gone, 8.1 square miles of Osaka, and 4.3 square miles (one-half) of Kobe were gone. In fact, Japan's six major industrial cities were virtually wiped off of the map. Every city with a population over 50,000 was extensively burned. The naval arsenal at Kure was destroyed; the Osaka army arsenal was gone. Mining by the 504th Bomb Group, based on Tinian, had eliminated coastal shipping. The Japanese aircraft industry was inoperative. But the Japanese refused to surrender.

On August 8, 1945, I flew my thirty-fifth mission, and among those thirty-five had been sixteen incendiary raids. At this point I want to provide a few brief details of these incendiary raids. The planes took off individually at two-minute intervals. Each aircraft flew alone all the way to Japan, over the target, and back. We would take off at about 5:00 PM, and after about a six-hour flight, we would arrive over the target around 11:00 at night. So, here are all those airplanes taking off two minutes apart, and all going to the same place in the dark. That alone could be scary because we did have instances of planes running together.

The pathfinder crews, which were the lead crews, took off a half-hour before us. They approached the target at low altitude and started fires in various parts of the targeted city. Our job was then to come in and approach from the opposite direction in order to confuse the Japanese. We had certain assigned targets, but the pathfinders had already started the fires. We flew in very low through the fiery holocaust that was taking place below. When we got there, it was every bit as scary as we thought it would be.

I do not get excited very easily, but my heart was beating very rapidly because I had never seen anything like this before, I'll tell you. First of all, you are in an airplane 5,000 feet in the air, and you can smell the smoke, which was so dense that it actually permeated the aircraft. We were flying through black clouds of smoke that were so rough that they were throwing the plane all over the sky. The turbulence was just crazy. The ultimate description of all this is that, if one can imagine Dallas, Texas, being totally on fire, it was like looking at the mouth of Hell.

In looking back, I did not have any feelings about what I had seen, other than that I was glad to get away from it. I think that that is the reason why the higher-ups like young men to fight wars. I did not worry at all about the social or moral implications of what we were doing. I recently read a new book entitled *Flames Over Tokyo* [by Bartlett Kerr, published in 1991], which describes these raids from the point of view of what happened to the people on the ground. I just shook my head and said, "My God! Did we do that?" On March 9, 1945, we killed 84,000 people in that one raid on Tokyo. The only difference between the crew of the *Enola Gay* and us was that it took us 300 planes to do what they did with one plane and one atomic bomb.

Because of these conditions, when we started in on the target, we would strap ourselves in our seats as tight as possible. We wore night-vision goggles, which had red lenses. We also wore "Mae Wests," flak jackets, and steel helmets. The Japanese searchlights, which were radar-operated, were just all over the sky in broiling smoke, and we did see some of our aircraft running together and falling apart. Night fighters also were out there, and we did not know where they were coming from. Their flak, also radar-operated, was ineffective, but it was still a concern, so we would throw out "rope" [strips of aluminum foil] to confuse their radar system. Again, we had no armament because LeMay had ordered that the guns be removed to allow us to carry a larger bomb load.

Prior to my arrival, the 497th had flown seventeen combat missions. After my arrival, it flew fifty-six more. Of those, we flew on thirty-five, plus some aborts caused by engine failures. The 73rd Bomb Wing suffered about 50 percent of all losses because it was the first there. Of the 709 aviators who ditched at sea, only 40 percent were found alive, meaning I am lucky to be alive.

By the end of the war, there were five B-29 wings, plus the atomic bomb group, based on Saipan, Tinian, and Guam. General LeMay had over 700 bombers at his command. It is perhaps ironic to note that the B-29, which was conceived as a scalpel-precise, high-altitude strategic bomber—and was certainly one of the most notably sophisticated weapons of World War II—because of the jet stream became a low-altitude bludgeon and then the delivery system for the most awesome weapon of all: the atomic bomb.

Fifty years later, the use of the atomic bomb still stirs controversy. I find the campaign to make every American over the age of sixty-eight feel guilty about this event to be ludicrous. As Russell Baker wrote in the *New York Times* the other day, "History is written by the winners and then re-written by their children—and it is a rare child who thinks his parents are almost as smart as he is." Revisionist historians argue that the atomic bombings and the fire bombings were unnecessary and reason that America was simply being cruel to Japan in a war of vengeance.

This experience fifty years ago was a central moment in my life, but today, with all the controversy surrounding the dropping of the atomic bombs on Hiroshima and Nagasaki and the end of World War II, it seems to me that America is having an identity crisis. The bomb was simply proof that war is deadly—terribly so—and that total war is ended only by the use of superior weaponry. America, or at least the part of it that was never there, or even born yet, seems to have overlooked the fact that our entry into the war began with an unprovoked sneak attack on Pearl Harbor, which severely damaged the U.S. Navy's Pacific Fleet and killed 2,400 unsuspecting sailors, soldiers, and civilians. The war ended with 100,000 American dead from the Pacific Campaign alone. In 1945, the dropping of the atomic bomb was applauded as a way to end the horrors of four long and weary years of war that killed 50 million people.

We should remember that Japan started the war, pursued it aggressively, and fought it in a particularly brutal fashion. The German atrocities and the Holocaust were terrible, but those of the Japanese were just as bad, or worse. In China, they killed 5 million. In Nanking, for example, they killed 200,000 Chinese civilians. In the Philippines, there was the Bataan Death March. There were more deaths in the construction of the Burma-Thailand Railroad. There were biological experiments. Prisoners of war were starved. We were fighting a fanatical enemy in a war that had to be won, no matter the cost. By the end of the war, the Japanese people through their War Ministry were responsible for the deaths of 17,222,500 people! Japan was a nation that had to be thoroughly defeated, occupied, and disarmed. Their entire system had to be disassembled, their leaders brought to justice, and their people reeducated. Questions today as to how we should have brought this war to an end are sheer speculation and, after the fact, often uninformed judgment calls.

We know that the basic objective of the Japanese was to seize the oil resources of the Dutch East Indies. Their war strategy was eventually divided into three phases. Phase 1, from 1941 to 1942, was successful. Phase 2, from 1942 to 1943, was one of retreat. They were checked in the Coral Sea, defeated at Midway, and defeated at Guadalcanal. Phase 3, from 1944 to 1945, was one of fanatical defense, fought with a fanaticism unique in military history, all to die for Emperor Hirohito. At Tarawa, 5,000 Japanese were killed; only seventeen were captured alive. At Iwo Jima, 23,000 were killed; only 212 were captured alive. At Okinawa, 117,000 were killed; 7,000 surrendered, but at a cost of 50,000 American casualties. They simply would not give up, even in the face of obvious defeat. They made the decision to inflict as much pain and casualties as possible on America. Their purpose was to end the war on their own terms: to keep the emperor with no occupation of Japan or war crimes trials, and to keep as much territory as possible. The "Trinity of War" required that the military, the government, and the people be defeated. One must fall to begin to bring down the others.

So, we had a Japanese military that would not give up, and they were not helpless at the time of the bomb. On the Japanese mainland, they had massed 2 million troops, with 2 million more in reserve. They had 10,000 aircraft, 5,000 of which would be used for *kamikaze* missions, and 3,000 suicide boats prepared to wreak havoc on any invading force. As for the Japanese people, their religious beliefs would inspire them to fight to the death. Thus, it remained for the emperor to surrender, which he did when he faced up to the reality presented by the atomic bomb. Continuing the war meant the total destruction of Japan as a nation. Prior to the emperor's decision, Generals George C. Marshall and Douglas A. MacArthur had made a professional judgment. They had to invade Japan. A blockade would not work. The casualty predictions for the American and Allied invaders varied. The Joint War Plans Committee predicted 131,000; MacArthur's staff, 105,000. But by June 7, Japanese forces on Kyushu numbered 280,000, and by August 6, they numbered 600,000: a force so large that it led to estimates that the invader's casualties would be in the neighborhood of 300,000 American boys.[2]

I want to conclude this presentation on a lighter note. Somehow, that seems a good thing to do after I have talked about war. As always, I must close with thanks to the gallant U.S. Marines, who suffered 20,000 casualties and had to kill the entire garrison of 21,000 Japanese soldiers in the process of taking Iwo Jima to make a safe harbor for B-29 airmen in deep trouble on their way home. As I have already noted, our crew in *A-32* landed there four times, each time in a life-threatening situation. There is no doubt that I would not be here today except for those Marines, and the crew of the Navy PBY "Rivet Popper," who saved my life the first time. Between them, they left me four more lives of my allotted nine, and I am living and enjoying them to the fullest!

The only complaint I ever had is that in the fifty years since World War II ended, I never had a parade. Probably not very many did. So, I close with a story that began when the Admiral Nimitz Museum in Fredericksburg, Texas, invited a group of World War II Pacific veterans to come together to participate in the V + 50 Celebration on September 2 and 3, 1995.

I got my parade—a marvelous affair! The parade marshals were President George Bush and the then Governor George W. Bush. We had all four branches of the service—Navy, Army, Marines, and Air Force—marching military bands, World War II and modern military

---

[2] Editor's note: According to Secretary of War Henry Stimson, his General Staff estimated Japanese military strength as follows: in the home islands, slightly under 2 million; in Korea, Manchuria, and China proper, slightly over 2 million; in French Indo-China, Thailand, and Burma, over 200,000; in the East Indies area and the Philippines, over 500,000; in the by-passed Pacific islands, over 100,000. The total strength of the Japanese Army was estimated at 5,000,000 men. These estimates proved to be in very close agreement with official Japanese figures. See Henry L. Stimson, "The Decision to use the Atomic Bomb," *Harper's Magazine* 194 (Feb. 1947): 97-107.

vehicles, a Confederate Air Force warbird flyover—the whole works! All of us vets were wearing whatever pieces of uniform we had left that still fit—mostly caps and tarnished silver wings. We rode in trucks with signs identifying our outfits. Lining the streets of little Fredericksburg were 50,000 people waving flags, yelling "Thank you!" and giving the old "V-for-Victory" sign. It was an emotional experience! We B-29 guys were riding down the street when my friend, Fiske Hanley, a B-29 flight engineer, and former POW of the Japanese, from Fort Worth, pointed and said, "Look down there!" On the curb was my entire family—my wife of fifty years, my three daughters, my sons-in-law, and all eight grandchildren—all wearing red, white, and blue and holding up a giant red banner: "David Braden, Our Hero!" That really grabbed me! Two days later, Helen McDonald from the museum called me all excited. She said, "Dave, your family made the front page of the *Fredericksburg Standard*, and I'm sending you a copy. I know you can't see this, but next to a photo of Governor Bush and his father, President Bush, is one of your family with the sign!"

Well, this is not the end of the story. Last Friday night, my wife and I attended a reception for Governor Bush and his family after the formal opening of the State Fair of Texas. I asked the governor if he had seen the front page of the *Fredericksburg Standard* after the V + 50 Celebration. He said, "You mean that picture of me and the 'Old Man' leading the parade?" Little did he know that I had known his dad for many years and that I was a little bit offended. President Bush and I were born in the same week of November 1924, and he's calling him an old man! But I said, "No, that picture next to it of that family holding up a sign that says: 'Our Hero, David Braden!'" He said, "Oh, yeah! I saw that." I said, "Well, that's my family. I'm David Braden." He said, "Glad to know you, Dave." I said, "Glad to know you, too, Governor. Please tell the 'Old Man' that General Braden sends his regards!"

My near-death experiences have made World War II one of the defining moments of my life. I am happy to call myself a survivor, and I am grateful to those who played a role in helping me survive.

DR. ROBERT A. DIVINE (UNIVERSITY OF TEXAS)

ENDING THE WAR WITH JAPAN: THE DECISION TO USE THE ATOMIC BOMBS

Robert A. Divine, George W. Littlefield Professor Emeritus in American History at the University of Texas at Austin, received his Ph.D. from Yale University in 1954. A specialist in American diplomatic history, he taught from 1954 to 1996 at the University of Texas, where both the Student Association and the Graduate School honored him for teaching excellence.

His extensive works include *The Illusion of Neutrality* (1962); *The Reluctant Belligerent* (1965); *Second Chance: The Triumph of Internationalism in America During World War II*; and *Blowing in the Wind* (1978). His most recent work is *Perpetual War for Perpetual Peace* (2000), a comparative analysis of twentieth-century American wars. He is also the author of *Eisenhower and the Cold War* (1981) and editor of three volumes of essays on the presidency of Lyndon B. Johnson. His book, *The Sputnik Challenge* (1992), won the Eugene E. Emme Astronautical Literature Award for 1993.

He has been a fellow at the Center for Advanced Study in the Behavioral Studies at Stanford University and has given the Albert Shaw Lectures in Diplomatic History at the Johns Hopkins University.

As a people, we seem to be unusually fond of anniversaries. We ignore history year after year until suddenly, as if to make up for decades of neglect, we indulge in an orgy of celebration. In the 1960s, it was the Civil War Centennial; in the 1970s, the Bicentennial of the American Revolution. Our latest national binge has been the fiftieth anniversary of the end of World War II.[1]

The formula is familiar. There are books by well-known authors, like Stephen Ambrose's *D-Day*,[2] newspaper accounts filled with reminiscences of veterans and their loved ones recalling wartime experiences with nostalgia, and the inevitable television documentaries that both celebrate the events of the war and stir up old controversies in an effort to gain the attention of a jaded public.

We have just survived the latest phase of this national pastime with the controversy over the use of the atomic bomb in ending the Pacific War. It began last year, in 1995, with the debate over a planned Smithsonian exhibit of the *Enola Gay*, with veterans groups charging that revisionist historians were portraying the Japanese as innocent victims of American nuclear aggression. The Smithsonian finally gave up its ambitious plans, but much of the media's coverage this summer raised doubts and questions about the morality of President Harry S Truman's decision to drop the bomb.[3]

---

[1] Editor's note: Dr. Divine presented this paper at the UNT Military History Seminar on October 7, 1995.

[2] Stephen E. Ambrose, *D-Day, June 6, 1944: The Climactic Battle of World War II* (New York: Simon and Schuster, 1994).

[3] Editor's note: On June 28, 1995, the Air and Space Museum of the Smithsonian Institution opened a scaled-down exhibit featuring the *Enola Gay*, the B-29 bomber that dropped the atomic bomb on Hiroshima on August 6, 1945. This exhibit had been at the center of a public controversy for more than a year. Originally, the federally funded Smithsonian Institution planned a major exhibit with extensive pictures and documentation that would have raised many questions about the decision of President Harry Truman to drop the atomic bombs on the Japanese cities of Hiroshima and Nagasaki. However, a campaign by American veterans groups supported by Democratic and Republican members of Congress succeeded in modifying the museum's originally planned exhibit.

I would like to offer some perspective on this controversy, so my goal is to try to place the atomic bomb decision in the context of World War II. It is easy to make sweeping moral judgments about the nuclear age after fifty years of experience, but it is much more difficult to try to go back to the situation in 1945 and examine it without the luxury of 20/20 hindsight.

When Harry S Truman unexpectedly took office in April 1945, he and his advisers faced a difficult situation. Within a month, Germany was defeated, but Japan remained a powerful, if weakened, adversary. The Japanese still had 5 million troops under arms and controlled vast territory in Asia, stretching from China and Korea to Burma and the Dutch East Indies. Her proud navy was virtually destroyed, and her cities were open to bombardment by American B-29s from bases in the Mariana Islands. In March 1945, firebomb raids had wiped out large sections of Tokyo and killed more than 80,000 people.

There was no question that Japan would be defeated, but at what cost? Her use of *kamikaze* planes in defending Okinawa had sunk twenty-seven ships and taken the lives of 5,000 American sailors. Japan was a proud nation that boasted of never losing a war, and her more fanatical leaders called on all 80 million Japanese to engage in suicidal resistance to an American invasion on her soil. Listen to the words of one Japanese army officer writing in the summer of 1945:

> We will prepare 10,000 planes to meet the landing of the enemy . . . We will smash one-third of the enemy's war potential with this air force at sea. Another third will also be smashed at sea by our warships, human torpedoes, and other special weapons. Furthermore, when the enemy actually lands, if we are ready to sacrifice a million men, we will be able to inflict an equal number of casualties upon them. If the enemy loses a million men, then the public opinion in America will become

> inclined toward peace, and Japan will be able to gain peace with comparatively advantageous conditions.

The dilemma facing Truman was how to achieve the goal he had inherited from Franklin Roosevelt—the unconditional surrender of Japan—in the shortest possible time and at the least cost in American lives.

There were three different paths the United States could follow to end the war. The first alternative was a military solution. We could end the war in the Pacific the same way we had in Europe: invade the Japanese home islands and force the enemy to surrender. The Joint Chiefs of Staff had approved this approach in 1944. Gen. Douglas A. MacArthur, who had been advancing from New Guinea to the Philippines, would join with Adm. Chester Nimitz's Central Pacific forces, which had recently seized Okinawa in the bloodiest battle of the Pacific War. The combined American forces would then carry out D-Day in the Pacific, Operation Downfall, in two stages. The first was an invasion of the southernmost Japanese island, Kyushu, in November 1945, to be followed by the landing near Tokyo on Honshu in March 1946.

The scale of the American planning was immense. Ten divisions would land on the beaches at Kyushu in Operation Olympic (compared to just five at Normandy), with three more in floating reserve; Operation Coronet, the 1946 landing on the Tokyo Plain, called for twenty-five divisions, including many fresh veterans from the European Theater of Operations.

A key concern at the time, and the source of much later controversy, was the estimate of casualties. After the war, President Truman and Secretary of War Henry Stimson gave exaggerated estimates, ranging from 250,000 to as high as 1,000,000 American casualties, to justify the use of the atomic bomb.

There is no evidence to back up these claims. In his careful study based on all the Army's plans for Downfall, John Ray Skates points out that when George Marshall asked for figures on the likely casualties for Olympic, the Kyushu invasion, General MacArthur estimated that they would run as high as 50,000 in the first thirty days and might total over 100,000 in the first four months. Previous experience in the Pacific indicated that the death toll would be between 15,000 and 30,000, which was high, but not unreasonable in light of the 13,000 killed at Okinawa and 16,000 at Normandy. These figures related only to Olympic and did not include Coronet, the Honshu landings scheduled for 1946. It was on this basis that Truman gave his preliminary approval for Olympic in mid-June 1945. (He never did give his assent to Coronet. He instead preferred to await the outcome of Olympic before making that decision.)[4]

Throughout June and July 1945, both sides prepared for the coming battle for Kyushu. There was no element of surprise, for the Japanese expected the Americans to invade Kyushu as a staging ground for the eventual landings on Honshu. Between April and the end of July, they moved seven divisions onto the southern part of the island, raising their troop strength there from 150,000 to over a half-million. Having studied earlier operations in the Pacific, they correctly surmised that the Americans wanted air and naval bases on Kyushu to ensure the success of Coronet. As one Japanese officer later explained to his captors, "It was strategic common sense," not a security leak as had been rumored, that led Japan to defend Kyushu so heavily.

The Japanese had several advantages beyond their large numbers. The terrain favored defense. The three broad beaches where the landings had to take place all gave way to easily defended bluffs,

[4] See John R. Skates, *The Invasion of Japan: Alternative to the Bomb* (Columbia, SC: University of South Carolina Press, 1994).

giving the Japanese the high ground. Moreover, the Japanese military allocated 5,000 *kamikazes* to the defense of Kyushu. Instead of targeting American warships, as they had at Okinawa, these suicide missions were aimed at the troopships in hopes of wiping out much of the invasion force before it could land. The Japanese navy also had more than a hundred *kaiten*, manned torpedoes that could deliver 3,000-pound warheads,[5] as well as suicide motorboats designed to blow up American vessels on contact.

Yet there were also serious Japanese weaknesses. Constant American air attacks forced them to scatter the *kamikaze* planes to

---

[5] Editor's note: In the Japanese language, *kaiten* means "Turning of the Heavens." By late 1944, the war situation had deteriorated for Japan to the point where extraordinary measures were seen as offering the only way out of an increasingly grim military predicament. Thus with the invasion of the Philippines, the Japanese first formulated and implemented "Special Attack" tactics in the form of suicide aircraft attacks: the *kamikazes* ("Divine Wind"), named to commemorate the coming of a typhoon that destroyed a Mongol invasion force in the twelfth century, thus saving Japan from foreign conquest. The objective of the *kamikaze* pilot was to dive his explosive-laden plane into an American ship, particularly a capital ship, to inflict maximum damage. These attacks first started during the American invasion of the Philippines and reached their peak in the battle for Okinawa.

In short order, Japan began applying the same doctrine to the creation of new weapons systems. Notable among these was the *kaiten* suicide submarine. The *kaiten* was not so much a vessel as an insertion of a human being into a very large torpedo. The innards of this weapon was a standard Type-93, 24-inch torpedo, with a mid-section elongated to create a pilot's space. He sat on a canvas chair practically on the deck of the *kaiten*, a crude periscope directly in front of him and the necessary controls close at hand in the cockpit. The nose assembly was packed with 3,000-plus pounds of high explosives; the tail section contained the propulsion unit. The normal attack method was for the mother ship carrying four to six *kaitens* to approach the target area, locate the target vessels, and then release her *kaitens* to attack at a range of between 6,000 and 7,000 meters. The *kaitens* would then close to tactical range, come to periscope depth for a brief re-targeting at around 1,000 meters, make course corrections, and then dive and run at the calculated position of the target until a hit was obtained. Once launched from the mother ship, the pilot was on his own; regardless of the outcome of the mission, there could be no return to the mother ship, which would have been submerged and unobservable in any case.

bases in Honshu and even Korea, so it was questionable whether they could mass enough of these suicide planes when the invasion occurred. Most of the pilots, unlike the veterans at Okinawa who had been so effective, were young volunteers without any experience and thus easier to shoot down. Similarly, most of the units of the home army were filled with recent volunteers and were poorly trained and equipped. The Japanese failed to build a network of fortifications behind the bluffs overlooking the beaches. The high command had decided to stake everything on defending the beaches and wiping out the invaders as they landed. Yet the intense naval and aerial bombardment that would precede the invasion was likely to devastate the Japanese defenses. (In contrast, at Okinawa the Japanese had deliberately refused to defend the beaches, retreating instead to strongholds inland where they resisted so stubbornly and inflicted such heavy casualties on the American invaders.)

Professor Skates, exploring the Army's postwar analysis of a battle never fought, concludes that Operation Olympic would have resulted in a quick but bloody American victory. The high number of Japanese forces and their suicidal determination, even though offset by poor training and flawed tactics, was likely to have caused between 60,000 to 75,000 American casualties and 15,000 to 20,000 deaths, about the same as Normandy. Moreover, Skates agrees with the postwar Army analysis that Japan would have used all its military assets at Kyushu and would have been forced to surrender, thus sparing the United States the even higher casualties of Operation Coronet.

In his recent book, *The Last Great Victory*, Stanley Weintraub offers some sobering evidence of the human cost of Downfall. He points out that the numbers projected by MacArthur's planners were optimistic, and their estimates were designed to win presidential approval for the operation. He cites estimates by Admiral William D. Leahy, FDR's and Truman's Chief of Staff and also *de facto* Chair of the Joint Chiefs of Staff, who used a figure of over 250,000 casualties, more than twice MacArthur's number. (In a lecture in 1994 in Austin, Stephen Ambrose claimed that Colonel Andrew Goodpaster, who was then in the War Department Operations Division and who would later serve as President Dwight D. Eisenhower's aide and as NATO commander, used the Okinawa figures to estimate American casualties at Kyushu at 500,000.) Moreover, someone in the Pentagon must have been even more pessimistic. Weintraub reports that the Army ordered so many Purple Heart medals for those expected to be wounded in action that the United States had enough on hand for the Korean and Vietnam Wars, with some left over![6]

One can gain another perspective on Operation Olympic from a general who became indignant when he found that he would be commanding the second wave at one of the Kyushu beaches. His anger quickly evaporated when he found out the reason: his troops would have exactly the same objectives as those who landed first. "It was clear to me then," he recalled later, "that they expected the first echelon to be wiped out in the invasion. The second echelon would get the thing done."

Noted *Washington Post* reporter Chalmers Roberts offers an equally chilling observation. As a member of the United States Strategic Bombing Survey, he found himself flying over one of the three landing beaches at Kyushu on November 1, 1945, the very date set for the invasion. Miyazaki Beach, he wrote,

> was perhaps forty miles long and at first glance appeared to be an ideal landing spot, long and gently sloping into the sea, the biggest beach on a rugged island, where the mountains looked like hooked-up rugs. But the beach was terribly shallow, and

[6] Stanley Weintraub, *The Last Great Victory: The End of World War II, July/August 1945* (New York: Talley, 1995).

> behind it rose a range from which murderous fire could have been poured down upon the men debarking from landing craft. My notes say that the estimate we got at the time was that there were 56,000 troops dug in nearby, with another 70,000 in reserve. The Japanese told us they had figured we would land in Miyazaki beach: "Where else?" they asked.

Twenty-five years later, Roberts concluded, "Flying over Miyazaki Beach on the day the landing was to have taken place there, I could not doubt or dispute Truman's decision [to use the atomic bomb]."[7]

The military alternative would almost certainly have brought about the defeat of Japan, but at a very high cost in American and Japanese lives. It is no wonder then that President Truman and his advisers looked for other ways to bring the Pacific War to an end.

The second alternative pursued by American leaders in the summer of 1945 was diplomatic: an attempt to end the war by negotiation. The great stumbling block was the policy of unconditional surrender, which was announced by President Roosevelt after the Casablanca Conference with Winston S. Churchill in January 1943. The problem was how to convince the Japanese to surrender without violating this inheritance from the fallen commander-in-chief.

Undersecretary of State Joseph Grew believed he had the answer. He had served as the American ambassador to Japan for the ten years preceding Pearl Harbor and knew Japanese culture and politics very well. The key to gaining Japan's agreement to surrender, he suggested, would be to give a public commitment that the institution of the emperor would not be abolished. Grew knew that Emperor Hirohito was a figurehead. Everything was done in his name, but he had no input into the policies decided upon by the civilian leaders. Yet the

---

[7] Chalmers Roberts, *First Rough Draft: A Journalist's Journal of Our Times* (New York: Praeger, 1973).

Japanese people considered the emperor a deity. Grew argued that assurances the emperor would continue to serve as figurehead would be enough to persuade the war-weary Japanese leaders to give up.

Grew also wanted to include a statement in the proposed Potsdam surrender declaration directed to the Japanese in July 1945, guaranteeing that the United States would respect the institution of emperor. American military leaders quickly concurred in this approach. They faced the difficulty of securing the surrender of millions of Japanese troops in China and Southeast Asia and the problem of postwar occupation rule of Japan itself. The cooperation of the emperor in ordering his loyal subjects to stop fighting and obey the orders of the victors would be vital to an orderly end of the war.[8]

The new Secretary of State, James F. Byrnes, disagreed. Impressed by the arguments of Cordell Hull, the man who had received the Japanese envoys in Washington in 1941 as the bombs were falling on Pearl Harbor, Byrnes argued that the American people viewed Hirohito as a war criminal on the same level as Benito Mussolini and Adolf Hitler (which in fact was the way the Japanese emperor was portrayed by American wartime propaganda). He bluntly told Truman that the press would crucify the president if he violated the unconditional surrender policy and gave public assurances that the emperor would not be punished. Byrnes prevailed on this point. Thus when the Potsdam Declaration was issued, it promised the Japanese that if they surrendered they would not be enslaved nor their nation abolished. But nothing was said about the future of the imperial institution.[9]

The Japanese leaders chose to ignore the Potsdam Declaration. We have no way of knowing how they would have responded if

8 Joseph C. Grew, *Turbulent Era: A Diplomatic Record of Forty Years* (Boston: Houghton Mifflin, 1952).

9 James F. Byrnes, *Speaking Frankly* (New York: Harper Brothers Publishers, 1947).

assurances had been given concerning the emperor. By July 1945, a group of civilian leaders, realizing the war was lost, was pushing for peace against the strong opposition of the military. The peace faction made a crucial mistake, however, by trying to use the Soviet Union as the third party in their negotiations. Josef Stalin was preparing to enter the Pacific War to reap the gains he had been promised at the Yalta Conference, primarily control of Manchurian ports, railroads, and industry, so he had no interest in seeing the war end early. And there was no indication that the Japanese militarists would have given up short of a last-ditch battle on Japanese soil.

The latest historical research suggests that Hirohito was not as innocent as he is often portrayed. He had willingly gone along with the militarists throughout the war. Those advising him in the summer of 1945 began to fear that the brutal suffering of the Japanese people would finally cause them to blame the emperor for their travail. By July, Hirohito and his advisers were far less concerned with the plight of his subjects than they were with the survival of the imperial institution. Herbert Bix writes,

> An internal power struggle was going on [within Japan], making it immaterial to the players if one hundred thousand or two hundred thousand people died as long as they could get their desired outcome, an end to the war that left the monarchy intact, available to control the forces of discontent that defeat would undoubtedly unleash.[10]

An American offer to guarantee the continuation of the imperial institution might have been tempting to Hirohito and his advisers, but they still faced the adamant opposition of the die-hard militarists.

[10] Herbert P. Bix, *Hirohito and the Making of Modern Japan* (New York: HarperCollins Publishers, 2000).

There was no assurance, even if the United States had made the commitment Grew wanted included in the Potsdam Declaration, that Japan would have surrendered. Hirohito was still casting about for a way to end the war and yet escape blame for the terrible suffering of his people. It was the third American alternative that would finally provide him with what Bix has termed "a face-saving excuse to surrender."[11]

Ending the war by shock became the third alternative, and a real possibility, by the spring of 1945. The Manhattan Project, which was begun by President Roosevelt just after Pearl Harbor, was on the verge of success. Scientists at Los Alamos were perfecting ways to transform the enriched uranium produced at Oak Ridge and the radioactive plutonium created at Hanford, Washington, into bombs of unprecedented explosive power.

The atomic bomb was a closely guarded secret, and even Harry Truman did not learn of its existence until the day after he became president. American military leaders had made their plans without any knowledge of the bomb.[12] MacArthur also was not informed about the bomb until late July 1945. The question of using the bomb was a political one, kept entirely separate from the military decision-making process. And the military would even be slow to grasp its strategic significance, viewing it as just another weapon in their arsenal. After the war, Gen. George C. Marshall told interviewers that

---

[11] Ibid.

[12] Editor's note: According to Adm. Donald M. Showers, who was at that time a twenty-six-year-old lieutenant commander compiling casualty estimates for JICPOA [Joint Intelligence Center Pacific Ocean Area], "Those of us working on the [casualty] figures didn't even know about the bomb. These were genuine figures. In fact, in looking back at them today, the figures were too conservative." The question of deliberately inflated casualty estimates was posed to Admiral Showers by an interviewer in March 1998 in light of the Smithsonian's display of the *Enola Gay*. See OH1257, "Interview with Admiral Donald M. Showers," University of North Texas Oral History Collection, Willis Library, Denton Texas.

he was planning to use as many as six atomic bombs on the beaches at Kyushu, part of the bombardment designed to soften up the Japanese defenders before the invasion.

Truman relied heavily on the advice of Secretary of War Stimson, who had overseen the bomb's development under FDR. In May an Interim Committee chaired by Stimson considered the question of how the bomb could be used. After brief discussion, the group ruled out both a peaceful demonstration on an uninhabited island to which the Japanese would be invited as witnesses and advance warning to the Japanese of its awesome power. In part, they did not see how to arrange such a demonstration in wartime; in part, they feared the bomb might prove to be a dud. The Interim Committee's final recommendation to the president was that the bomb be used against a military target, defined as a Japanese industrial city.[13]

By the time the bomb was tested successfully in the New Mexico desert on July 16, the Air Force had come up with a slim list of possible targets. B-29 attacks had already wiped out most of the larger Japanese cities; only a few were intact long enough to demonstrate the explosive force of the atomic bomb. After removing Kyoto, a city of unique cultural treasures, from the list, Stimson approved five cities. At Potsdam, Truman informed Stalin in vague terms of the new American weapon and then gave his final approval for the bomb's use. Weather conditions on August 6 made Hiroshima the fateful target for a weapon designed to shock the Japanese into an early surrender.

Two days later, the Soviet Union declared war against Japan, honoring a commitment made at Yalta but acting a week earlier than planned. The next day, August 9, the United States dropped a second

---

[13] Henry L. Stimson with McGeorge Bundy, *On Active Service in Peace and War* (New York: Harper and Row, Publishers, 1948); Henry L. Stimson, "The Decision to Use the Atomic Bomb," *Harper's Magazine* 194 (February 1947): 97-107.

atomic bomb on Nagasaki and then waited for Japan to give up in face of this terrible devastation.

For the next four days, a strange series of events unfolded in Tokyo. With his cabinet still deadlocked on whether to surrender or fight to the bitter end, the emperor broke with all precedent and ordered his ministers to arrange for the surrender of Japan. Military hardliners, despite the obliteration of Hiroshima and Nagasaki, wanted to fight on, but its leaders deferred to the divine will of the emperor. Japanese diplomats, however, still sought to spare the throne, and at the last minute the United States relented. Secretary of State Byrnes now approved compromise language that allowed the emperor to remain but made clear that his authority would be "subject to the Supreme Commander of the Allied Powers, who will take such steps as he deems proper to effectuate the surrender terms." As Truman noted in his diary about the emperor, "We told 'em we'd tell 'em how long to keep him, but we'd make the terms."[14]

Even then, many in the lower ranks simply could not accept the thought of surrender. On August 14, a group of army rebels seized control of the imperial palace, searching for the tape recording of the imperial rescript in which the emperor called on all his loyal subjects to end their resistance and cooperate with their conquerors. Fortunately, loyal troops regained control of the palace and allowed the imperial surrender rescript to be broadcast as scheduled on August 15, effectively ending the fighting. The atomic bomb had had the desired effect, shocking the emperor into action to bring about the defeat of Japan in just over a week's time.

In retrospect, there were few doubts about the use of the bomb in the summer of 1945, but over the years the debate has swelled as people began to ponder the significance of Truman's wartime

[14] Harry S Truman, *Memoirs: Years of Decisions* (Garden City, NY: Doubleday, 1955).

decision. Much of that concern is legitimate, and much of it relates to the broader issue of the dawn of the nuclear age and the course of the subsequent Cold War. I am sure that many will want to raise those issues.

I will conclude, however, with three observations. First, the atomic bomb did end World War II. Ever since, there have been claims that we could have ended the war by other means short of a bloody invasion. Some claim that blockade and continued conventional bombing would have quickly brought the Japanese to their knees. Others believe that Soviet entry into the war destroyed Japan's last hope and made surrender likely. Still others argue that if we had only made a forthright promise regarding the emperor in the Potsdam Declaration, we could have easily negotiated a peaceful surrender.

All these judgments are from hindsight, retrospective judgments based on later perspectives. This is history as might-have-been, not history as it was. The fact remains that the atomic bomb worked just as Truman thought it would because it shocked the Japanese into an early surrender. It is hard to believe that the other alternatives short of invasion would have led the emperor to enter into the political process and break the deadlock within the government. Whether Hirohito acted to save his throne or to spare his people further suffering, the undeniable fact is that the atomic bomb proved remarkably effective, for it brought the war to an end in just over a week's time.

Second, I strongly object to the charge of some revisionist historians, notably Gar Alperovitz, that Truman used the bomb primarily to frighten the Soviets, make them more manageable in Europe, and limit their postwar gains. These historians cite documents indicating that Truman, Byrnes, and Stimson were worried about postwar relations with the Soviets and realized the bomb would help offset the huge Russian advantage in conventional military manpower. But there is no evidence that concern with the Soviet Union was ever a major consideration in the A-bomb decision.[15]

The atomic bomb was used to end World War II, not as the first shot in the Cold War. As historian Barton Bernstein, a former revisionist himself, has argued recently, the bomb was a godsend for Harry Truman, for he viewed it as a way to end the war without the heavy casualties of an invasion. The casualties might not have been as heavy as Truman feared, and Japan might have given in without the use of the bomb, but in 1945 U.S. leaders were intent on only one thing: ending the war as soon as possible with the least loss of American life. Not a single one of the president's advisers dissented from the decision. To them it was the obvious way to bring a long and bloody war to a swift conclusion.[16]

Finally, I would offer a moral justification for what many see as a totally immoral act by the United States. Using the same retrospective argument of many critics, I claim that the dropping of the atomic bombs, intended only to save American lives, also spared many hundreds of thousands of Japanese civilians. On Okinawa, the civilian casualties ran to more than 200,000, nearly one-third of the island's population. The heavy aerial and naval bombardment to precede Olympic and the devastating firepower we planned to use against Japanese defenses would have resulted in the killing and maiming of hundreds of thousands of Japanese civilians: in the long run, many more than the casualties at Hiroshima and Nagasaki.

The other moral calculation is more cold-blooded. It is sad, but I think true, that the world could never fully understand the devastating power of nuclear weapons without the horrible examples provided

---

[15] Gar Alperovitz, *Atomic Diplomacy: Hiroshima and Potsdam* (New York: Simon and Schuster, 1965).

[16] Barton J. Bernstein, "The Atomic Bombs Reconsidered," *Foreign Affairs* 74 (Jan./Feb. 1995): 135-152.

by the two Japanese cities the bombs obliterated. In that sense, those who died at Hiroshima and Nagasaki were martyrs for all mankind. Their suffering helped keep the subsequent Cold War cold. It was the graphic pictures and accounts of the victims of the atomic bombs that restrained later leaders—men like John F. Kennedy and Nikita Khrushchev during the Cuban Missile Crisis—and thus prevented the conflict between the United States and the Soviet Union from ending in a nuclear catastrophe.

Yet this retrospective judgment does not absolve the United States from the responsibility of being the first, and, thank God, so far the only nation to use nuclear weapons against other people. Whatever the justification for Truman's decision, the United States is obligated to take the lead in trying to limit the spread of these weapons and work toward their ultimate abolition. The end of the Cold War has helped by halting the nuclear arms race, but we still have a long way to go toward the goal of freeing the world of the nuclear danger. Only when we have reached that objective can we finally be reconciled to Truman's wartime decision.

Section III
THE EARLY COLD WAR

The Cold War spans most of the chronology of this work, commencing in the days of Allied victory in 1944–45 through the Korean War and the Vietnam conflict and into the 1990s. The section on the Cold War has been divided into two parts, one on the early Cold War and a second entitled "The Late Cold War." The papers fit better in a chronological organization with other U.S. conflicts. The early Cold War section will focus on the period from 1945 into the 1960s when the conflict raged largely between the United States and the Soviet Union and their respective allies. Both sides grappled with the full meaning of the nuclear age and how to employ military force under the ever-present threat of escalation to thermonuclear war. During these years the strategy of deterrence evolved, and a new breed of military leader emerged in all the military services.

The paper presented by retired Gen. Russell Dougherty provides a fascinating view of military leadership in the nuclear age. General Dougherty was known and respected as an aviator, combat leader, and attorney who served primarily in the Strategic Air Command, a major command of the newly independent United States Air Force. Dougherty describes his own career but also pays tribute to the special contribution of Gen. Curtis LeMay, naming him the best of the military leaders of the Cold War period. LeMay, as first commander of the Strategic Air Command, made deterrence a credible option. He selected and trained aircrews to the very highest level of excellence. LeMay demonstrated to the Soviet Union that the democratic West could survive a nuclear first strike and then could deliver a devastating blow that would destroy their civilization. The Triad, including a combination of manned bombers, submarine-launched ballistic missiles, and land-based ballistic missiles, ultimately prevailed.

Dougherty managed forces through all the changes in warfare in the post-World War II period. It was an age of new leadership, strategy, and technology. He and his colleagues created a credible force and helped to keep the world free from nuclear war in an age when each side retained the capability to destroy the other. The free world is indeed fortunate that men of Dougherty's quality were in positions of leadership during this challenging age.

GENERAL RUSSELL E. DOUGHERTY, USAF (RET.)

LEADERSHIP DURING THE COLD WAR: A FOUR-STAR GENERAL'S PERSPECTIVE

At the time of his military retirement in 1977, Gen. Russell E. Dougherty was Commander in Chief of the Strategic Air Command and Director of U.S. Strategic Target Planning. He had previously served as Chief of Staff of NATO's Supreme Headquarters Allied Powers, Europe (SHAPE), as commander of the 2nd Air Force, and as Deputy Chief of Staff for Operations, U.S. Air Force.

General Dougherty began his military career as a member of the 123rd Cavalry, Kentucky National Guard. At the outbreak of World War II, he became an Aviation Cadet in the U.S. Army Air Forces. He has served in the Far East Air Forces Command, U.S. European Command, Air Training Command, the Air Force Logistics Command, and the Strategic Air Command. He completed two tours in the Pacific and three in Europe. General Dougherty retired with thirty-five years commissioned service on August 1, 1977.

General Dougherty is a graduate of Western Kentucky University, the Law School of the University of Louisville, and the National War College in Washington, DC. During his military career, he served as an Air Force Judge Advocate

Officer; he was an Assistant Judge Advocate Officer for the Far East Air Force; and he concluded his legal assignments in 1952 as an Assistant Air Force Trial Attorney. He is a member of the Bar of Kentucky and the Bar of the Supreme Court of the United States. General Dougherty is currently an attorney with McGuire, Woods, Battle, & Booth, one of the nation's largest law firms, with offices in Virginia, Baltimore, and Washington, DC.

The United States Air Force, from which I retired in 1977, is celebrating its fiftieth anniversary this year (1997), having been created through congressional legislation in the summer of 1947, with its first secretary, Stuart Symington, sworn in on September 18, 1947.[1] The forty-five-year period in our history that we call the "Cold War" can be overlaid almost exactly with the first forty-five years of the United States Air Force, since its birth in 1947.[2]

Unlike the U.S. Air Force, however, the beginning of the Cold War cannot be established with precision. Its beginning is a subjective date, a date that will vary with an individual's perception of post-World War II events. Not only is the beginning of the Cold War subjective, but its end is also subject to individual interpretation of the events following the breach of the Berlin Wall in 1989 and into the early 1990s. We have our own views on this, of course, but forty-five years is a good layman's consensus as to the Cold War's duration.

[1] Editor's note: The National Security Act of 1947 authorized the creation of a separate U.S. Air Force, which began operating on September 18, 1947. The Department of the Air Force would operate as an executive agency headed by the Secretary of the Air Force, a civilian appointed by the president with the advice and consent of the Senate. In addition, there would be appointed for four years by the president, with the advice and consent of the Senate, a Chief of Staff, United States Air Force, from among the officers of general rank who are commissioned in the U.S. Air Force.

[2] Editor's note: General Dougherty presented this paper at the UNT Military History Seminar on October 11, 1997.

Historian Adam Ulam wrote that Josef Stalin, intoxicated by the post-World War II survival of his nation and his own role as wartime leader, "could not long withstand the logic of his position as the ruler of a totalitarian society and as the supreme head of a movement that seeks security through constant expansion."[3] Then Dean Rusk, in his "Reflections on Containment," said that, in keeping with Ulam's assessment of Stalin's imperative for expansion:

> we ourselves bear some responsibility for launching the Cold War, because it may well be that we exposed Josef Stalin to intolerable temptation through our own weakness . . . Just after V-J Day we demobilized almost completely, and almost overnight. We in the State Department were being told by officers on the Joint Staff that we did not have one division in the Army, nor one group in the Air Force, that should be considered ready for combat.[4]

One could take a few specific exceptions to these dismal postwar assessments by the Joint Staff as reported by Secretary Dean Rusk, but my observations were that, in the main, they were just about right. That was the situation in the 1946–47 period. We were not focused on any external threat, for we were still basking in the complete victories in Europe and the Far East, and concerned with garrison and occupation duties. There was no compelling reason to maintain combat readiness; no country dared challenge us. We felt no impulse of fear—we were asleep.

By and large, we were totally preoccupied with getting back to

---

[3] Adam B. Ulam, *The Rivals: America and Russia since World War II* (New York: The Viking Press, 1971).

[4] Quoted in George F. Kennan, "Reflections on the Containment Doctrine," in *Consensus at the Crossroads: Dialogues in American Foreign Policy,* ed. Howard Bliss and Maurice Glen Johnson (New York: Dodd, Mead, 1972).

peacetime pursuits, to getting rid of mountains of wartime supplies in bases and depots throughout the world, downsizing or closing unneeded installations, and building a relatively small regular military establishment for our future needs, whatever they were. President Harry S Truman had explicitly laid out a plan for the creation of relatively large Reserve and National Guard forces, and the services were screening the wartime ranks in an attempt to identify and build a relatively small, young cadre of qualified officers for integration into the depleted ranks of Regular Air Force, Army, and Navy officers.

We had no imperialistic ambitions. Though left in a position where we could have done so, we had no desire to expand, to dominate other regions, or to seize and rule other parts of the world. While we reluctantly accepted our obligation to occupy and stabilize certain areas in the Pacific and Europe for a short period, we had absolutely no intention of becoming the "world's policeman."

This was the early Cold War period, but as a relatively young captain, I had no real feel for it. I had only the prevailing and popular notion, shared by all of my youthful colleagues, that we could never really be confident of cooperation with the Soviets. I was completely occupied with crew duties, base legal officer's "legal work," and caring for my family in remote, ill-equipped habitats. I had no knowledge of the extent of Soviet encroachment into Central Europe and its postwar domination of non-Soviet Europeans. Like my contemporaries, I had no illusions concerning productive international cooperation between the Soviet Union and the Western Allies, but I had an inadequate understanding of what this meant for our future peace and security, and I was not alone in my ignorance!

Not until I read and studied former UK [United Kingdom] Prime Minister Winston Churchill's "Iron Curtain" speech at Fulton, Missouri—and the commentary surrounding it in the nation's press—did it hit me personally that there were serious complications to our uneasy relationship with the Soviets.[5] Then came the reports of what we later came to know as George Kennan's famous "long telegram" from Moscow and the policy of "containment" that it spawned.[6]

[5] Editor's note: On March 5, 1946, nine months after Winston Churchill lost reelection as Britain's prime minister, he traveled by train with Harry Truman to make a speech at Westminster College in Fulton, Missouri. This is widely known as the "Iron Curtain Speech." In this speech, Churchill used the very descriptive phrase that surprised people in the United States and Great Britain: "From Stettin in the Baltic to Trieste in the Adriatic, an iron curtain has descended across the Continent." Before this speech, the U.S. and Britain had been concerned about their postwar economies and had remained extremely grateful for the Soviet Union's role in the winning of World War II. It was Churchill's speech, which he titled "The Sinews of Peace," that changed the way the democratic West viewed the Soviet-dominated eastern bloc. Churchill's phrase received widespread publicity, and it was generally recognized as signaling the beginning of the division of Europe into East and West. Thus, many people consider Churchill's "iron curtain speech" the beginning of the Cold War.

[6] On February 22, 1946, George Kennan, the U.S. *charge d'affaires* in Moscow, sent his famous five-part "Long Telegram" to the State Department. This document became a major factor in shaping U.S. grand strategy in the Cold War era. He sent the "Long Telegram" to Washington shortly after Soviet Premier Josef Stalin's speech about the inevitability of conflict with the capitalist powers, and the capitalist encirclement of the Soviet Union. His analysis began with the thesis that the Soviet leadership conceived world politics as a split into capitalist and socialist societies, in which the "USSR still lives in an antagonistic capitalist encirclement" with which there could be no "permanent peaceful coexistence." Kennan came to the conclusion that Soviet policy was aimed primarily at strengthening the relative power of the USSR in the international environment. Of far greater importance, he argued, the Soviet rulers would attempt to accomplish their goals through the "total destruction of rival power." To this end, they would use every direct and indirect means, and they would do everything in their power, to undermine and infiltrate the political, social, and moral edifice of western states by exploiting what they perceived as the contradictions inherent in the capitalist system. In summing up his view, at the beginning of the fifth and last section of the Long Telegram, he underlined emphatically and in quite alarmist language that the U.S. had to confront "a political force committed fanatically to the belief that with the U.S. there could be no permanent *modus vivendi*." Therefore, Kennan argued that under these urgent circumstances, the most overriding task of the U.S. grand strategy should be the stopping of Soviet expansion. He cautioned that in dealing with the USSR, American officials should approach it with objectivity, thoroughness, and calmness. He was convinced that it was within American capabilities to solve the problem without direct confrontation or a "general

My personal international naïveté, and that of many of my contemporaries in the Regular officer ranks of the services, was rapidly disappearing. The Air Force initiated serious studies of the Soviet Union for us to pursue. Then, of more practical importance, the Soviets themselves closed ground access to the jointly occupied city of Berlin, and the necessity for the Berlin Airlift was upon us. Though I was in the Pacific at the time, all of our airlift squadrons were involved, and our people affected. My introduction to the vicissitudes of the Cold War was underway, and was to continue and intensify for some forty years.[7]

Now, let me move ahead some twelve years into the Cold War period. In the fall of 1959, as a colonel coming out of one of Strategic Air Command's [SAC] operational air forces, I became a resident stu-

military conflict" for two basic reasons: first, the Soviet leaders, unlike Hitler, were "neither schematic nor adventurist," in the sense that they were extremely "sensitive to the logic of force" and, therefore, they could easily withdraw when strong counterforce and sufficient resistance was applied at any point; second, the Soviet Union continued to lag economically far behind the West. See George Kennan, *Memoirs, 1925–1950* (Boston: Little, Brown, 1967).

[7] Editor's note: In May 1948, the United States, Great Britain, and France took steps toward organizing a separate West German state and introducing a new currency for West Germany. These actions led the Soviets to impose by late June 1948 a complete blockade of all surface routes through eastern Germany to West Berlin, which since the war had remained an enclave under the three Western powers' control inside East Germany. An outpost of relative economic prosperity and political freedom more than one hundred miles inside the Soviet sphere, West Berlin was, as Nikita Khrushchev later described it, a "bone in the throat" of Russia. Fearing above all else a strong and rearmed West Germany, Stalin apparently believed that the blockade would force the West to negotiate with Russia a settlement of the German issue as a whole. President Truman, who was not disposed to accommodate the Soviets, responded with a massive and continuing airlift of supplies to the more than two million West Berliners and the Allied personnel stationed there. Their blockade having failed either to isolate Berlin or to change western policy elsewhere in Germany, the Soviets in early 1949 signaled their interest in ending this dangerous stalemate. See Ralph B. Levering, *The Cold War, 1945-1987* (Arlington Heights, IL: Harlan Davidson, 1988).

dent in the National War College at Fort McNair, in Washington, DC. My classmates and I—all Army, Air Force, and Marine colonels and Navy captains—ranged in age from the late thirties to mid-forties. All of us stemmed from the college and Academy classes of 1939 to 1943, and we all had reasonably good records and potential, else we would not have been selected for the National War College. Though well beyond the World War II years, all of us dwelled, with nostalgia and endless anecdotes, on our World War II experiences, often with excessive hyperbole and exaggeration. Several of my classmates had heroic episodes in their records—Congressional Medal of Honor, Navy and Army Distinguished Service Crosses, etc.—but all earned in war as junior officers, not as major unit commanders.

The post-World War II turbulence and uncertainties of mission and organization, which, to put it mildly, had been a sorry state of affairs, were behind us. In my case, Lt. Gen. Curtis LeMay, the forty-two-year-old, gutsy combat commander in Europe and the Pacific in World War II, had left Europe, where he was running the Berlin Airlift, to take command of the newly created Strategic Air Command in October 1948, and move its headquarters to Offutt Air Force Base in Omaha, Nebraska. He is quoted upon arrival at SAC as saying: "We didn't have one crew—not one crew—in the entire command who could perform a professional job . . . we would need to rebuild the organization completely before we would be ready to fight." And General LeMay proceeded to rebuild it completely and make it ready to fight. His creed was: "A force that cannot fight and win will not deter."

The extent to which General LeMay succeeded in his rebuilding and training efforts with SAC through the next decade—and his incomparable example to other commands—must be evaluated as one of the (if not *the*) most significant command actions of the Cold War. I would say today that he was for over ten years the consummate Cold

War commander. General LeMay's demands were: "You must train as you plan to fight"; "Every training mission must be as intense and demanding as an actual combat mission"; "There is no room for second best"; "Measure up or get out."

We began serious, all-source intelligence collection on potential targets and on Soviet equipment, tactics, and command constructs. We knew our enemy. LeMay instilled in all of us a sense of purpose: a sense of *mission*, a mission in which every one of us, from the lead pilot to the ground crewman pulling the chocks from under the wheels, believed that he had an absolutely integral role in the success of our efforts. This was carried down through the organization with an intensity and zeal that inspired excellence. General LeMay was tough. He was uncompromising, but he was not sadistic. All of us knew where he was coming from and what he was trying to do, and we wanted to be part of his team.

To get back to 1959, as I entered the National War College, the Korean War was a recent, but traumatic, memory for most of us, a memory in which our forces fought valiantly but lacked the military professionalism that was to be demanded in the Cold War years that were ahead of us, both in our strategic forces and in our deployed theater forces. The Suez Crisis was also still fresh in our minds, and, to some degree, a bone in the throat of most of our State Department colleagues. At this time, I did not appreciate just how much this episode had affected our cooperation with our allies, particularly the French, but I saw the fallout later in my days with NATO [North Atlantic Treaty Organization] in Europe.[8]

[8] Editor's note: In late October 1956, only days before the Soviets moved into Budapest to quell the Hungarian revolution, Israel, France and Great Britain launched coordinated attacks against Egypt, a former British protectorate. The Anglo-French aim was to repossess the Suez Canal and, apparently, to overthrow Egyptian President Gamal Abdel Nasser. Furious that he had not been informed in advance and disapproving of an action reminiscent of nineteenth-century colonialism, President Dwight D. Eisenhower announced that the United States

In Europe, the early estimates of NATO's force size and the conventional weapons needed to counter and stop a full-scale Soviet attack to the West were absolutely staggering. The SHAPE [Supreme Headquarters Allied Powers, Europe] staff estimated hundreds of divisions and several dozen air armies. Conventional blocking—using conventional weapons for deterrence—was seen to be inadequate. Then came the economical promise of "nuclear deterrence." The relative economy in force size, cost, and basic structure for a nuclear countering force to deter any Soviet aggression was adopted with enthusiasm by our NATO allies, and by us. We adopted NATO's newly fashioned nuclear strategy in the mid-1950s with alacrity.[9]

We who had come from SAC [Strategic Air Command], as well as a few persons from our tactical and naval units, were proficient and experienced in handling nuclear weapons and in the procedures for their delivery. We had mastered radar navigation and all-weather bombing, plus the air refueling tactics and techniques, that gave us

---

would not accept "one code of conduct for those who oppose us and another for our friends." The administration then took strong and successful diplomatic action at the United Nations and elsewhere to force the removal of the foreign forces in Egypt. Meanwhile the Soviets made strong threats against France and Britain, and even proposed to Eisenhower that America and Russia conduct a joint military intervention to restore peace in the Middle East. Faced with hostile world opinion and pressure from the two world superpowers, Britain and France halted their attack and removed their troops by December, and Israel, under intense American pressure, followed suit by the following March. The American hand in the affair left some bitterness among officials in London and Paris that harmed NATO and still rankled when the United States asked for help in Vietnam a decade later. Finally, the Suez Crisis damaged Soviet-American relations, despite their common opposition to the attack. See Levering, *The Cold War, 1945–1987.*

[9] Editor's note: The financial savings were to come from the Eisenhower administration's "New Look" defense strategy, which was designed to lessen reliance on conventional forces and to favor nuclear weapons and bombers and missiles capable of delivering them. Secretary of State John Foster Dulles argued that this approach would allow the West "to retaliate instantly by means and at places of our own choosing," and thus keep the Soviets off balance. By spending less on expensive ground forces, the U.S. could achieve, to use the term of the time, "more bang for the buck." See Levering, *The Cold War, 1945-1987.*

an intercontinental, all-weather capability with our B-47 jet bombers and the emerging eight-engine B-52s. We knew how to handle and employ nuclear weapons.

As we entered the War College, ICBMs [intercontinental ballistic missiles] and IRBMs [intermediate-range ballistic missiles] were proliferating at a rapid rate, some becoming obsolete and being retired within a few years from inception. Ballistic missile technology was racing ahead. We had just mastered the technology for employing solid fuel in our big rockets, making both silo and submarine basing of ballistic missiles feasible and affordable.

The exotic technology of guidance systems for our ballistic missiles and that of our air- or surface-launched cruise missiles was making great strides, as was the SENS [small extension node switch] system of accurate navigation for our ballistic missile submarines. We were now thinking of accuracy in hundreds of feet rather than thousands; we saw that we could develop a "triad" of nuclear delivery systems to ensure survival and reliability: air-delivered bombs, silo-based ICBMs, and submarine-launched SLBMs. We could beef up and enhance our deterrent position with these survivable forces, which were external to the theaters.

Unfortunately for us, the same thing was happening on the Soviet side. In some respects, it was even more dramatic. They had demonstrated the technology of building huge nuclear weapons and delivering them by air-, sea-, and land-based missiles at all ranges from theater areas to intercontinental. Their numbers of weapons were expanding exponentially, particularly their theater-range nuclear weapons with which they could hold Europe hostage to their mid-range forces. We were acutely aware that we were entering a period where there would be a plethora of nuclear weapons on both sides of the Iron Curtain, and effective deterrence would become ever more difficult, even questionable. We no longer held most of the cards in our deck.

We achieved significant military command successes during these days, but these command achievements were largely in the fields of research, development, and logistics, not in the classic "combat leader" roles. Some of these men were: Adm. [William F.] "Red" Raborn, in the development of the missile-carrying Polaris submarines; Gen. Bernard ("Benny") Schriever, the production genius who was responsible for the intercontinental ballistic missiles and early space achievements; Adm. Hyman Rickover, who was building nuclear propulsion for submarines and surface ships with a legendary, uncompromising intensity. These individuals' accomplishments were comparable to General LeMay's success with SAC.

On the military/political scene, both in writings and in lectures, trenchant comments, quotes, articles, and books on the nuclear weapons milieu were coming out in record numbers. Bernard Brodie, Albert Wohlstetter, Henry Kissinger, and others of the military/political world were producing the literature faster than one could absorb it.[10] Our political and diplomatic leadership was becoming steeped in the overall strategy of deterrence.

We War College students were trying to soak it up like blotters. We wanted to master everything available in this arcane area of nuclear deterrence, and to understand the interactions of nuclear forces, the Soviets' and ours. We knew that most of us were on the threshold of senior positions in our services, when the direct military responsibilities of Cold War command were going to be dumped directly in our laps.

It was a sobering time for all of us. A new appreciation of the importance of precluding conflict between the major powers—of

[10] Bernard Brodie, *Strategy in the Nuclear Age* (Princeton, NJ: Princeton University Press, 1959); Albert Wohlstetter, *et al.*, "The Delicate Balance," in *Nuclear Policies: Fuel Without the Bomb: A Policy Study of the California Seminar on Arms Control and Foreign Policy* (Cambridge, MA: Ballinger Publishing Company, 1978); Henry Kissinger, *Nuclear Weapons and Foreign Policy* (New York: Council on Foreign Relations, Harper, 1957).

fashioning reliable firebreaks to the onset of war, particularly in the areas of direct confrontation in Europe and Asia—weighed heavily on all of us. In 1947 George Kennan had given us the idea of containment in our approach to burgeoning Soviet communism, and, by and large, containment had become our central political theme.[11] Professors Brodie, Wohlstetter, and others had coupled political and military containment with a military strategy of deterrence, which was made vital when one weighed the costs of a global catastrophe from a major nuclear conflict, or a nuclear war in Europe.

Into this environment, there came a distinguished lecturer to our National War College podium from the U.S. Military Academy at West Point. This person was Permanent Professor and Head of the Social Science Department [George A.] "Abe" Lincoln, one of the most distinguished and respected academics in the nation. Many of Professor Lincoln's prior students were in the audience. Those of us who had not gone to the Military Academy knew all about his prescience and

[11] Editor's note: In July 1947, George Kennan, perhaps the government's leading expert on the Soviet Union, and at the time head of the State Department's Policy Planning Staff, published an article entitled "The Sources of Soviet Conduct," which appeared in the prestigious journal *Foreign Affairs*. His article, written under the pseudonym "X" (soon identified as Kennan), provided the theoretical underpinnings for American policy in dealing with the Soviets in the early postwar period. Given the tense Cold War atmosphere at the time, Washington policymakers paid more attention to his scathing indictments of the Soviet system and its alleged tendency toward expansion than they did to his calls for restraint and balance in American policy. The "X" article, which first used the word "containment" in advocating a policy toward Russia, focused on the evils of Soviet communism and urged "a long-term, patient but firm and vigilant containment of Russian expansive tendencies" to be achieved by the "application of counterforce at a series of constantly shifting geographical and political points." Kennan later regretted his failure "to make clear that what I was talking about. . was not containment by military means of a military threat, but the political containment of a political threat." Regardless of what he meant, his "X" article contributed to the increasing hostility toward the Soviet Union in 1947 and 1948. See George Kennan, "The Sources of Soviet Conduct," *Foreign Affairs* 25 (July 1947): 566-82; George Kennan, *Memoirs, 1925-1950* (Boston: Little, Brown, 1967); George Kennan, *Memoirs, 1950-1963* (Boston: Little, Brown, 1972).

wisdom. His lecture was profound. All about the importance of fresh water, as I recall.[12]

After his lecture, we scrambled to get a seat in the smaller, more intimate seminar session for the informal question-and-answer period that followed. I made it into the session. Someone asked him about the strategy of deterrence. Professor Lincoln walked to a chalkboard in the center of the room and wrote in big letters: "Capability X Will = Deterrence." Then he proceeded to emphasize that he had written a political/military problem as one of multiplication and not addition. He said that deterrence must be thought of as a product, not as a sum. No matter what "capability" one had, if the factor of "will" to employ it was seen to be lacking, the "deterrent" product was sure to be "zero." On the other hand, one could have the most vital and intense "will" imaginable, but if multiplied with little or no "capability," the product, i.e., "deterrence," would not be consequential. Professor Lincoln said that, to produce the product of deterrence, the military capability underlying it had to be *real*. It could not be ersatz or phony. In a like vein, the will had to be recognized and accepted as a serious and believable intention to employ the capability.

I have thought about this simplistic but profound analogy a thousand times since that day in 1959, and I have played it over and over again in my mind throughout my times as an operational unit commander and as a commander-in-chief of a major U.S. command. I cannot fault it. This was exactly what General LeMay had created in SAC. Professor Lincoln simplified a major problem with all of its implications, while General LeMay gave it substance. I share it with you for assistance in understanding some of the things that will follow.

---

[12] Editor's note: Professor George A. Lincoln was a member of the Department of Social Sciences at the United States Military Academy, West Point, NY. See George A. Lincoln, *et al.*, *Economics of National Security: Managing America's Resources for Defense* (New York: Prentice-Hall, 1954).

Now, back to my story. Late in my year, I was tasked by the War College to produce a formal dissertation on the validity and utility of a military strategy based on deterrence, but to cast it *not* in a situation where we held all of the trumps and an overwhelming nuclear arsenal, but in a world situation where there was an abundance—a "plenty," if you will—of nuclear weapons of all sizes and shapes available on both sides of a military deterrent equation. To spare you the pages and pages of text in my dissertation, I concluded that "containment" of the Soviet Union was the only feasible, short-term objective and that our deterrent strategy and posture, to be effective in such a situation, required: (1) a rational (probably misguided, but not insane) antagonist who could assess, with reasonable accuracy, the probable effect of his attacks; (2) a confident assessment by this antagonist that, no matter what the circumstances of his attack, he could not succeed, could not achieve his objectives, and would assuredly pay a penalty far beyond any possible gain he might achieve; (3) a need to make sure that any enemy was convinced that our capacity to inflict such a penalty was real and in being, that this capacity was adequate, no matter what he did, and, importantly, that our nation had the unquestioned will and intention to mount such a response to any threat or challenge he might impose.

So, I took into my command years a real appreciation of what my first commander-in-chief, Gen. Curtis LeMay, had done in SAC during the early years when he said, "Everything we do must be real, consequential, and meaningful, and it must be recognized as such by the Soviet Union. No bluff, no smoke and mirrors, just raw and recognizable capability to exact unacceptable punishment, and with the unquestioned ability of our forces to employ it effectively under all circumstances."[13]

[13] See also Curtis LeMay, *Mission with LeMay* (Garden City, NY: Doubleday, 1965).

But, I also took from the National War College a more balanced view of the essential synergy of our nation's strengths required by an overall strategy of deterrence. We and our allies needed strong forces, but much more. We needed the political, the economic, the psychological strengths, and the focus on all of these to make deterrence work.

Let me share with you a memorable event that occurred when I assumed the command of Strategic Air Command in 1972, thirteen years after my War College experience. I was flattered that General LeMay was going to join us for the change-of-command ceremony when my predecessor, General J. C. Meyer (our top World War II ace still on active duty at the time), retired and I took command of SAC. Immediately after the change-of-command ceremony, there was a full-scale reception in the officers' club. When General LeMay arrived to go through the receiving line, the protocol people brought him up to the front of the line, and he stood for a relatively lengthy period looking directly at me. He said, "Russ, I hope you are fully aware of the implications of your command responsibilities." I assured him that I was aware of my role and authority, and sobered by the scope and potential of SAC's extensive nuclear arsenal.

Then General LeMay asked me point blank: "Who do you remember from Pearl Harbor?" The question was so surprising that I was taken aback, and I did not give a quick, direct response. When General LeMay pressed me to answer the question, I gave him the only reply that came immediately to mind: "Sir," I said, "I remember General Short and Admiral Kimmel." (After the Pearl Harbor disaster, Lt. Gen. Walter Short, U.S. Army, and Adm. Husband E. Kimmel, U.S. Navy, were relieved of their commands in Hawaii for dereliction of duty, notwithstanding the contributory failures of others.) "You are exactly right," he said. "The responsible military commanders are the ones that history remembers in the aftermath of disasters and defeats." He emphasized that history does not record, nor do people remember, all those others who may have abetted, or even caused, the debacle. It is the one with command responsibility who is charged with the failure! He warned me that my nuclear command responsibilities to this nation were such that I could not afford to fail, that I could never do anything wrong myself, nor ever condone mistakes on the part of others, that affected the mission of my command. "Don't you be remembered in history for a single mistake," he concluded. I shall remain forever grateful for this trenchant advice and the memorable way he gave it.

The "kick the tires and light the fires," "damn the torpedoes," and "follow me" élan of the World War II period gave way over the Cold War years to more sober and thoughtful acts of major commanders whose arsenals brooked no mistakes, because mistakes, once made, could cause a global catastrophe. Training in the nuclear commands of the Cold War was intense. Our training scenarios were designed to be as rigorous, as realistic, and as demanding as they could be made in peacetime, even when such training exacted penalties and incurred hazards, as it did. Such training permeated the last thirty-five years and paid off for us in the end.

Every single procedure and requirement for employing those weapons—from communicating the national command authorities' order to launch, to the actual delivery, penetration, and impact on designated targets—had to be seen to be believable, robust, and reliable. And, by and large, it was seen in just that light. Crew procedures in all of our nuclear delivery systems had to be well thought-out and followed explicitly. Throughout all the nuclear commands, we had what was known as the "human reliability program" to ensure that what must be done was done and, likewise, what was not to be done was not done.

I had a missile control officer in my command who was asked routinely if, upon receipt of a properly authenticated and valid execution order, he would have any doubt or hesitation concerning his ability to turn the activation key and fire his missile. It was reported to me that he hesitated, professing that he really would turn his key if he thought the order was legal, if he thought the circumstances required a missile launch, if he was convinced that it was rational and moral, and so on. Every affirmative action was qualified by a personal subjective decision. This just would not cut it in a nuclear command, for we had designed our command and control system so that these conditions had to be fulfilled to the satisfaction of the national command authorities before the launch order was issued, and that subjective "what-if-fing" after the order was given had no place in the execution chain. Throughout the Cold War, in all the commands in which I served, I found it essential that people be disciplined "to do their country's thing," and found no place for those who insisted on "doing their own thing" with the nation's nuclear arsenal.

The real challenge confronting all of us exercising command responsibilities throughout the years of the Cold War was that of keeping our people and our equipment in a state of peak readiness for instant deployment, without ever employing those capabilities. The command challenge was to ensure that we were equipped, trained, and ready to fight a war that we recognized must never be fought.

Then, in the 1960s and 1970s, we were faced with the sociological, human challenges occasioned by the liberal revolution among our young people: the "Flower Child" years.[14] We had to form our commands from volunteers recruited from a new sort of society and had

[14] Editor's note: The counterculture, or hippie, movement mainly through example wanted to transform society by promoting such ideas as peace, love, community, and freedom from serious employment. The worship of youth, the use of marijuana and other hallucinogenic drugs, the promotion of civil rights, and opposition to the Vietnam War as well as all things military were important components of this movement. Everyone was urged to wear flowers in their hair and to "make love, not war," hence the coining of the phrase "flower children."

to turn them into a truly disciplined force. If we had lost society's support and understanding during those years, we could not have had the continuing flow of trainers and recruits required to maintain a relevant size force. But we did not lose it!

Another unique aspect of military command during those years was that of leading and inspiring our forces without being in the van of their employment, and that continues today. Technology now demands absolute proficiency in our warriors; senior leaders lack this finely honed proficiency. I well remember a night early in the 1950s when, as the squadron commander of fifteen B-47s, I was alerted and required on a "no notice" basis to deploy those fifteen aircraft and crews to England from Arizona. My wing commander got the squadron commanders together and said, in effect, "Now, fellows, ours is a new ball game. It is your command responsibility to get those fifteen aircraft and crews off the ground in a combat-ready condition, not to be in the first aircraft yourself. Forget the World War II commander, gallantly leading his forces into combat. Today, it is up to you to get them ready and launch them in perfect condition for combat, not to lead them off with dash and daring." He said, "That is the way it is going to be in the new Air Force. Our excellence will be measured on our overall performance as a unit, not on individual acts of heroism." My observations are that this absence of individual acts of heroism has been the hallmark of our Cold War success.

I plan to discuss the key attributes of military commanders during the Cold War. In preparation I have searched my mind and my recollections of the Cold War years to compile a list, and an analysis, of the brilliant, bold, and effective commanders through these years. But such commanders just do not jump out for me as do those great commanders of the hot war periods: George Patton, Omar Bradley, Jimmy Doolittle, Arleigh Burke, Ira Eaker, Douglas MacArthur, and the like.

I asked myself, "Why not?" Why do no single commanders during the Cold War years come to mind?"

I continued to provoke my recollections. Surely effective command in the Cold War years must have been maintained, for I knew that it was, having been a part of those years. Of course, we had superb field commanders throughout the war, men such as Lyman Lemnitzer, Lauris Norstad, Andrew Goodpaster, David Jones, Bernie Rogers, Robert J. Dixon, "Ike" Kidd, Earle Wheeler, George S. Brown, Alexander Haig, and Bill Creech. And they go on and on. The Cold War commanders of our nation's forces are legion, and they were, by and large, superb leaders. Nevertheless, in the short term, they are not found to dominate our history of that period. They are not prominent in our recollections, or in our biographical tributes. Why not? Why are they not given accolades for having won the Cold War?

Obviously, the reason is that the Cold War victory was not just a military campaign. It was a total campaign waged by the totality of our nation and our key allies. It was a total victory of all of our nation's attributes, not just its military side. Slowly it began to take shape in my mind that these Cold War military commanders, albeit effective, were not the *sine qua non* of our Cold War achievements. Our Cold War victory, if victory is the right word, was not occasioned by the actions of a few heroic military commanders, but rather the result of the effective actions of all of us throughout our democratic, capitalist society, actions that were sustained over a period of years by our allies and us. Our system had worked, and worked well, notwithstanding our stops and starts and the turbulence often accompanying the acts of our society. No doubt, our military preparedness was critical to Cold War success, but it was only a part of the total posture of the West.

Our political leaders had stayed the course and had kept us second to none, even though there were periods when many of us doubted what the future would bring. We had stayed the course from the early

1950s "long haul" commitment to military development and equipment promised by President Dwight D. Eisenhower during the Korean War years and through the technological revolution associated with the space program of the John F. Kennedy administration. We had recovered from General [Edward] "Shy" Meyer's shocking exposé of a "hollow army."[15] We had supported President Ronald Reagan's vigorous commitment to technological achievements, military modernization, and space defense technology. We did this to the recent period when, just as the Berlin Wall was coming down in 1989, our weapons were finally modernized and procured in quantity and of such consequence that they were the envy of the world.

Witness the Gulf War activities. We had built a modern military system, based on democratic principles and in the midst of a peace-loving, capitalist society, a force that, when employed, exploited modern technology rather than battlefield slaughter, a force that leveraged our strengths and preserved our people through the Cold War years. Our research and development technology was second to none. Our innovations in all aspects of command, control, intelligence, and military equipment were superior. Our production genius (no matter how

---

[15] Editor's note: After withdrawing from Vietnam, the American military went through an abrupt downsizing similar to that experienced at the end of World War II. In 1980, General Edward C. Meyer, then Army Chief of Staff, used the term "hollow Army" in congressional testimony to describe the imbalance that existed between the number of Army divisions and the combat personnel available to fill those divisions. Soon after his testimony, the term "hollow force" became widely used to characterize not only shortages of experienced personnel, but also shortages of training, weapons, and equipment. These conditions undermined military readiness during the mid- and late 1970s.

The Defense Science Board Readiness Task Force, created in 1993 by then Secretary of Defense Les Aspin, and chaired by General Meyer (Retired), in its report dated June 1994, characterized the military of the late 1970s and early 1980s as "hollow forces," and Service members during this period as "on average less well educated, more involved in drugs, less well trained, less well equipped, less well sustained, less strategically mobile, and less highly regarded by the American public."

we joke and malign it) provided equipment that could not be matched. Our space achievements gave us unchallenged control of the "high ground" of intelligence, communications, and command and control. Our gross national product continued to grow and meet the test of these improvements and military equipping. Our political leaders exploited our strengths wisely and effectively. Our military leadership subsumed itself into the whole to achieve total victory. I could go on and on, but suffice it to say, we not only contained the Soviet Union, but we drove it to the wall, and we broke its back. We proved the political fallacy of the Soviet communist system.

I will conclude with the argument that there were no truly heroic military commanders of the Cold War period. Only Gen. Curtis LeMay comes up on my screen as a Cold War commander of truly unusual stature, not only because of his combat exploits (And, in World War II, General LeMay's combat exploits were legion!), but because of his unusual wisdom and skill in the art of applying force to support a deterrent strategy. I think it was he who set the military stage for the full impact of our overall democratic, capitalist system to pin Soviet communism to the wall. He championed the military actions that made military deterrence work over the Cold War years, whether it was in the forces of the Army, Navy, or Air Force. He deserves our commendation, and not the trite condemnations so often seen in the tabloids and shortsighted op-ed criticisms of our national press. I think he was exactly right when he cautioned me, as I assumed command of SAC: "Russ, make sure that you are not remembered in history."

Section IV
KOREA

In a short span of five years, the victorious Allied coalition that had defeated the fascist powers unraveled and became a distant memory. In its stead, a Cold War had developed pitting two great alliances of nations against each other under the threat of nuclear war. Winston Churchill called it an Iron Curtain separating the Soviet Union and its Eastern European satellite states from the western powers led by the United States. The Berlin Airlift, the fall of China to communism, and the explosion of a nuclear weapon by the Soviet Union were all symbols of a very dangerous world in the late 1940s. Despite the threats and fears of war, the United States had reduced its military and permitted its conventional units to deteriorate as a combat-ready force.

In the early hours of June 25, 1950, the North Korean Army attacked across the 38th Parallel against a weak South Korean force. In Washington, President Harry Truman had to make another of the short-notice, major decisions that characterized his administration. Truman opted to oppose the aggression from the north. Acting quickly and decisively, he alerted U.S. forces for combat and immediately sought and won the support of the United Nations to repel the invasion. Korea was a frustrating conflict for the troops as well as for the diplomats.

Two warrior/ historians have contributed articles to this section. Brig. Gen. Edwin H. Simmons served as Director of Marine Corps History and Museums for twenty-four years. As a young officer, he was involved in some of the most difficult fighting in Korea, including the Inchon invasion and the historic evacuation of Allied forces from the Chosin Reservoir in late 1950. His paper provides an overview of the conflict, including the early decisions by Truman to intervene, the lack of preparedness of the military, the Truman-MacArthur controversy, and the ensuing stalemate and ceasefire. Simmons also reviews the contributions of the naval and air forces during the first "jet" war. The forces still face each other across a demilitarized zone, and the security issues involving the Korean people remain in the forefront to the present day.

Col. Henry Gole entered the Army as a volunteer for the draft in 1952 and went on to become one of its brightest teachers and thinkers in the years to follow. His perspective on Korea is that of the young infantryman fighting in the bitterly cold, difficult terrain of that land. The war soon shifted from a fast-moving conflict to a static duel almost reminiscent of World War I. Included were a long series of trenches that reached across the more than 150-mile front. Periodic patrols and sporadic artillery fire relieved boredom for the troops spending their tour in Korea. Gole was struck by the general unpreparedness of the Army of the Korean War era. Occupation duty in Japan did not provide adequate preparation for the intense combat of Korea. Gole left the Army in 1954 only to return seven years later to serve in the Special Forces during the Vietnam War.

In many ways, the Korean conflict served as a transition from the great world war of the 1940s to the limited, guerrilla campaign in Vietnam in the 1960s and 1970s. Korea provided many lessons to be learned, ranging from the proper role of the military in a democracy to the recruiting and training of a ready force prepared to fight in the nuclear age. Too few of the lessons were learned, as the United States would once again find itself in a difficult land war on the Asian periphery.

KOREA

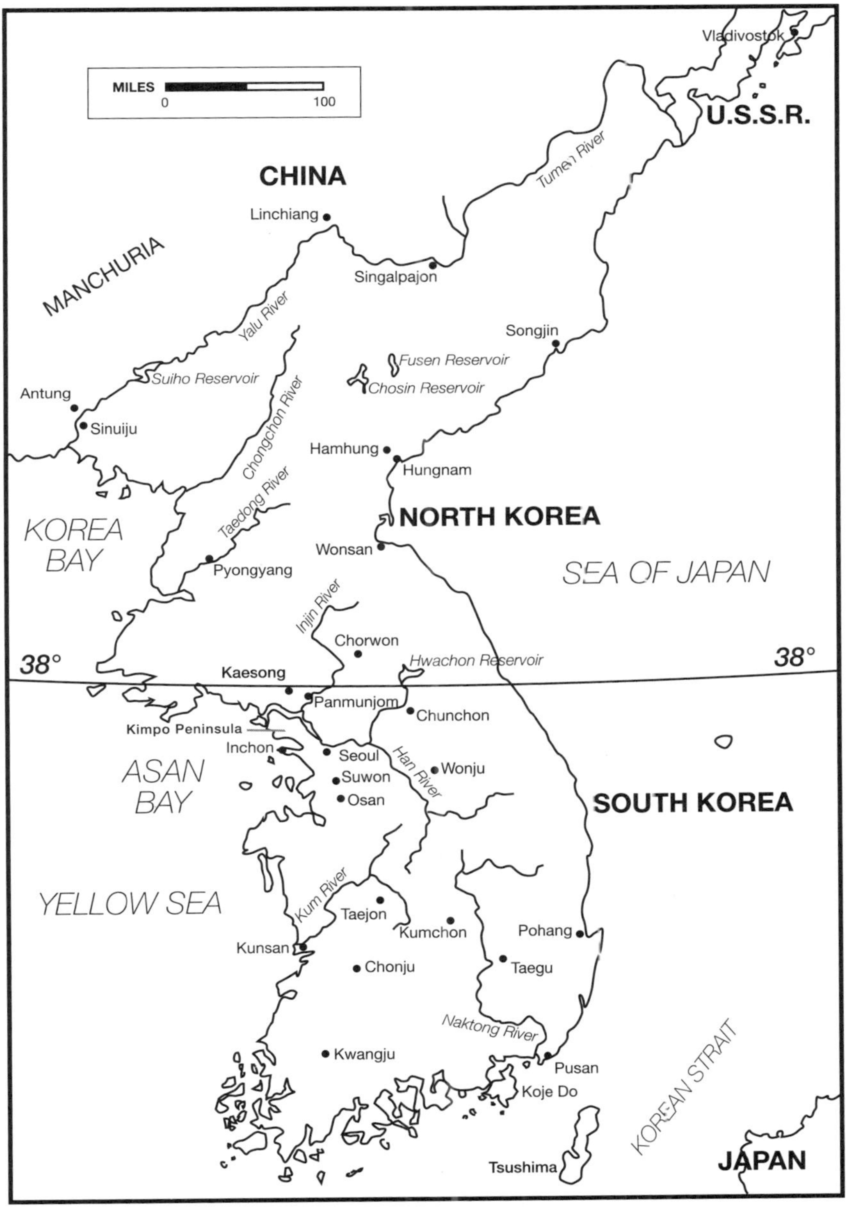

MILES
0
100
U.S.S.R.
Vladivostok
Tumen River
CHINA
Linchiang
MANCHURIA
Singalpajon
Yalu River
Songjin
Fusen Reservoir
Chosin Reservoir
Suiho Reservoir
Antung
Sinuiju
Chongchon River
Hamhung
Hungnam
Taedong River
NORTH KOREA
KOREA BAY
Wonsan
Pyongyang
SEA OF JAPAN
Injin River
Chorwon
38°
Hwachon Reservoir
38°
Kaesong
Panmunjom
Chunchon
Kimpo Peninsula
Inchon
Seoul
ASAN BAY
Suwon
Han River
Wonju
Osan
SOUTH KOREA
YELLOW SEA
Kum River
Taejon
Kumchon
Pohang
Kunsan
Chonju
Taegu
Naktong River
Kwangju
Pusan
Koje Do
KOREAN STRAIT
Tsushima
JAPAN

BRIGADIER GENERAL EDWIN H. SIMMONS, USMC (RET.)

THE KOREAN WAR: ARE THERE STILL MILITARY LESSONS TO BE LEARNED?

Brig. Gen. Edwin H. Simmons is a veteran of three wars: World War II in the Pacific, Korea, and Vietnam. Born in 1921 in Billingsport, NJ, he received his commission in the Marine Corps through the ROTC program at Lehigh University in 1942. He later earned the MA degree from The Ohio State University and is also a graduate of the National War College.

In the Korean War, as a twenty-nine-year-old major in command of Weapons Company, 3rd Battalion, 1st Marines, Simmons participated in the Inchon landing and the recapture of Seoul. He continued in this command during the epic breakout at the Chosin Reservoir. Simmons left Korea in spring 1951 after being wounded.

General Simmons's fourteen military decorations include the Distinguished Service Medal, Silver Star, three Legions of Merit with Combat V, two Bronze Stars with Combat V, and a Purple Heart.

In 1972, General Simmons began serving as Director of Marine Corps History and Museums. He held this position for twenty-four years, six years in uniform and eighteen years as a civil servant. He currently holds the title of Director Emeritus.

General Simmons is the author of five books and more than three hundred articles and essays. Two of his books deal with the Korean War, and another is a general history of the Marine Corps. In June 2000, he published his Korean War novel, *Dog Company Six*, which won the Samuel Eliot Morrison Award for Naval Literature.

In this paper, I propose to review the American military experience at the operational level in the Korean War and from that review to suggest that there are still some military lessons to be learned from that war.[1]

The North Korean invasion of South Korea was a veritable *blitzkrieg,* both in technique and in time. It began at 4:00 AM on June 25, 1950. After a thunderous forty-five-minute artillery bombardment, six North Korean infantry divisions, an armored brigade, and three border constabulary brigades crossed the 38th Parallel into South Korea. On the following day, two more North Korean divisions moved south. The North Korean People's Army [NKPA], some 165,000 men in all, had managed to achieve complete tactical surprise, although there had been strategic indications that should have been noted.

First word of the invasion, a report from U.S. Ambassador John J. Muccio, sent at 11:45 AM on June 25, reached Washington, because of the time differential, at 9:26 PM on June 24. The war was then seven hours old. At 3:00 PM on June 25, the United States government requested a meeting of the United Nations Security Council, and, on June 27, the Security Council called upon all member nations to assist the Republic of Korea.

On June 26, President Harry S Truman had authorized Commander-in-Chief, Far East, General Douglas A. MacArthur, to use

[1] Editor's note: General Simmons presented this paper at the UNT Military History Seminar on September 19, 1987.

Navy and Air Force elements "to attack all North Korean military targets south of the 38th Parallel" and to use naval forces "in the coastal waters and sea approaches of Korea without restriction."[2] The *casus belli* was clear and incontrovertible, and President Truman's decision to commit American forces to the defense of South Korea was a popular one.

From an American viewpoint, and quite probably from the viewpoint of any popularly based government, how a war begins is very important. A clearly discernible immediate cause is essential to the marshalling of American public opinion and support. Without such support, the conduct of lengthy or extensive combat operations by the American military becomes increasingly impossible. So it is that most of America's wars—I might better say America's successful wars—have begun with a triggering device, an immediate cause for war so compelling that it brings an instant, and possibly lasting, coalescing of American public opinion. The best example of this, of course, was the Japanese attack on Pearl Harbor on December 7, 1941.

When World War II ended in 1945, the United States was without argument the strongest military power in the world, but by the summer of 1950, our armed forces had declined to the point of being disastrously unprepared for war, and particularly for war in South Korea.

As had happened after every one of America's wars, peace in 1945 had brought immediate demobilization, a process that, if anything, was accelerated by the attitudes of the new president, Harry S Truman. As a National Guard officer, he had commanded a battery of field artillery in France in World War I, wartime service of which he was vastly proud. He had a visceral distrust of large standing armies;

[2] Editor's note: See "Classified Teletype Conference, dated June 27, 1950, between the Pentagon and General Douglas MacArthur Regarding Authorization to Use Naval and Air Forces in Support of South Korea," Papers of Harry S Truman: Naval Aide Files, Truman Presidential Museum and Library.

he saw little excuse for them in the context of American affairs. In his view, the peace of the world, or at least the prevention of larger conflicts, was guaranteed by the American monopoly of atomic weapons. Such forces as the United States had to maintain as an occupying authority in such places as Japan and Germany were made deliberately unready for combat.

The American armed services were further debilitated by the so-called "unification" debates that led to the eventual passage of the National Security Act of 1947.[3] This act created the office of the Secretary of Defense, and the first incumbent, Louis Johnson, a politician with much the same background as Truman, became the president's primary agent for further reductions of the armed forces in the name of economy.[4]

---

[3] Editor's note: During World War II, competition among the components of the country's armed forces had increased the expense of conducting the war and affected combat efficiency. What was needed, some observers thought, was the unification of those forces. But, any suggestion that the armed forces be unified stirred fierce opposition, particularly among leaders of the Navy, for the admirals feared that the Army would dominate a unified armed service, and the result might be the elimination of the Marine Corps and discrimination against sea-based airpower. Despite the misgivings of the admirals, Truman was appalled by interservice rivalry and duplication, so he pushed through Congress a unification measure. The result was the National Security Act of 1947, which recognized the Army, Navy, and Air Force as coequal departments, all under a civilian Secretary of Defense. The act established the Air Force as a branch independent of the Army and replaced the War Department with two new departments, those of the Army and Air Force. The secretaries of the new departments did not have cabinet status, as had the Secretary of War, and the Secretary of the Navy lost his cabinet rank. The legislation also formalized the institution of the Joint Chiefs of Staff, which was established by executive order during the war, and directed the service chiefs to work together in the preparation of defense plans and consideration of strategy. See John E, Wilz, *Democracy Challenged: The United States Since World War II* (New York: Harper and Row, 1990).

[4] Editor's note: Johnson's personal style and mode of operation made him a figure of extreme controversy. His first move as Secretary of Defense was to evict several high-ranking officers from the largest office in the Pentagon and make it his own. Responding to what Truman wanted, Johnson then suddenly canceled construction of naval ships and, to the disbelief of the Joint Chiefs, slashed another $1.4

Korea received scant American attention in those years. The closest ground troops were the four U.S. divisions making up the Eighth U.S. Army in Japan. These divisions were in no way ready for active operations. The Air Force, which had just become the independent Air Force in 1947, and the Navy were somewhat better prepared.

At the time of the North Korean invasion, the army of the Republic of South Korea numbered about 98,000 men. Only four of its eight divisions were at anything like full strength. They had neither tanks nor heavy artillery. Both the ROK [Republic of Korea] Navy and ROK Air Force were inconsequential. The ROK Air Force, for example, consisted of twenty-two training aircraft. This was not a force that could be expected to stop or contain a cross-border invasion by an army that was superior in numbers, weapons, equipment, and training.

Conjure up a mental map of Korea. The most striking characteristic is that it is a peninsular appendage to the East Asian mainland. This suggests that, as a theater of operations, it might be readily isolated from the mainland, which included Red China and just a bit of the Soviet Union. To the east of the Korean peninsula is the Sea of Japan; to the west is the Yellow Sea. These two watery sides to the peninsula presented an opportunity for a dominant naval power.

Korea is about 650 straight-line miles from its northernmost to southernmost extremities and is shaped like a funnel, a funnel that opens out into a very wide top. This northern boundary is very clearly delineated for almost all of its length by the Yalu and Tumen rivers. All of its northern border fronts on China except for a tiny land link with Soviet Russia at its extreme eastern end. Across Peter the Great

---

billion from the defense budget. To those who charged that he was weakening the country's defense, Johnson responded that the United States could "lick Russia with one hand tied behind our back." One historian observed that Johnson was possibly the worst appointment that Truman ever made. See David McCullough, *Truman* (New York: Simon and Schuster, 1992).

Bay from this land link is Vladivostok. In 1950, the name "Vladivostok" had a very ominous ring. It was synonymous with the Soviet threat to U.S. naval operations.

The boundary with China was approximately 450 miles long. Could this very wide mouth to the funnel be sealed off by air operations? That would be one of the big questions of the war, and the results would be disappointing. That is an exceedingly simplified geographical description of the Korean Theater of Operations. An adequate description would also have to include the effects of terrain, climate, and weather.

Now, to move from geography to leadership and command, we must first consider that towering figure, General of the Army Douglas MacArthur. Whatever might be its other inadequacies, William Manchester's highly readable biography of MacArthur has the perfect title: *American Caesar*.[5] No other two words can better sum up MacArthur. In 1950 he was CINCFE: Commander-in-Chief, Far East. His military authority within his assigned geographical area, which included Korea, was almost total and virtually identical to that enjoyed by the Allied theater commanders of World War II.

On July 10, two weeks after the crossing of the 38th Parallel by North Korea, his mantle of authority was embroidered with another title, CINCUNC: Commander-in-Chief, United Nations Command. His operations in Korea and surrounding waters would be fought under the light blue and white flag of the United Nations. Subject to political constraints, geographic limits, and major strategic decisions, he was quite free to conduct military operations as he saw fit, or so he thought. Eventually, there would be the cataclysmic conflict with President Truman over their respective powers to control or direct military operations.

[5] See William Manchester, *American Caesar: Douglas MacArthur, 1880–1964* (Boston: Little, Brown, and Company, 1988).

On June 28, just three days after the North Koreans crossed the 38th Parallel, Seoul, the capital of South Korea, fell. It soon became apparent, however, that the loss of the capital did not mean the end of the war.

Truman ordered a naval blockade on June 30. The instrument for this would be the U.S. Seventh Fleet with subsequent substantial help by Britain's Royal Navy. Next in the chain of command above the Seventh Fleet was Naval Forces Far East, headquartered in Tokyo and a component command subordinate to MacArthur. Vice Adm. C. Turner Joy was Commander Naval Forces, Far East. Vice Adm. Arthur D. Struble commanded the Seventh Fleet. At the war's beginning, however, the U.S. Navy had only one cruiser, four destroyers, and a few minesweepers in the Sea of Japan.

MacArthur had flown to Korea on June 29 to make his own reconnaissance, and he returned to Tokyo with two ideas fixed firmly in mind. First, American troops had to be committed immediately to the land battle. He gained Truman's approval for this recommendation during the early hours of June 30, and immediately the U.S. 24th Division, the best of his under-strength, under-trained divisions, began moving piecemeal from Japan to Korea. Second, he argued that, to seize the initiative, the U.S. had to use its amphibious capability to land behind the North Koreans. Seoul would be the target of the operation. Macarthur organized a conference on July 4 in Tokyo to consider the implications of such a landing.

On July 13, Lt. Gen. Walton H. Walker, one of Gen. George Patton's corps commanders in World War II, arrived as commander of the Eighth U.S. Army in Korea [EUSAK] and was given command of all ground forces, including South Korean units. The 25th Infantry Division and the 1st Cavalry Division followed the 24th Infantry Division to Korea in mid-July.

At the end of July, Walker ordered all of his troops to fall back behind the Naktong River. The defensive line, manned by about 47,000 American troops and some 45,000 South Koreans, was called the Pusan Perimeter.[6] Reinforcements began to arrive from the United States, including the 1st Provisional Marine Brigade.

In an otherwise completely dismal situation, Walker enjoyed one great advantage, and that was airpower. At the war's outbreak, the only immediate combat support that could be given the retreating ROK Army was that which could be provided by the U.S. Far East Air Forces [FEAF] augmented by the carrier arm of the Seventh Fleet. FEAF, the Air Force component of MacArthur's Far East Command, was commanded by Lt. Gen. George C. ("Strat") Stratemeyer, who had the demeanor, it was said, of a jolly college professor. Largest of FEAF's subordinate commands was the Fifth Air Force, primarily a fighter and fighter-bomber command, based in Japan. Initially, Fifth Air Force fighters and bombers were ordered to attack North Korean forces moving south from the 38th Parallel.

At a greater distance, but also subordinate to FEAF, were the Twentieth Air Force on Okinawa and the Thirteenth Air Force in the Philippines. On July 8, 1950, General Stratemeyer organized the FEAF Bomber Command, with headquarters at Yokota Air Base in Japan, to take operational control of three B-29 bombardment groups, which were being diverted from their primary missions with the Strategic Air Command.

During World War II, U.S. Army Air Forces doctrine had spoken of the "isolation of the battlefield." In practical terms "isolation" had proved impractical, and by the time of Korea, the term "interdiction," implying something less than complete isolation, had come into use. In Korea the interdiction effort began on August 2, 1950. Also begin-

[6] Editor's note: It was called the Pusan Perimeter because it was MacArthur's defensive line that protected Pusan, the major South Korean port for the entry of men and supplies.

ning in August, the fighter-bomber squadrons of the Fifth Air Force and the carriers of Task Force 77 were heavily committed to the defense of the Pusan Perimeter.

MacArthur's amphibious assault on Korea's west coast was made on September 15 with the X Corps, spearheaded by the U.S. 1st Marine Division, landing at Inchon in the face of almost overwhelming technical problems. The outskirts of Seoul were reached on September 21, and in another week of heavy fighting, the city was retaken.

MacArthur's masterstroke had turned the war around, and at the same time Walker's troops had come bursting out of the Pusan Perimeter. The collapse of the North Korean People's Army [NKPA] was at hand. To ensure its destruction, MacArthur asked for authority to go north of the 38th Parallel. This authority was given him with the caveats that he must halt if there was an entry into North Korea of major Soviet or Chinese Communist forces and that he under no circumstances was to cross the Chinese or Soviet borders. Most significantly, the North Koreans had no base of popular support in South Korea. The inconsequential guerrilla activity in South Korea was chiefly the work of scattered and by-passed members of the shattered North Korean Army.

By this time, the UN Command had grown to 315,000 of whom 200,000 were ground combat troops, half American and half South Korean. Also, the 27th British Infantry Brigade and a Philippine battalion combat team had arrived. All five of the U.S. divisions had had their under-strength ranks filled out with KATUSA [Korean Attached to the U.S. Army]. There were some 22,000 KATUSA loosely integrated into American units under the "buddy" system. MacArthur speaks highly of the KATUSA in his *Reminiscences*.[7] Actually, it was an unworkable system at first. These recruits had just three weeks of training, and most could speak no English. Unprepared for com-

[7] Douglas A. MacArthur, *Reminiscences* (New York: McGraw-Hill, 1964).

bat, the KATUSA were easily demoralized, and many hid in foxholes, never firing their weapons. These problems contributed to the breakdown of the "buddy" system in some of the American divisions.[8]

The Eighth Army was given the mission of seizing the North Korean capital of Pyongyang, and the still-independent X Corps moved in amphibious ships to land at Wonsan on the east coast. On October 10, MacArthur had his famous Wake Island meeting with Truman at which he confidently predicted that the Chinese would not intervene. Moreover, MacArthur assured Truman that if the Chinese were to try to cross the Yalu, the slaughter by American airpower would be so great that not more than 50,000 to 60,000 of them would get into North Korea. For two very different accounts of the Wake Island meeting, I suggest the reading of MacArthur's *Reminiscences* and Truman's *Memoirs.*[9]

Pyongyang was taken on October 19, and the much-delayed landing of the 1st Marine Division at Wonsan was made on October 26. The reason for the delay was mines. Historically, Russia had been known for its interest in mines. For Imperial Russia, mines and mining operations played an important part in the Crimean War, the Russo-Turkish War, and the Russo-Japanese War. This interest and use continued through World Wars I and II. In addition to the venerable contact mine, World War II saw the development of the magnetic mine, the acoustic mine, the pressure mine, and various combinations such as the magnetic-acoustic mine. Mines could be moored to the bottom or set afloat as drifters. Even today virtually every Soviet combatant ship has a mine-laying capability. It was very logical for

---

[8] Editor' note: The first British unit to arrive at Pusan on August 28, 1950, was the 27th British Infantry Brigade. The 28th British Infantry Brigade Group followed in September 1950.

[9] MacArthur, *Reminiscences*; Harry S Truman, *Memoirs*: *Years of Trial and Hope, 1946-1952,* vol. 2 (Garden City, NY: Doubleday, 1956).

Soviet Russia to aid her client state by providing the means for mining virtually every suitable beach to forestall another Inchon and to interfere with shore bombardments. Mines are passive weapons that complement other naval weapons. Properly employed, they can deny or make difficult access to harbors and other ocean areas. Much of the Korean coastal region, with constricted channels and shallow muddy water, was ideal for mines.

The job of the minesweeper is difficult, dangerous, and unglamorous. During World War II, the Navy had as many as 550 minesweepers in the Pacific, but by the beginning of the Korean War, the Navy had just four steel-hulled fleet minesweepers (and three of these were in caretaker status) plus six wooden-hulled auxiliary sweepers in the Far East. Although our naval forces sighted a minefield in the approach to Inchon, Flying Fish Channel, the North Koreans had failed to use mines effectively at Inchon. During the last week in September, however, three U.S. Navy ships operating off the east coast struck mines. Two South Korean minesweepers also hit mines during the same period.

The task of sweeping the Wonsan minefield was exceedingly dangerous. It was afterward learned that there were 3,000 mines, a mixture of magnetic and contact mines, in a 400-square-mile area. The North Koreans had sown these 3,000 mines in just three weeks, mostly by simply dumping them off the sterns of wooden barges.

By coincidence, Admiral Struble had commanded Mine Force Pacific, so he knew mines and the threat they posed. Two of his precious minesweepers, the *Pirate* and the *Pledge,* were lost in the process of sweeping the approaches to Wonsan. The commander of the Advance Force sent a woeful message that began: "The U.S. Navy has lost command of the sea in Korean waters . . ." It was not quite that bad, for by the evening of October 25, a channel leading into Wonsan was cleared of mines. However, it had taken fifteen days to accomplish what had been planned as a five-day sweep. The main lesson of Wonsan, said Admiral Joy, "is that no so-called subsidiary branch of the naval service, such as mine warfare, should ever be neglected or relegated to a minor role in the future."[10]

On the same day that the Marines finally landed at Wonsan, a Chinese ambush destroyed a South Korean battalion sixty miles south of the border. After three days of fighting, the parent ROK 6th Division was finished. The enemy was identified as the CCF [Chinese Communist Forces] 39th Army.

By the end of October, the CCF Fourth Field Army, consisting of the 38th, 39th, 40th, and 42nd Armies, was south of the Yalu and was about to be joined to the east by the CCF Third Field Army, consisting of the 20th, 26th, and 27th Armies. Each of these numbered Chinese armies had about 30,000 men and was roughly the equivalent of a U.S. corps, so with seven numbered armies, the Chinese now had at least a quarter-million men in the field.

By November 6, MacArthur was forced to admit to the Joint Chiefs of Staff that "men and materiel are pouring across all bridges over the Yalu from Manchuria." However, MacArthur, still confident of complete victory, ordered Walker to regain the offensive. Substantial reinforcements had arrived, including the British 29th Brigade, which arrived in September 1950, the Turkish Brigade, and battalions from Thailand, the Netherlands, and Canada. Ultimately, fourteen members of the United Nations, in addition to the United States, sent troops to South Korea. The United Kingdom sent two brigades. Canada and Turkey each sent a brigade. Australia sent two battalions, and Belgium, Colombia, Ethiopia, France, Greece, the Netherlands, the Philippines, and Thailand each sent one. Air squadrons came from Australia, Canada, Greece, South Africa, and Thailand. Twen-

[10] See James A. Field, *History of Naval Operations: Korea* (Washington, DC: United States Government Printing Office, 1962).

ty-two naval ships came from Australia, Canada, Colombia, France, the Netherlands, New Zealand, Thailand, and the United Kingdom. The effort of the United Nations, other than that of the U.S., totaled around 40,000 ground troops, more than 30,000 naval personnel, and some 1,100 air force personnel.

China's entry into the war brought MiG-15 interceptors into the equation, imperiling the U.S. bombers, particularly the B-29 Superfortresses, which were pounding North Korea in what was essentially an interdiction campaign. B-29 Superforts, now classified as medium bombers, were used tactically simply because they had soon destroyed their strategic targets and were available for other uses. The threat posed by the MiG-15s, however, was quickly countered by the introduction of the superior F-86 Sabre jets. The air war, in so far as aerial combat was concerned, had become a jet war.[11]

Walker's offensive began on November 24. Two days later, the CCF Fourth Field Army launched a counterattack, and the two forces collided. The CCF Third Field Army moved simultaneously against X Corps. Both Chinese offensives were successful. X Corps was extricated by an amphibious withdrawal from Hungnam, completed on Christmas Eve. The evacuation of Hungnam was the last significant use of the U.S. Navy's great amphibious capability.[12] From time to

[11] Editor's note: Shortly after its introduction, the MiG-15 entered combat over Korea. Flown by Russian, Chinese, and North Korean pilots, the swept-wing MiG struck fear into USAF B-29 bomber crews flying strategic bombing missions over North Korean cities. The MiG-15's speed, maneuverability, and heavy armament allowed it to brush aside escorting fighters and rip through the B-29 formations. B-29 losses to MiGs reached such high levels that the USAF stopped using this airplane for daylight bombing raids and flew all future strikes under the cover of darkness. Only the North American F-86 Sabre was the MiG's equal in combat.

[12] Editor's note: Generally described as an "amphibious operation in reverse," the evacuation of Hungnam from December 10-24, 1950, encompassed the safe withdrawal of the bulk of UN forces in eastern North Korea. It was the largest sealift since the Okinawa operation in 1945. In barely two weeks, over 100,000 military personnel, 17,500 vehicles, and 350,000 tons of cargo were pulled out. Though the Chinese did not seriously interfere with the withdrawal, the

time, further amphibious assaults of the Inchon pattern would be proposed, but they would not be implemented.

Meanwhile, the Eighth Army, which had broken into large fragments, fell back to a line north of Seoul, where on December 23 General Walker was killed in a vehicle accident. Lieutenant General Matthew B. Ridgway was flown out from Washington to replace him, arriving in Korea the day after Christmas. The Chinese resumed the offensive on January 1, 1951, and by January 4, Seoul was again under Chinese Communist control. The UN line fell back but did not shatter, and by January 24 the Chinese offensive had stalled.

The second great American military commander in Korea, after MacArthur, was Gen. Matthew Ridgway, who was quite possibly the finest operational commander in the twentieth century. On January 25, Ridgway began his counterattack, which would continue until mid-April, rolling unrelentingly forward until the UN lines were just north of the 38th Parallel. MacArthur, who initially had not been confident of Ridgway's chances of success, once again began arguing for complete victory. This put him at cross-purposes with Truman and the Joint Chiefs of Staff, who sought to limit the conflict and to maintain strict control of the operations of MacArthur's forces. An increasingly exasperated Truman, with the endorsement of the JCS, finally dismissed MacArthur on April 11. This created a political crisis in the United States but did not greatly affect events in Korea.[13]

---

potential threat they represented necessitated a vigorous bombardment by aircraft from nearby Yonpo Airfield until it was abandoned, artillery ashore, and naval gunfire provided by two heavy cruisers and a battleship plus several destroyers and rocket ships (LSM (R)).

[13] MacArthur was determined to press forward and achieve the victory that had eluded him the previous summer. Ignoring Truman's directive that military commanders make no public statements on political or military policy without obtaining clearance from Washington, MacArthur spelled out his views to news correspondents. And, after learning that Truman was about to make a peace proposal, he issued on March 24, 1951, an incredible statement threatening the Chinese with nuclear annihilation if they did not leave Korea. Because of the

Ridgway moved up to MacArthur's position as CINCFE and CINCUNC, and Gen. James Van Fleet came out to take command in the field in Korea. The full fury of the Chinese spring offensive came down on the UN lines on April 21. This offensive reached a climax with the Battle of the Imjin River, which pitted the Chinese 63rd Army against the British 29th Brigade. As would be repeatedly the case, the Chinese could not sustain a full-fledged offensive, and by the end of April, it was clear that the Chinese attack had lost its momentum. The Chinese paused for two weeks and then on May 15 attacked again. The spring offensive, by American estimates, cost them 90,000 men.[14] Van Fleet then launched a general counteroffensive on May 22. The Chinese appeared to be at the point of complete defeat when orders reached Van Fleet forbidding a further advance to the north.

Less dramatic than the jet-versus-jet aerial combats being fought in the North Korean skies was the introduction by the United States of helicopters into combat. Casualty evacuation had been its first use, but, as the lines began to harden, Army and Marine helicopters were increasingly used for frontline troop movement and resupply.

Truce talks began in July 1951. The lines were at the narrow waist of the peninsula, and here both sides settled down to entrenched posi-

---

confusion generated by the general's threats, Truman felt compelled to withhold his peace proposal. Then, on April 5, Representative Joseph Martin, Republican from Massachusetts, read to the House a letter he had received from MacArthur. The letter summarized the general's views about driving the communists from Korea, and concluded, "There is no substitute for victory." Five days later, Truman relieved MacArthur of his various commands, replacing him with Ridgway. See Wilz, *Democracy Challenged*.

[14] Editor's note: Peng Dehaui (Peng Te-huai) commanded the Chinese People's Volunteer Army (CPVA) in Korea. From October 1950 to June 1951 the Chinese launched five major "counterattacks" under Peng's direction. On April 22, Peng launched his fifth campaign with the aim of retaking Seoul, but U.S. forces under General James A. Van Fleet broke the Chinese offensive north of the city. By May 21, 1951, the front line was at a standstill. See Spencer C. Tucker, ed., *Encyclopedia of the Korean War: A Social, Political, and Military History*, vol.2 (Santa Barbara, CA: ABC-Clio), 2000.

tions. The fighting would go on for two more bloody years, but essentially the war had become a stalemate. A "No Man's Land" 155 miles long stretched across the waist of Korea. The Communist forces now numbered 850,000 troops, but lacking in airpower and lighter in fire support than the 700,000 UN troops, they dug in more deeply.

The United Nations navies had been overwhelmingly successful in the blockading of the two coasts of North Korea, but efforts to seal off the northern border by airpower were much less rewarding. By June 1951, an estimated 55,000 Soviet-built trucks had crossed over into North Korea. A great air interdiction effort, Operation Strangle, was launched to cut Communist lines of communication from the Yalu River south to the front. This massive American air effort ultimately failed as attacks mounted by the Communists demonstrated in the fall of 1952. In a way, it presaged the failure of airpower to halt the flow of supplies down the Ho Chi Minh Trail during the Vietnam War.[15]

The stalemated war continued until the armistice was signed on July 27, 1953. By then the strength of the United Nations forces approached a million men with something over 300,000 of them being Americans. The ROK Army, at first of dubious quality, had grown to sixteen divisions and over 600,000 men.[16]

---

[15] Editor's note: Operation Strangle was launched on May 31, 1951, for the aerial interdiction of the Communists' seven main transportation and communication highways leading to the front. At first Operation Strangle was very successful, but by mid-June the Communist forces were able to resupply and regroup their frontline troops more easily, and the aerial campaign bore diminishing results. As would be repeated in Vietnam, the difficulty in destroying trucks, the ease in repairing vehicles, and the vast number of new trucks supplied to the North Koreans by the Soviet Union made interdiction almost impossible. On a positive note, senior North Korean prisoners captured later confirmed that their leaders had called off a major August offensive because of the destruction of 40,000 trucks. However, never in the six months did the FEAF ever effectively stop Communist resupply of their combat forces nor isolate the battlefield. See Tucker, *Encyclopedia of the Korean War,* vol. 2.

[16] Editor's note: As 1953 opened, the ROK Army was a steadily improving fighting force, having added heavy artillery and armor. Its training centers were more

Korea was by our own choice a "limited war." The enemy was given virtual guarantees that there were both geographic boundaries and thresholds of military action that we Americans would not cross. After the first year, the enemy knew almost with certainty that the war would not be carried into the Chinese homeland.

Korea was a conventional war fought with conventional uniformed forces using conventional weapons in a conventional way. It was a war of east-west lines moving up and down a north-south axis until equilibrium was reached. The pattern of operations was roughly analogous to the pattern of World War I as fought on the Western Front. The first year was a war of movement characterized by sudden and dramatic successes and reverses as new impulses of force were introduced. After the truce talks began, the fighting settled down to a stalemated war of position, during which neither side risked a general offensive, until the armistice was signed. At this point, the analogy of the Korean War to World War I breaks down. Germany, of course, did not consent to an armistice until its Western Front had been broken.

The taking of the enemy's capital has always been the classic way of winning a war, rather like checkmate in chess. But, in the Korean War, Seoul was twice taken by the enemy and twice recaptured. Similarly, Pyongyang was taken by UN forces and retaken by the Communists. Capture and loss of these respective capitals neither won nor lost the war for either side.

U.S. Air Force analyses of the Korean War accept it as one more historical justification of the overriding priority USAF doctrine gives to achieving air superiority. This was achieved rather cheaply. During the first weeks of the war, FEAF easily destroyed the North Korean Air Force, catching most of it on the ground at its airfields, which is

---

than meeting the requirements for replacements and men for newly activated commands. When the ceasefire was signed ending hostilities, the South Koreans possessed a large, new, and strong army of which they could be proud. See Tucker, *Encyclopedia of the Korean War,* vol. 2.

the best place to destroy aircraft. From then on American air "owned" the air space north to the Yalu. But, at the Yalu this air superiority ended because UN aircraft were not permitted to violate the sanctity of the Manchurian borders. Once enemy aircraft began operating solely from the sanctuary of the Manchurian airfields, attacks on airfields were no longer possible. About one thousand enemy aircraft were destroyed in aerial combat. Of this number, USAF Sabres destroyed the lion's share, 810 enemy aircraft including 792 MiG-15s. The ratio of kills was ten-to-one in the Sabres' favor.

America's supremacy in airpower was offset by the enemy's passive and active defenses growing out of his long-learned experience going back to his wars with the Japanese. Tactical airpower, particularly close air support, was of great importance in that many times it tipped the balance in UN favor, offsetting Communist superiority in numbers. Interdiction, on the other hand, was a qualified but not complete success. However, by the war's end, the Air Force concluded that "air-interdiction attacks against the rear of the Communist ground armies undoubtedly had a decisive significance that was secondary in importance only to air-superiority operations." Complete isolation of the battlefield was not claimed. In the words of the Air Force's official history of the war, "Korea's peninsular conformation and its scarcity of good transportation arteries simplified interdiction, but the relatively short distance from the front lines to the Yalu and the modest supply requirements of Red troops hindered the effort."[17]

However, many Army and Marine Corps officers were less appreciative of interdiction as compared to close air support. Interdiction was something much more remote and distant than close air support, whose effects could be immediately perceived from the ground. As MacArthur reported to the Congress, "It is quite evident to anybody

[17] See Robert F. Futrell, *The United States Air Force in Korea, 1950-1953*, rev. ed. (Washington, DC: Office of Air Force History, U.S. Air Force, 1983).

who is acquainted with war that determined ground troops cannot be stopped by air alone."[18]

By World War II standards, the Far East Air Force was not a large air force. During the course of the war, FEAF controlled an average of nineteen aircraft groups totaling sixty-two squadrons. On any given day FEAF would control about 1,250 aircraft of which about 850 would be combat-ready. U.S. Air Force aircraft delivered about 476,000 tons of ordnance, carrier-based U.S. Navy aircraft about 120,000 tons, the Marines about 82,000 tons, and friendly foreign air forces about 20,000 tons.

America's naval near-monopoly was used most effectively during the first year of the Korean War. Control of the seas, taken for granted, made possible the movement of UN military strength to Korea. Six out of seven UN personnel who fought in Korea went there by sea. Seapower made possible the amphibious assault at Inchon and the amphibious withdrawal at Hungnam. After that first year, however, there were virtual guarantees that there would be no further amphibious operations against the North Korean coasts. Once the land fighting settled down into stalemate, the primary uses of naval forces were for blockading and carrier-based air interdiction. The close blockade of North Korea's coast denied the Communists easy resupply by sea and helped contain the theater of operations. And, it must also be remembered, seapower kept the United Nations Command supplied throughout the war.

On the ground, we allowed the enemy to shift the nature of the war from a war of maneuver, in which we had all the advantages, to a war of position, wherein most of our advantages were neutralized. Even so, we can conclude that the American military experience in Korea, viewed in operational terms, was a qualified success. At sea and

[18] U.S. Congress, Senate Joint Committee on Armed Services and Foreign Relations, MacArthur Hearings, 1951.

in the air, we prevailed completely. On the ground, territorial *status quo ante* was achieved. Behind the wall of the fortified Demilitarized Zone, South Korea has flourished. The ultimate cost for Americans in Korea was 157,530 casualties of whom 33,629 were battle deaths and 20,617 were other deaths.

Twelve years after Korea, we would be involved in another long East Asian war, one that would have a much less satisfactory outcome than the Korean War. There are many parallels that can be drawn between Korea and Vietnam, but also many differences. In some ways, Vietnam was a rejection of Korea and the lessons it had to offer. Both wars demonstrated that America is in truth a Pacific power, not an Asian power. In projecting force across the Pacific, our greatest strengths are our air and naval capabilities. These capabilities were underused in the Korean War and misused in the Vietnam War. I hope this is a lesson that has been learned just as it is to be hoped that we have learned that America is at a great disadvantage whenever it engages in a ground war in East Asia.

COLONEL HENRY G. GOLE, USA (RET.)

COMBAT IN KOREA: REFLECTIONS BY A ONCE-YOUNG SOLDIER

Col. Henry G. Gole's initiation to combat came as a draftee during the Korean War, where he served in 1953 as a rifleman and BAR (Browning automatic rifle) man before being promoted to sergeant and squad leader.

After receiving his bachelor's degree from Hofstra University in 1957, he served a three-year stint as a high school history teacher and coach. In the meantime, he found time to earn a master's degree from the Fletcher School of Law and Diplomacy in 1958 and a master's degree in education from Hofstra in 1960.

Gole reentered the Army in May 1961 and remained until 1988. He continued his formal education while in the Army, earning a master's degree in history from Stanford University in 1969. After completing infantry, airborne, and ranger training at Fort Benning in 1961, Gole served two Special Forces tours in Vietnam (1966–67 and 1970–71), the latter with MACV-SOG (Military Assistance Command Vietnam-Studies and Observations Group), an unconventional warfare task force engaged in highly secret operations throughout Southeast Asia. He had earlier completed a Special Forces tour in

Germany (1963–65).

Gole was assigned to the Special Assistant for the Modern Volunteer Army, Department of Army Staff, 1971–72, and played a role in planning for the all-volunteer Army as conscription was phased out. Colonel Gole is also a scholar of national repute. He taught European history at the U.S. Military Academy, 1977–80, and served at the U.S. Army War College, 1980–84 and again from 1986 to 1988 as Director of International and West European Studies.

He earned his Ph.D. from Temple University in 1991 and is the author of numerous articles and book reviews on history, military education, the Bundeswehr, NATO, war planning, and special operations. He continues to teach on an adjunct basis at the Army War College. His book, *The Road to Rainbow: Army Planning for Global War, 1934–1940,* was published in 2003. His *Soldiering: Observations from Korea, Vietnam and Safe Places* (Brasseys) is due out in early 2005. His current project is the biography of Gen. William E. Depuy.

Combat has been described as 1 percent terror and 99 percent boredom, but I found it to be low-grade fever, fatigue, blackheads, and defecating in the woods, usually at a time and a place not entirely of one's own choosing. I intend to convey my sense of being a combat soldier in Korea. The essence of the experience is in the details within the spirit of the time, but mostly it is about the men.[1]

I left college to volunteer for the draft in 1952 because I wanted to be the Audie Murphy of the Korean War. Since I was born in 1933, the war-in-my-head was World War II. I followed that war like a sports fan, keeping scrapbooks, mostly of sleek aircraft and beautiful ships. Who would, after all, save pictures of grown men rolling in mud and

[1] Editor's note: Colonel Gole presented this paper at the UNT Military History Seminar on September 26, 1998.

snow? I cheered on my uncles and the other guys who fought it, for they were heroes to me. In 1952, it was my turn to serve.

Basic training was fun and filled with the stock characters I had seen in the Hollywood version of the Army. Discipline in that brown-shoe Army was arbitrary, and our training cadre was third-rate. Most of them were ignorant drunks. Further, this NOO YAWKER was stunned to see in the bus station at Blackstone, Virginia, signs at water fountains and toilets declaring: WHITES ONLY and COLORED. Camp Pickett was integrated; Virginia was not.

After basic training, there was no doubt concerning my ultimate destination. I crossed the Pacific Ocean to Korea via Japan with 4,500 souls at nine knots aboard the good ship *Montgomery Meigs*. Some twenty-five years later, one of my colleagues in the History Department at West Point was then-new Major, and now four-star General, "Monty" [Montgomery] Meigs. His family has been littering American battlefields with its bodies for several generations. Nice man. Good family. Rotten ship. Life in Compartment 4-C above the engine room and below the galley and waterline is not an ideal topic for a luncheon talk. We were stacked four high in pipe-framed canvas bunks. The showers were saltwater, so no one used them more than once on the trip across the pond. Many of the landlubbers were constantly seasick. Vomiting in a confined area caused a chain reaction. In all, it was an unpleasant voyage.

We disembarked at Yokohama, Japan, boarded a train, and spent a couple of nights at Camp Drake, outside of Tokyo. There we were issued M-1 rifles, zeroed them in, turned in our stateside gear, got our "go-to-war" equipment, and climbed aboard another troopship, destination Pusan, Korea. We soon had the impression that this was a serious business that we were undertaking.

Those who have shared my experience will affirm that one could smell Korea long before it was sighted, the consequence of fertilizing fields for millennia with human waste. Lined up for hours, we sounded off the last four digits of our serial numbers when the man with the clipboard called our names as we came off the gangplank. Into the windowless train cars with wooden benches we went. The trip north took over twenty-four hours, as we were frequently shunted off to the side so that priority trains could clatter through. There were also many tunnels along the way. By the time we left the coal-burning train, our blackened faces suggested that a minstrel show was in town.

I was deposited at the 25th Infantry Division Replacement Center where an officer told us that we were in the Army's "best" division. I was sent to the 27th Infantry [Wolfhound] Regiment, which was in squad tents in reserve. There an officer told us that we were in the "best" regiment. Then we went on to the 1st Battalion, which, of course, was the "best" battalion. An officer said so.

Finally, I was sent to Choppin' Charlie Company. After fifty years I recall the scene with absolute clarity. Someone aimed me at the Charlie Company orderly room, which was nothing but a squad tent. Somebody told me to report to Sergeant "X," who was the platoon sergeant of the 1st Platoon. I trudged down the muddy company street in the rain with rifle, duffel bag, steel pot, and pack to the designated tent. My awkward entrance was greeted with a growl: "Close the [blanking] flap!" The adjective that he used was alliterative. Variations of that multi-purpose word served as gerund, noun, verb, and adverb. Nevertheless, I reported. The next time my platoon sergeant spoke to me was on line when he said, "You're a big kid," and he tossed me a BAR. That's how personnel decisions were made in a rifle platoon.

Memories of my first night on line are vivid. Despite removing the Tropic Lightning[2] patches from our shirts and jackets and despite

[2] Editor's note: The shoulder sleeve insignia for the 25th Infantry Division features a lightning bolt on a red taro leaf with the stem up, surrounded by a yellow border. The taro leaf is indicative of the origin of the 25th Division in the Hawaiian Islands, while the lightning flash is representative of the manner in which the division performs its assignments.

covering the truck bumper markings with mud or tape, as we relieved the ROK [Republic of Korea] Marines, a voice came over the public address system from the Chinese lines: "Welcome, Woofhounds! Welcome, Charie Company! Welcome, Rootenant Kramer!" So much for our secret troop movement.

As we filed through the trench, three of us were directed to occupy a bunker: Anderson, Amborn, and Gole, the three new guys. Instead of mixing the replacements with old hands, there we were: HEAR-NO-EVIL, SEE-NO-EVIL, and SPEAK-NO-EVIL. No one had prepared us for the normal battlefield sights and sounds: artillery, mortars, and the irregular popping of illumination rounds. Worse still, no one had prepared us for the penetrating scream from what I later learned was a "quad fifty," four .50-caliber machine guns mounted on a halftrack vehicle. This one was located a half-mile behind us and fired directly over us at irregular intervals. It had the charm of tin being dragged across a chalkboard.

The demonstration of amateur leadership continued into the wee hours of the next morning. At about 2:00 AM, I was awakened and taken to a machine-gun bunker that I manned until 4:00 AM. I was to report every thirty minutes by sound-powered telephone to the platoon command post, wherever that was. After an hour or so of a noise and light show that revealed concertina wire reaching from my .30-caliber machine gun out to infinity, I heard footsteps in the trench approaching my position. I stepped into the shadows at the rear of the bunker from where I could see the trench, knowing that I was invisible to anyone in the trench looking into the black on black of the bunker's interior. I pounced on a Chinese or Korean, slapped his weapon away, kicked him into a leaning position, and pressed my bayonet into his back, thus getting his undivided attention. With the safety off my M-1, which was leveled at my prisoner, I whistled into the telephone and reported. A disembodied voice told me to ask my prisoner his name. "Kim See Yong," I reported. "Congratulations," said my platoon sergeant, "you have captured a KATUSA from our 1st Squad." KATUSA was the acronym for Korean Attached to the U.S. Army. So it went. The only instruction that I recall came from the other BAR man, Ismael Rios Rodriguez from Naranjito, Puerto Rico. His advice was first-rate, and so was he.

In the spring and early summer of 1952, I was engaged in the routine functions on line: trench guard, patrolling, and manning a squad-sized outpost, or OP, about a mile from the front of the MLR [Main Line of Resistance]. Those of you who are familiar with the trench warfare of World War I have a picture in your head that approximates what I experienced. By day we rested, improved fighting positions, and from time to time dove into bunkers to avoid incoming artillery or mortars. The latter normally happened when our tanks, on Hill 155 to our left, pulled forward, put direct fire rounds on the Chinese, and then backed to the reverse slope of the hill. We cussed the tanks and the Chinese in that order. Tanks pulled forward; tanks fired; tanks withdrew; and Chinese shot at me.

Our patrols were another example of amateurs playing at war. Since I could read without moving my lips, I had read a little manual filled with valuable tips. It was entitled *Combat Patrolling and the Individual Soldier*, which, among other things, cautioned that soft hats, not helmets, should be worn on patrol and that individual equipment should be taped or tied down to avoid the characteristic sounds of troops moving. It also stressed that patrol routes should be varied. Nevertheless, we wore helmets and used the same routes out and back, and our equipment was not muffled in any way. At the same time, we wore clumsy armored vests and laid communications wire all the way out and back, miles each way. Frequently, our patrol route was thicker than my arm with communications wire from earlier patrols. Our noise and the use of the same routes invited ambushes and booby traps, and that is what we got.

On one occasion we conducted an afternoon rehearsal for an ambush planned for that night. It included formations to be used, actions at danger spots, and the positioning of each man at the ambush site. Then we rested. We were about to leave the friendly front lines when Rodriguez said to me, "Gole, look!" and he pointed to my BAR. Since the BAR was old and worn, a retaining pin had fallen out unnoticed. I told the patrol leader and suggested that I either get another pin or grab an M-1. He thought that over and directed me to join the alert squad, which would go to the rescue of the patrol if needed.

We were not called upon that night, but a U.S. artillery round rigged as a mine by the Chinese on one of those too-often used routes ripped the patrol. Amborn, my companion of that first night on line, had a leg blown off, and I never saw him again. Three others were injured by shrapnel but returned to duty. My buddy, Rodriguez, praised "Doc" Mitchell, the medic, who somehow patched Amborn, controlled his bleeding, and got serum albumin into his bloodstream to save his life, if not his leg. Rodriguez pointed out that my position in the formation was closest to poor Amborn, and he said I was down to eight lives. Amborn and I had been on line for about a month.

I went on some twenty combat patrols that were wildly exciting and stupidly executed. I did not think much of the leadership skills or guts of my platoon leader nor of the platoon sergeant, but perhaps they were told to avoid casualties. In any event, they always played it safe. In my own case, I think I was suspect for being too "gung-ho." It is my impression that some 10 percent of the troops—the Audie Murphy aspirants—shared my views. The majority of the troops, including the leadership, concentrated on survival and getting home.

I spent about three weeks with my squad at an outpost called COW, which was approximately a mile directly forward of where we had been on line, and I have a distinct recollection of a searchlight—code-named "Sally"—over Panmunjom some five to ten miles to our left front. It indicated to both sides the neutral place where armistice talks were being conducted. It was also a good reference point for navigation at night.

Once, at first light I saw a firefight. The tracers streamed both ways, and ricochets were visible. But I could not hear a thing due, I suppose, to the direction of the wind. More than once I watched, like a tennis fan, artillery exchanges between our side and Chinese guns, literally over my head.

"Bedcheck Charlie," a small enemy aircraft that made a loud noise, flew overhead almost nightly to drop a bomb on troops to our rear. We found that amusing and cheered "Charlie."

One night I popped a hand grenade at a sound I had heard. Since there was no body spread on the wire in the morning when we checked, I had probably disturbed a hungry rat. On another occasion, our OP [observation post] fired in support of one of our patrols that was in contact with a Chinese patrol near us. Cummings was killed. He was the first KIA [killed in action] I knew.

I also remember that I took four of us to a listening post in "no-man's land." I suppose I was assigned to take them because I was a "veteran" private.

We were always tired on OP COW. An assault was expected, so we were on 100 percent alert at night, and we deepened our trenches by day. One night, after being awake for forty-eight hours, I told Andy to give me his M-1 so I could walk trench guard. My normal post was an uncovered fighting position that overlooked the path leading to our OP, a path we closed at night with concertina wire to which we attached flares and tin cans for early warning. My fighting position was a notch in the trench. It consisted of sandbags and ammo boxes inserted in the walls of the position to hold hand grenades and extra magazines for my BAR. On a quiet night, while peering into the darkness from my perch on the stack of sandbags, it was very hard for this nineteen-year-old to keep his eyes open, so I walked trench guard.

When I got to my friend Rodriguez on the far side of the OP, he was surprised to see me. Hearing about my struggle to remain alert, and knowing that I was a non-smoker, he thought a cigarette would stimulate me. So, on the floor of the trench and under a poncho, I smoked a C-ration cigarette. It worked. With tears in my eyes, I was alert for about an hour. Within a week, I was smoking from one to two packs a day, a habit that lasted until 1988, when I retired from the Army.

On line we received two cans of beer per day. At first I gave mine to my buddies, but then I learned to like beer. I saved my beer and cooled it in the stream that ran by our bunker. Coming off a patrol at 3:00 or 4:00 in the morning, John Plunkett, my assistant BAR man, and I would drink a few cans to get a buzz before getting a few hours of sleep.

While on line, we got various goodies on an irregular basis: toilet articles, pocket books ranging from classics to trash, sewing kits, cigarettes, and candy. Why do I remember Chuckles, Tootsie Rolls, and Mary Janes? We shared everything, so I have no recollection of bickering. And we appreciated the goodies.

Another amenity was the shower point. One day while I was at the OP, the squad leader shouted, "Who wants a shower? One man!" When no one sounded off, I said I'd go. I left my BAR at the OP, and I borrowed an M-1. Then I walked two miles to the company orderly room and hopped on a truck. After some thirty minutes, I dismounted in the vicinity of several tents joined together like a hobo camp. A pump pulled water from a stream into showers in several of the tents. One entered a dry tent to peel off fatigues, underwear, and socks that were never to be seen again. Boots, wallets, and dog tags were left in a secure place.

After exiting the shower, the procedure was to dry, put on clean fatigues, underwear and socks that more or less fit, collect boots, dog tags and wallet, and hop back on the truck. Within minutes we were covered with red dust not unlike that found from Georgia to Virginia. By the time I had walked back to the OP, sweat and dust had become mud covering the me exposed to the world. Some of my nether regions, however, had been sanitized. The next time the squad leader asked for a volunteer "scrubie," I declined.

After returning to our position on line after two weeks at the OP, John Plunkett and I occupied "Lakeview Manor," a bunker that doubled as a sleeping and fighting position. It was constructed of a timber frame covered with stacked sandbags to absorb small-arms fire, mortars, and artillery rounds. An aperture for my BAR was about a foot high and three feet wide. Chicken wire on the outside was defense against hand grenades. Our bunker was like the others, except that the main trench ran through it. John slept on one side, and I slept on the other. Our bunks consisted of engineer stakes as a frame, communications wire for makeshift springs, and C-ration boxes for a crude mattress.

Very big rats and tiny mice shared our "home." A stream from our rear flowed under our trench and fed a rice paddy to our front. The rest of the squad joined John and me in damming the stream, thereby creating a pool that both the rats and we used. The rats drank the water, and we bathed in it, obviating the need to visit the shower point. Hence, the name "Lakeview Manor" that graced the entry to our abode, and I think it was home for about a month.

I can still see the ROK soldiers who were with us in Charlie Company. Kim Yong Kil! Kim See Yong! Pak Yong Wu! Um Chuk Sup! Just saying the names rings of the exotic to this hopeless romantic.

Um was from Pusan, and he asked GIs en route to Japan for R&R [rest and recuperation] to bring back Japanese books. He had studied at a university, was very bright, and constantly read Japanese publications. He was also the permanent point man for Lieutenant Kramer's platoon. Kramer, who was on his third tour in Korea, had been promoted through the ranks until he got a battlefield promotion. He was a war lover. At first I wondered why Um lounged about reading while the rest of us did the dirty details, but that was part of the deal he had made with Kramer for being the lieutenant's point man. Kim Yuk Kil served in the North Korean Army, was captured, and then served in my squad. We used a combination of Pidgin English, Korean, and Japanese but were unable to get to the nuances of his story. At six feet tall and weighing 195 pounds, he probably came from somewhere in North Korea near Manchuria. He had a wonderful sense of humor and a volatile personality. Another of the KATUSAs had been impressed into the Imperial Japanese Navy in the Second World War. He told me about firing at U.S. aircraft at Saipan.

We were never quite sure how to interpret the bedding habits of our Korean comrades. We wondered whether they bundled up together for warmth when it was cold, with temperatures at times twenty to thirty degrees below zero Fahrenheit, or if they were simply open about homosexuality. My later experiences with Vietnamese men holding hands in public and Montagnards sleeping in heaps on chilly nights in the Central Highlands of Vietnam raised the same questions. I think I observed displays of innocent friendship and shared body heat against the cold with regard to the Koreans, but I am not certain.

Discipline in the Korean Army, however, was unambiguous. American leaders were required to bring KATUSA discipline problems to the senior Korean in C Company, Sergeant "Tommy." A brief exchange in Korean was followed by Sergeant "Tommy" beating the hell out of the KATUSA, beating as in a punch to the groin, followed by a knee to the face, followed by some serious combat-booted kicking. Then he brought the offending soldier to attention, and the process was repeated. It was generally enough to say, "We go to Sergeant 'Tommy'" to adjust attitude. It was alleged that Korean officers had "Article .45" authority, literally a license to kill.

I can testify as an eyewitness that Korean discipline was similar to that in the Turkish Brigade assigned to the 25th Division. Officers and NCOs simply called the soldier to attention and proceeded to kick and punch. I never saw a Turk or a Korean raise an arm to protect himself. He stood at attention until knocked to the ground, and then he returned to the position of attention until dismissed.

My connections to activities outside the company were few. We lived in an area devoid of civilians. As I recall, we had to go some twenty miles (presumably out of artillery range) to the rear to see Koreans engaged in normal civilian pursuits. The only civilians we saw on a regular basis were the kids or old-timers hired as kitchen helpers and officers' houseboys. Lieutenant Kramer's "house boy," however, turned out to be a girl, a discovery regarded with amusement by the troops. I have no idea how the dignitaries up the chain of command regarded that situation.

I was in Seoul twice, both times via the back of a "deuce-and-a-half." Much of the city was rubble. We drank Japanese beer and chased girls; and on one occasion, an MP told me to square away my field cap. That is really all I can report about my visits to the capital city.

Combat veterans will recall that in the U.S. Army on Thanksgiving Day and Christmas Day, Americans got the full holiday meal with all the "fixins," literally from soup to nuts, including shrimp. It occurred no matter where the troops might have been at the time, even on a remote OP. This is a tradition that I hope we will maintain despite its obvious inefficiency. However caustic a GI may be on occasion, he always appreciates the effort at Thanksgiving and Christmas.

All GIs liked payday, and on payday in Korea, the troops were paid, period. One reported to the platoon leader in his CP bunker: "Sir, Private Gole reporting for pay." "How do you want it?" "Sir, I want $5.00 in cash and the rest to ride." The amount of money was $78 base pay, $9.00 overseas pay, and $45 for combat pay. That amount combined entitled Private Gole to $132. I took $5.00, and the rest was in the hands of the Army, available to me on the next payday. My options were to write a postal money order to send home or to take some or all of my money. I took $5.00 to demonstrate to myself that I actually had money. Even then it was like Monopoly money: military scrip, not greenbacks. I would give the $5.00 to one of my friends going on R&R to Japan with careful instructions to buy anything, just to show that the money was real. For months on line, I literally had no need for money.

We received copies of *Stars and Stripes* that were two or three days old. Some American newspapers mailed free copies to GIs. The *Chicago Tribune* did that, and I remember a buddy's "*Trib*" that was a week or two old.

For reasons that bear analysis, I found that bonding among peers in Korea was intense, but generally not durable. The bonding I experienced in Vietnam, however, was intense and lasting. I have had contact with men I knew as young fellow soldiers in Korea, but with one or two exceptions that association eventually ended after five or ten years. On the other hand, friendships formed in Vietnam some thirty-five years ago are still strong. I think that has to do with our going separate ways after Korea in contrast with the shared memories and common profession of those I served with in Special Forces in Vietnam. The latter, Special Forces men, comprised a kind of fraternity even before our Vietnam days. I must emphasize, however, that in squads, crews, and teams in both Vietnam and Korea, we were as thick as thieves.

One night at the outpost, Rodriguez came around to my position to share his hot chocolate. It was not a complicated matter to him. He had drunk half his canteen cup, and he offered the other half to me. I absorbed the lesson. Since we were normally filthy and running low-grade fevers from a combination of exposure to the elements and irregular sleep, we had many opportunities to nurse one another and do the dirty job for a buddy who was ill.

In late 1953 the Army decided to upgrade the education of all soldiers to the fourth-grade level. I was shocked to find out how many illiterates there were in the company, so I tutored them informally, reinforcing what they had done in *Ding Dong School*. A grandfather had raised one of the men in a logging camp in northern California, and this soldier had never gone to school. At the age of twenty-four, he had already lost all his teeth, a matter that he attributed to a diet of sourdough when he was a child. He was quite bright and learned easily. Another buddy was a Portuguese from Rhode Island. His family fished. He too had never attended school. One day I asked him for a status report on school. He demonstrated competence at adding and subtracting and told me that his group had begun multiplication. I drew up the multiplication table on a piece of—what else—C-ration box, and the feat earned me the reputation of being a genius. All those numbers! I showed him how to multiply, and once he had broken the code, he was delighted with his knowledge. When he discovered that he had to learn the tables, however, he grew sullen and refused. Hell hath no fury like a thwarted pedagogue! I strangled him just a little bit and banged his head a tad to encourage him. Thereafter, he worked his way from the twos to the tens. I doubt that he teaches at Brown University or MIT, but I know he can multiply to ten.

In Korea I gained an appreciation for American good fortune. An unforgettable memory for me and for people like me was the abject poverty I saw in Korea and later in Vietnam and what happens when indigenous poverty and American wealth exist side by side. Two episodes will suffice to make my point.

Late in my tour, when I was a sergeant sipping coffee in the mess hall, the mess sergeant, a decent man with whom I had served earlier in a squad, entered pale and in near shock. I put a cup of coffee in front of him and asked what was wrong, and here is what he told me. On a daily basis, Charlie Company dumped slops from the mess hall into a sump about two miles from the company tents. A village arose around the sump. The villagers lived in shacks built from scrap sticks, canvas, and flattened beer cans. As the village grew, competition for the slops became keen. As the mess sergeant backed up his three-quarter-ton truck to the sump on this rainy day, an eager father slipped from the moving truck after jumping on, and it ran over him. A man died attempting to feed his family on the slops from our mess hall.

At the end of my tour, I left Korea from the port of Pusan. Before boarding the ship, we spent a night there in a compound surrounded by barbed wire. In the morning of a hot and sunny day, I watched children two to four years old playing. They were pushing a sled in the deep dust ten feet from where I watched. All of them were filthy, almost naked, and they were laughing. The blond-haired, blue-eyed boy with Oriental eyelids caught my attention and made me profoundly sad. We Americans have serious race problems, but a blond-haired, blue-eyed Korean national—if he survived—could tell you about prejudice. Perhaps we have some sense of that problem from the publicity given to so-called Amerasians fathered by GIs in Vietnam. We had no such catchy word for Amerasians then, but I recognized a poor little bastard when I saw one.

The relationships between officers and enlisted men have undergone a major change in the years since 1952. I had little contact with officers in basic training or later with Charlie Company in Korea, and that suited me fine. By and large they were an unimpressive lot. My company commander, First Lieutenant Kelly, wanted me to get a commission. When I indicated my intention to leave the Army to attend civilian college, he said some visionary things about army aviation, many of which I later saw realized. He suggested that I might become a pilot and ride the wave of the future. I later thought of him in Vietnam where the helicopter was the "deuce-and-a-half" truck of that war.

Earlier that year, I was ordered to report to the first sergeant. As I moved out smartly for the orderly room, I examined my conscience for insufficiently concealed sins that might have been uncovered by duly constituted authority. "Report to the Company commander," said the FIRST SHIRT, and I did. Captain Senger was a West Point officer, and the youngster that I was thought he was a very old man. I later found out that he was twenty-nine. He put me at ease and explained that the Army selected some soldiers to attend West Point, perhaps after some time in a special preparatory school. He then asked me if I was interested. I asked if I could think it over. The next day I declined, but I did appreciate the captain's interest in me.

Later, Captain Senger did something else that I've never forgotten. The day we left Charlie Company to go home, I joined a group of about a dozen other Wolfhounds to pick up our records at Battalion S-1, the personnel shop. Captain Senger was the S-1. He sat us down, and in a five-minute talk he thanked us for our service. This was so totally out of keeping with the usual manner in which officers treated us that it made a deep impression on me and, I suspect, on the others. What followed, however, made an even deeper impression. He escorted us to a waiting truck, watched us clamber aboard, stood at rigid attention, and saluted us until he disappeared from our sight.

As we currently grumble about knee space and peanuts on contemporary commercial aircraft—and I include myself as a grumbler—it is good for the soul to recall life on a troopship. The crowding, boredom, and anxiety of the trip to the Far East became the crowding, boredom, and heightened anticipation of the trip home. We were looking forward to escaping the known arbitrary foolishness of military life and to enjoying the unknown arbitrary foolishness of civilian life.

We sailed from Pusan to Yokohama to Seattle. We were in Fort Lewis, Washington, long enough to eat the long-promised steak and ice cream and to visit the PX. There I bought some cheap civilian clothing, all the time anticipating cross-country adventures.

We climbed aboard a troop train that was to be our home away from home for the next five days. Two memories survive intact. One is of the farm women on the Great Plains hanging out wash and waving greetings to the passing soldiers. The other memory is of jumping off the train at a stop near Minneapolis-St. Paul, where a few of us—in civvies for the first time in over a year—ducked into a bar to drink beer until the train moved. Actually, it was moving toward the East Coast when we caught it.

We arrived at Camp Kilmer, New Jersey, where I had been issued my first uniforms almost two years earlier. Silly and officious "twits" herded us about for a couple days to accomplish what an average cretin could do in minutes. I barely suppressed a strong urge to feed them a "knuckle sandwich." Let us not forget that one of the less attractive features of the conscript Army is the blind leading the blind. On liberation day the silly "twits" who had successfully defended New Jersey continued their pettiness up to the moment they handed me my release and final pay. I shook the dust of the U.S. Army from my boots in July 1954.

Had someone ever told me that I would voluntarily return to the bosom of the U.S. Army seven years later, I would have laughed or slugged him. I was a very angry veteran, not yet twenty-one. But, after earning a couple degrees and being restless after three years as a high school teacher, in 1961 I responded to President John F. Kennedy's inaugural speech by returning to the Army. I think I missed the company of good men and the prospect of high adventure.[3]

My full career is a story for another day, but later experience stood in sharp contrast to what I have described today. First, the Special Forces soldiers with whom I worked in Vietnam were skilled, brave, and completely reliable. They knew what they were about, and many of them at the moment of truth laid down their lives for their friends. That approach to soldiering contrasted sharply with the playing at soldier that I saw in Korea, in an outfit that enjoyed a good reputation.

Finally, although I do not have the time to develop the point, as one reads about high-tech solutions to military problems, be dubious about the antiseptic, "gee-whiz" panaceas. Certainly, let us support our troops and put the best equipment in their hands, but the most important thing leaders can do to prepare soldiers for combat is to, first, train them, and, second, create a climate within which teams, squads, and crews become bands of brothers. Such bands win or die trying. And that is why we hire soldiers.

[3] In his inaugural address on January 20, 1961, John F. Kennedy stated: "And so, my fellow Americans, ask not what your country can do for you. Ask what you can do for your country."

Section V
VIETNAM

During the 1960s and 1970s, the United States was engaged in one of the most difficult conflicts in its history. Working to contain the spread of communism in Asia and motivated by the desire to foster democracy among the nations of the region, the United States became entangled in a difficult struggle on the periphery of Asia. Its actions were inhibited by the presence of nuclear weapons and the determination to keep the conflict limited and local. Further, the United States was involved in a series of domestic crises that only complicated its dilemma. A major civil rights struggle under the leadership of Martin Luther King was under way; a major movement to enhance the status of women in society emerged; and other minority groups such as Latinos and Native Americans began to organize and demand their full rights and opportunities in society. It was a turbulent time that shook America to its roots. Conducting a war in a distant land in the midst of its domestic challenges was difficult if not impossible for the United States. The effects of the conflict left deep scars upon the American political and social landscape.

Professor George Herring from the University of Kentucky is one of America's most prolific and respected authors on the war, especially its diplomatic elements. Herring concentrates on the role of President Lyndon Johnson as commander-in-chief during the conflict. He refers to LBJ as "The Reluctant Warrior," the beleaguered president, forced to conduct a distant war while his major priorities, the domestic agenda, suffered at home. Herring recognizes the difficult environment that Johnson confronted but ultimately concludes that he failed to address the major issues that the civilian leader in a democracy must deal with in wartime. He refers back to President Lincoln in the Civil War and the strong hand that he took in leading the nation through that difficult war. Herring calls Johnson one of America's weakest wartime presidents especially because he failed to provide a clear vision and strategy for the nation and the military waging the war.

The next paper, once again, takes the reader from the broad questions of national strategy to the warrior himself and his personal sacrifice. In this case, Brig. Gen. David Winn writes about the air campaign designed to hamper the resupply of the Communist forces in the south and persuade the North Vietnamese to negotiate a settlement to the conflict. Winn flew the F-105 Thunderchief from a base in Thailand against targets in North Vietnam. He describes the war and the bombing campaign as being led by "good men doing dumb things." He was shot down in 1968 and imprisoned in Hanoi for six years. His description of life in the POW camp provides a fascinating look at another aspect of warfare in addition to ground combat. The POWs, mostly from the Air Force and the Navy, had to prepare for a lengthy stay in the "Hanoi Hilton." They established an effective chain of command based upon rank, not service; created an imaginative communications system through a "tapping" code; and dealt with a myriad of problems such as the wisdom of escape attempts when great pain and suffering awaited those left behind.

The Vietnam War ended with the evacuation of the American embassy in Saigon in April 1975. The generation of military and civilian leaders who served during the Vietnam War were determined to avoid another conflict with ill-defined goals and a divided nation.

THE VIETNAM WAR, 1964-75

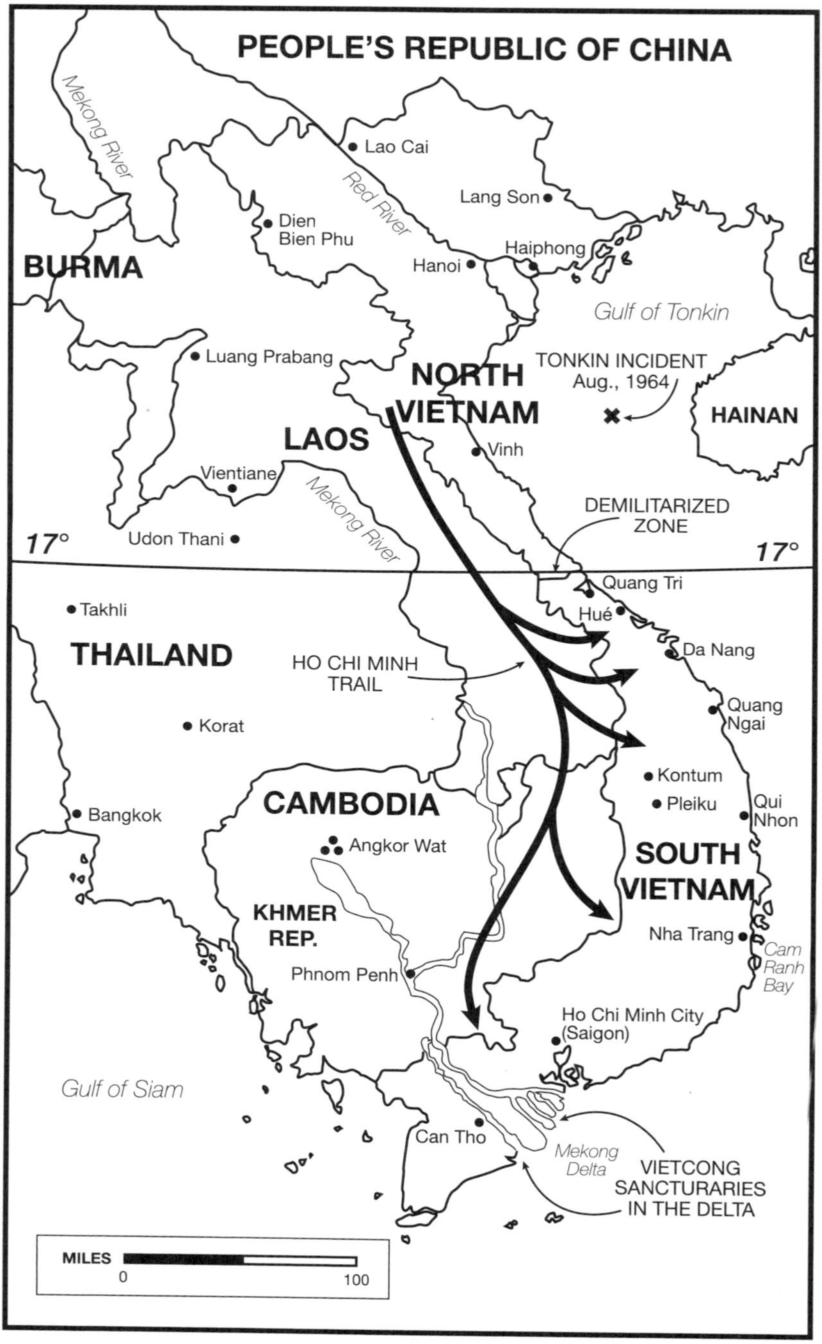

DR. GEORGE C. HERRING (UNIVERSITY OF KENTUCKY)

THE RELUCTANT WARRIOR: LBJ AS COMMANDER-IN-CHIEF

George Herring, a professor of history at the University of Kentucky, is one of the nation's foremost scholars of the Vietnam War. He is the author of three books on that war, and his monograph, *America's Longest War: The United States and Vietnam, 1950–1975,* is acknowledged as one of the best general works about that conflict. In addition to his books on Vietnam, Professor Herring has published three other books as well as scholarly articles in the *Journal of American History, Political Science Quarterly, Diplomatic History,* and *Military Affairs.*

On several occasions during his academic career, Professor Herring has been called to serve as chair of the Department of History at the University of Kentucky. His other honors at Kentucky include: Alumni Professor (1990); Distinguished Professor (1988); University Research Professor (1986–87); and Hallam Professor of History, (1985–87, elected by colleagues). Professor Herring also has served as president of the Society for Historians of Foreign Relations (1989).

Lamented Lyndon Johnson in 1965, "Every time we have gotten near the culmination of our dreams, the war bells have rung. If we have to fight, I'll do that. But I don't want . . . to be known as a War President."[1]

Whatever his wish, Johnson *is* remembered as a war president, and among America's commanders-in-chief, he generally rates with the least effective. He is, of course, popularly viewed as the only American president to lose his war, something he greatly feared and on more than one occasion vowed he would not let happen. He is scored, on the one side, as the stereotypical, shoot-from-the-hip Texan, the warmonger who destroyed Vietnam to save his own ego, and from the other side as a timid, all-too-"political" war leader who refused to do what was necessary to win an eminently winnable war.[2]

Such criticisms tell a great deal about the way Johnson fought the war, but they do not get at the fundamental problems of his war leadership. To be fair, of course, limited war is extraordinarily difficult to fight, especially within the American system, and Vietnam was a war that probably could not have been won in any meaningful sense. Still, the deficiencies of Johnson's leadership contributed to the peculiar frustrations of the Vietnam War and its outcome, and these deficiencies derived to a large extent from his personality and leadership style. Looking at such crucial issues as his handling of public opinion and the formulation of strategy, I will analyze the ways in which Johnson exercised the duties of commander-in-chief in America's longest war.[3]

In a limited war, the role of commander-in-chief is admittedly a most difficult one. In total war, the president can wrap himself in the

[1] Quoted in George Herring, *LBJ and Vietnam: A Different Kind of War* (Austin: University of Texas Press, 1994).

[2] Editor's note: Dr. Herring presented this paper at the UNT Military History Seminar on October 9, 1999.

[3] See George C. Herring, *America's Longest War: The United States and Vietnam 1950–1975*, 2nd ed. (New York: Alfred A. Knopf, 1986).

flag, rally the nation, and even suppress the criticism that in peacetime normally goes with the office. A fundamental principle of limited war, on the other hand, is that it should be waged without too much intrusion into the life of the nation. The commander-in-chief must set the tone and thus cannot appear preoccupied with the war to the exclusion of other things. But, with men and women dying in the field, he cannot appear indifferent, either. He must walk a very high and thin tightrope. From the beginning of the war to the end, Johnson struggled with this dilemma, but he never quite resolved it.

Most of his associates would agree with Clark Clifford that LBJ "was the most complex man I ever met."[4] He was prodigiously energetic, obsessively ambitious, proud, and outwardly vain. He was a driven man, single-minded, manipulative, overbearing, and capable of great meanness to those closest to him. Despite his huge achievements, he remained profoundly insecure, and he was sensitive to the smallest slight, real or imagined. At the same time, he could be compassionate and warm toward other people, and he was capable of great generosity. He was committed with every fiber of his being to large causes. "He had as many sides to him as a kaleidoscope," Dean Acheson once observed.[5] "He could be altruistic and petty, caring and crude, generous and petulant, bluntly honest and calculatingly devious—all within the same few minutes," recalled Joseph Califano.[6]

Johnson was in many ways miscast for the role of commander-in-chief in a limited war. He shared to some degree the yearning for military glory common to his generation. He took great pride in the Silver Star he won in World War II. Draping the Congressional Medal of Honor around the neck of a chaplain who had distinguished him-

[4] See Clark Clifford with Richard Holbrooke, *Counsel to the President: A Memoir* (New York: Random House, 1991).

[5] See Dean Acheson, *Present at the Creation* (New York: W.W. Norton, 1969).

[6] See Joseph A. Califano, *The Triumph and Tragedy of Lyndon Johnson: The White House Years* (New York: Simon and Schuster, 1991).

self in battle, he was overheard to exclaim: "Son, I'd rather have one of these babies than be President."[7] On the other hand, he had little of the boyish fascination with war of his idol Franklin Roosevelt. He had no lust for combat, and his one day under fire in World War II was contrived for political ends.[8] More important, much of his political career had been devoted to the cause of domestic reform, and he later complained that he had been forced to shun "the woman I really loved"—the Great Society—for that "bitch of a war on the other side of the world."[9]

In terms of personality, LBJ was particularly ill suited to be commander-in-chief in the confusing and intractable war in Vietnam. He was a flamboyant and impulsive man in a situation that demanded restraint, an emotional man given to wild mood swings in circumstances that required calmness and steadiness. He was a man with a passion for success and a yearning for greatness, whose whole life had been a single-minded quest for measurable achievement in the form of bills passed, wells dug, and schools built, fighting a war in which it was difficult to establish criteria for progress, much less measure it. He was a restless and impatient man waging war against an enemy

---

[7] Quoted in Herring, *LBJ and Vietnam.*

[8] Navy Lieutenant Commander Lyndon B. Johnson, the first member of Congress to enter active duty in World War II, was awarded the Silver Star in 1942 for gallantry in action on a flight over enemy territory in the Southwest Pacific. For most of his life as a politician, Johnson proudly wore a Silver Star pin identifying him as a war hero. Whether Johnson truly rated the Army's third highest combat award is a question his biographers have long debated. Robert Caro, in *The Years of Lyndon Johnson: Means of Ascent* (New York: Alfred A. Knopf, 1990), states, "the most you can say about Lyndon Johnson and his Silver Star is that it is surely one of the most undeserved Silver Stars in history." Robert Dallek, in *Lone Star Rising* (New York: Oxford University Press, 1991), believes LBJ's Silver Star was more about politics than bravery. Dallek concluded that there was a deal made between General Douglas MacArthur and Johnson. LBJ would get his medal in return for a pledge that he would lobby Roosevelt to provide greater resources for the Southwest Pacific Theater.

[9] Quoted in Doris Kearns, *Lyndon Johnson and the American Dream* (New York: Harper and Row, 1976).

who thought in terms of years, not days, and centuries, not decades. He was a man for whom defeat was intolerable, even unthinkable, ensnared in a conflict that probably could not have been won.

From the outset, Johnson dutifully grappled with the challenge. His credo from his youth had been that if you "do *everything*, you'll win," and in every personal crisis he had faced, he had pushed himself beyond his limits.[10] He thus brought to *his* war the same enormous energy and compulsive attention to detail that characterized his approach to life in general. From the outset, he demanded the final word on the tonnage, timing, and targets of air strikes against North Vietnam. "Those boys can't hit an outhouse over there without my telling them," he would boast with characteristic hyperbole.[11] He insisted on being informed of every troop movement. He stopped drinking in 1966 the scotch he so loved for fear he would not be at full capacity in some crisis.

Whatever public image he sought to convey, during most working days, he could not escape the burdens of war leadership. His mornings usually began with edited summaries from a National Security Council staffer of cables reporting the latest developments in Vietnam. It was not unusual for him to call the White House Situation Room at midnight, 4:30 AM, and 6:30 AM and ask in a concerned voice, "What's going on?"[12] In October 1968, he convened a meeting of his top advisers at 2:30 AM, which his wife Lady Bird conceded was "bizarre behavior even for him."[13]

His passion for information was legendary. In the morning, he would devour several major newspapers and the *Congressional Record*

---

[10] Quoted in Lawrence J. Korb, *The Joint Chiefs of Staff: The First Twenty-Five Years* (Bloomington: Indiana University Press, 1976).
[11] Quoted in Herring, *LBJ and Vietnam.*
[12] Quoted in Herring, *LBJ and Vietnam.*
[13] Lady Bird Johnson, *A White House Diary* (New York: Holt, Rinehart, Winston, 1970)

while watching three television networks simultaneously. Despite conscious efforts to do so, he was not able to balance Vietnam with other concerns, and his absorption in it became near total.

He faithfully and at times eloquently executed his public, ceremonial role as commander-in-chief. He regularly visited wounded war veterans, his voice sometimes sinking to a "barely audible whisper as he murmured over and over: 'Your country is grateful to you.'"[14] On one occasion he quoted an eve-of-battle prayer attributed to George Washington: "Good God, what brave men must I lose today."[15]

From early on, it is equally clear, Vietnam was a source of great frustration for him. When Senate dove George McGovern sought to explain to him why the United States had erred in intervening in Vietnam, he exploded, "Don't give me another goddamn history lesson . . . I've got to deal with where we are now."[16] As the war dragged on, opposition mounted, and as that elusive light failed to appear at the end of the tunnel, his frustration grew. "I can't get out," he complained. "I can't finish with what I've got. So, what the hell do I do?"[17]

For the emotional Johnson, the war became a source of great personal grief. "No man felt . . . more heavily the burdens . . . of the decisions he was called on to make," a sympathetic Secretary of the Treasury Henry Fowler later remarked. Fowler compared Johnson to Lincoln, a comparison the president himself used as a source of comfort, adding that "if the mothers of the men who went to Vietnam could have seen him on occasion as I saw him, reading their letters with the deepest emotion, they would have felt sorry for him, as I did, for the grief he had to suppress publicly, but gave way to privately, of carrying on this dreadful conflict."[18]

---

[14] *Time,* May 20, 1966.
[15] *Time,* May 24, 1968.
[16] Quoted in George McGovern, *Grassroots* (New York: Random House, 1977).
[17] Johnson, *A White House Diary.*
[18] Quoted in Henry Fowler, Oral History Interview, LBJ Library, Austin, TX.

Grief sometimes gave way to melancholy and self-pity, a device he had also used from his youth to force others to share his pain. He told a group of labor leaders in August 1967 that the first thing he reviewed each morning was a list of the men who had died in Vietnam the day before, and he added: "Remember that every time you criticize me it is just another rock of cement that I must carry."[19] His mentor and confidante, Senator Richard Russell, stopped going to the White House alone because, he explained, Johnson would start crying uncontrollably, and he could not stand to be subjected to that kind of emotionalism.

Although he took on the job of commander-in-chief with the greatest reluctance, Johnson gave it his full attention, applying himself with characteristic single-mindedness. He carried out the ceremonial aspects of the position with restraint and quiet dignity. He worked hard at managing the war, seeking to oversee each detail, agonizing over it, eventually suffering from it. His failure was not from want of trying. He can be more readily faulted for getting too involved in the day-to-day detail of the war, for letting the trees obscure his view of the forest.

One of the most important tasks for the commander-in-chief in the American system is to generate and maintain public support, and in limited war this is especially difficult to do. Unlike his counterpart in total war, the president cannot rally the nation. Yet he must sustain public support. How to balance these conflicting demands especially vexed Johnson, and as the war grew more unpopular, anything he did or did not do opened him to ridicule, abuse, indignation, or outrage. If he attempted to raise morale, as with his notorious injunction to the troops to "nail those coonskins to the wall," those who opposed the war pilloried him.[20] If he did nothing, he was charged with failing to lead.

[19] Quoted in Herring, *LBJ and Vietnam*.

[20] Quoted in Herring, *LBJ and Vietnam*.

Johnson never resolved this dilemma. At the outset, he and his advisers went by the book, playing it low-key, hoping to hold public support without exciting popular passions. This did not happen, of course, and by 1967 they were fighting a desperate rear-guard action to prevent collapse of the home front.

At least moderately concerned about public support, some administration officials in the summer of 1965 proposed a full-scale program to rally the nation. Johnson rejected all such proposals. Complacency may have been one reason. After World War II, within the larger confines of the Cold War consensus, the executive branch had mastered the art of analyzing and manipulating public opinion. Postwar administrations were never free from criticism, but in no case was a major foreign policy initiative frustrated by lack of public support.

More important, perhaps, the war posed a huge dilemma for the president's beloved domestic programs. He was deeply committed to the Great Society, and he knew that if the United States were driven out of Vietnam, his dreams of domestic reform would be crushed. He also feared that a public debate on Vietnam would jeopardize the Great Society legislation then pending in Congress, and he knew that if he revealed candidly to the American people what he increasingly realized to be the prospective costs of the war, his goals would be jeopardized.

But, there were larger and more important reasons for the administration's approach that derived from prevailing theories about the way limited wars should be fought. Johnson and his top advisers especially feared that mobilizing the nation for war would set loose irresistible pressures for escalation and victory that might provoke the larger war with the Soviet Union and China the commitment in Vietnam was designed to deter. As Dean Rusk later put it, "in a nuclear world, it is just too dangerous for an entire people to get too angry, and we deliberately tried to do in cold blood what perhaps can only be done in hot blood. . . ."[21]

They thus gambled that, without taking exceptional measures, they could hold public support long enough to achieve their goals in Vietnam. As a result, the United States went to war in July 1965 in a way that was uniquely quiet and underplayed. The president announced the major troop increase at a noon press conference instead of at prime time. He lumped it in with other items in a way that downplayed its importance.

With the exception of several hastily arranged, typically Johnsonian public relations blitzes, the administration persisted in this low-key approach until the summer of 1967. The president made few public appearances and fewer speeches. At first, his silence was justified in terms of strategic necessity, aides confiding that he feared statements of optimism might sway hawks to press for all-out escalation, doves for a negotiated peace. Increasingly, however, he was criticized for being the most aloof chief executive since Calvin Coolidge and for being unable to communicate to the nation a sense of what it was doing in Vietnam and why it was necessary. *Time* reported in August 1967 that he was holed up in a small study away from the Oval Office, "strangely insulated from his countrymen's doubts and fears."

Increasingly on the defensive, administration officials responded to the growing criticism in a way that was typically Johnsonian. If Ronald Reagan was the "Teflon President," to whom nothing stuck, Johnson—to a large degree by choice—was the "Flypaper President," to whom everything clung.[22] A compulsive reader, viewer, and listener, who took every criticism personally and to heart, he was at first intent on and then obsessed with answering every accusation, responding to every charge. When Gen. Matthew Ridgway came out against the war,

---

[21] See Dean Rusk, *As I Saw It* (New York: W.W. Norton, 1990).

[22] See Herring, *LBJ and Vietnam.*

the president ordered his aides to get statements of support from two other leading World War II generals. Reams of paper were devoted to proving how wrong critical columnist Walter Lippmann had been on so many occasions. White House staffers wasted thousands of man-hours compiling dossiers on critics like Senator J. William Fulbright and especially, of course, the despised Kennedy brothers.

By mid-1967, the administration belatedly recognized that its greatest crisis was at home. As the war dragged on with no end in view and as domestic unrest grew, the president's job approval rating steadily declined. More ominous, the number of those who thought that sending troops to Vietnam had been a mistake increased sharply, raising disturbing parallels to Korea. Still more unnerving was the mood of the nation, anxious, frustrated, increasingly divided.

Signs of waning support left the administration deeply troubled. Johnson and his advisers particularly worried about public perceptions, fed by the press, that the war had become a stalemate. The president groped for some magic formula to reverse the spread of disillusionment, on one occasion even longing for "some colorful general like McArthur [*sic*] with his shirt neck open" who could dismiss as "pure Communist propaganda" the talk of a stalemate and go to Saigon and do battle with the press.[23] Anticipating his dramatic decision of March 31, 1968, a despondent president wondered aloud at a top-level meeting in early October what the effect on the country would be if he decided not to run again.

Vietnam was not fundamentally a public relations problem, of course, and a more vigorous and effective public relations campaign would likely not have changed the outcome. Still, what stands out quite starkly is the strangely limited and notably cautious effort made by the Johnson administration between 1965 and 1967 to promote

[23] Quoted in Herring, *LBJ and Vietnam.*

public support for the war. The president and his advisers thought they were following limited war doctrine and hoped they could achieve their objectives without arousing popular passions. They failed, and by late 1967 their problem was magnified. "The temperament of our people seems to be, 'you must get excited, get passionate, fight it and get it over with, or we must pull out,'" Lady Bird Johnson confided to her diary. "It is unbearably hard to fight a limited war."[24]

The primary task of the commander-in-chief is to oversee the conception and implementation of strategy, to shape the objectives of the war and devise appropriate means to achieve them. Limited war, in particular, requires the most sophisticated strategy, precisely formulated in terms of ends and means, with special attention to keeping costs at acceptable levels. In Vietnam, as complex a war as ever fought by the United States, there was *never* any systematic discussion at the highest levels of government of the *fundamental* issue of *how* the war should be fought!

Simple overconfidence may be the most obvious explanation for this curiosity. Americans could not conceive that the United States would be unable to impose its will on what Lyndon Johnson once referred to as that "raggedy-ass little fourth rate country." There was no need to think in terms of strategy.[25]

But, the explanation goes much deeper than that. Unlike his predecessors, Polk, Lincoln, and Franklin Roosevelt, all of whom worked hard at the job of being commander-in-chief, Johnson never took control of his war. In contrast to Lincoln, Roosevelt, or even Harry Truman, he had no illusions of military expertise. He was fond of quoting his political mentor, Sam Rayburn, to the effect that "if we start mak-

---

[24] Johnson, *A White House Diary*.

[25] Quoted in George C. Herring, "Cold Blood: LBJ's Conduct of War in Vietnam," The Harmon Memorial Lectures in Military History, no. 33 (Colorado Springs, CO: U.S. Air Force Academy, 1990).

ing the military decisions, I wonder why we paid to send them to West Point,"[26] perhaps rationalizing his own ignorance and lack of security in an alien field. Johnson thus refused to do what the civilian leadership must do: he "did not define a clear . . . mission for the military and did not establish a clear limit to the resources to be allocated for that mission."[27]

He saw his primary task rather as maintaining tight operational control over the military. On Johnson's part, of course, a compulsive determination to micromanage everything was an essential part of his makeup. Even as a young congressman, he had insisted on overseeing the minutest detail, never sure "things would go right," an aide later recalled, "unless he was in control of everything."[28]

The tendency to micromanage also derived from other factors. Johnson brought to the White House the southern populists' suspicion of the military. Suspecting that generals and admirals needed war to boost their reputations, he was determined to keep close check on them. It also reflected the deep-seated and pervasive civil-military tension of the 1960s. In an age of profound international tension with weaponry of enormous destructive potential, civilians were determined the keep the military in check. The result in Vietnam was a day-to-day intrusion into the tactical conduct of the war on a quite unprecedented scale. The larger result was an unhappy combination of "high level indecision and micromanagement."[29]

Even more crippling, Johnson finessed rather than resolved the deep divisions among his advisers on how the war should be con-

[26] Quoted in General Andrew Goodpaster, Oral History Interview, LBJ Library, Austin, TX.
[27] Stephen P. Rosen, "Vietnam and the American Theory of Limited War," *International Security* 7 (Fall 1982).
[28] Quoted in Robert Caro, *The Years of Lyndon Johnson: The Path to Power* (New York: Alfred A. Knopf, 1982).
[29] Rosen, "Vietnam and the American Theory of Limited War," *International Security*.

ducted. Far more than has been recognized, no one in the administration really liked the way the war was being fought and the results that were being obtained. What is even more striking, however, is that despite the rampant dissatisfaction, there was no change of strategy or even systematic discussion of a change in strategy. Indeed, in many ways the system seems to have been rigged to prevent discussion, debate, and adaptation.

From July 1965, there were sharp differences over strategy within the administration. The running battle over the bombing of North Vietnam, especially between Secretary of Defense Robert McNamara and the Joint Chiefs of Staff, is well known. But there was also widespread and steadily growing dissatisfaction with Gen. William Westmoreland's ground strategy.

Divisions within the military paled compared to the growing conflict between military and civilians. The military bristled at Johnson's refusal to mobilize the Reserves and protested his micromanagement of the war. For their part, the civilians worried about relentless military pressure for escalation of the war. They increasingly pressed for cutting back or even stopping the bombing, putting a ceiling on the number of ground troops, and shifting to a less costly and wasteful ground strategy.

Despite these divisions, there was no change of strategy or even systematic and sustained discussion of a change of strategy. The explanation for this is complex and must be found in a number of areas. For one thing, the military tradition of autonomy of the field commander inhibited debate on any possible alterations of the ground strategy. More important was the leadership style of the commander-in-chief. Lyndon Johnson's entirely political manner of running the war, his consensus-oriented *modus operandi*, effectively stifled debate. On such issues as bombing targets and bombing pauses, troop levels and troop use, by making concessions to each side without giving any what it wanted, he managed to keep dissent and controversy under control.

The president and his top advisers also insisted on rigid standards of loyalty in an increasingly divided administration. Unlike his hero, Franklin Roosevelt, Johnson had no tolerance for internecine conflict, and he imposed on his government the "Macy's Window" variety of loyalty made legendary by David Halberstam.[30] Unfortunately, the two men who might have influenced him, McNamara and Rusk, shared his perverted notions of team play. In-house devil's advocate George Ball later recalled that McNamara treated his dissenting memos like "poisonous snakes." He was "absolutely horrified" by them, considered them "next to treason."[31] Rusk agreed. "When the president has decided what the policy shall be," he later wrote, "an officer should either support that policy or resign."[32]

Finally, and perhaps most important, is what might be called the MacArthur syndrome, the pervasive fear among civilians and military alike of a repetition of the illustrious general's challenge to authority in the Korean War. Johnson lived in mortal terror of a military revolt and did everything in his power to squelch the slightest tendency in that direction.

Themselves learning from Korea, the military carefully refrained from anything approaching a direct challenge to civilian authority. The approach of the Chairman of the Joint Chiefs of Staff, Gen. Earle Wheeler, emphasized short-term acquiescence and silence. Hopeful of breaking down the restrictions imposed by the White House, he

---

[30] Editor's note: The exact quote, according to Halberstam, was "I don't want loyalty. I want *loyalty*. I want him to kiss my ass in Macy's window at high noon and tell me it smells like roses. I want his pecker in my pocket." See David Halberstam, *The Best and the Brightest* (New York: Random House, 1972).

[31] George Ball, Oral History Interview, LBJ Library, Austin, TX.

[32] Quoted in Barry Rubin, *Secrets of State: The State Department and the Struggle over U.S. Foreign Policy* (New York: Oxford University Press, 1984); and Rusk, *As I Saw It.*

encouraged Westmoreland to continue to push escalation and accept half a loaf to "get his foot in the door."[33]

For a variety of reasons, then, the president kept a tight lid on dissent. Even in the spring and summer of 1967, with the now-dovish McNamara pressing for an end to the bombing and a negotiated settlement and civilians and military deeply divided, there was no change of strategy or even discussion of a change. Characteristically, Johnson avoided a confrontation between the positions of McNamara and the military. There was no debate on the issues at the highest levels. He delayed a decision for months, and when he finally decided, he did so on a piecemeal basis, carefully avoiding the larger strategic questions. When the air war became an open subject of dispute between the Joint Chiefs of Staff and McNamara during Congressional hearings in August, the president dealt with the problem by denying its existence. There were "no quarrels, no antagonisms" within his official family, he insisted, "I have never known a period when I thought there was more harmony, more general agreement, and a more cooperative attitude." "There have been no divisions in this government," he stated on another occasion. "We may have been *wrong* but we have not been *divided*."[34] What a *strange* observation, reflecting a distorted sense of priorities! Of course, it was not true. The administration was both wrong and divided, and the fact that the divisions could not be worked out or even addressed may have contributed to the wrong policies, at huge cost to the men themselves—and especially to the nation.

Writing to Johnson in late 1967, Undersecretary of State Nicholas Katzenbach posed the question: "Can the tortoise of progress in Vietnam stay ahead of the hare of dissent at home?"[35] Katzenbach's Aesopian analogy makes clear the dilemma faced by the commander-

[33] Quoted in Herring, *LBJ and Vietnam.*

[34] Both passages quoted in Herring, *LBJ and Vietnam.*

[35] Quoted in Herring, *LBJ and Vietnam.*

in-chief at this crucial point in his war. To stave off collapse of the home front, progress had to be demonstrated in Vietnam. Yet real progress in the war might not be possible without clear-cut indications of public support at home.

By late 1967, Katzenbach and other civilian advisers pressed Johnson to do what he had thus far staunchly refused to do: address head-on the issue of how the war was being fought. A now blatantly dissident McNamara, civilians in the State Department and Pentagon, and establishment figures outside the government urged the president to check dissent at home by changing strategy in Vietnam. They pressed for stopping the bombing, scrapping Westmoreland's costly search-and-destroy strategy, and shifting to a "clear-and-hold strategy" that might stabilize the war at a politically acceptable level. They also pushed for an incipient form of what would be called Vietnamization, shifting greater military responsibility to the South Vietnamese.[36]

Presidential adviser McGeorge Bundy got closer to the flaws of Johnson's leadership, pressing him to take control of the war. He should make a "basic command decision" to settle once and for all the issue of the bombing. Conceding that it was a "highly sensitive matter" to question the field commander, Bundy went on to say that if the strategy was not wise or effective, the work of the field commander "must be questioned." Now that the principal battleground was at home, he added, the "Commander-in-Chief has both the right and duty . . . to visibly take command of a contest that is more political in character than any in our history except the Civil War (where Lincoln interfered *much* more than you have.)"[37] It was essential to

[36] Quoted in Larry Berman, *Lyndon Johnson's War: The Road to Stalemate in Vietnam* (New York: W. W. Norton, 1989); for an excellent account of the role of Washington insiders in determining policy in Vietnam, see Walter Isaacson and Evan Thomas, *The Wise Men: Six Friends and the World They Made* (New York: Simon and Schuster, 1986).

end the conflict in government and steady the home front.

Johnson was not moved by these appeals of his closest advisers. He was unsympathetic to repeated military requests for expansion of the ground and air wars. He also doubted that McNamara's proposals for a bombing halt would work. "How do we get this conclusion?"[38] he scrawled on a memo where the secretary had predicted that stopping the bombing would lead to peace talks. As before, he refused to make the hard decisions, and he refused to take control of the war. He "resolved" the strategic questions politically without addressing the strategic issues. He kicked McNamara downstairs to the World Bank and tossed the military a bone in the form of a few new bombing targets. In regard to ground operations, he would go no further than privately commit himself to review Westmoreland's search-and-destroy strategy at some undetermined point in the future.

To resolve the dilemma posed by Katzenbach, Johnson attempted to slow down the runaway rabbit of dissent at home rather than speed up or shift the direction of the turtle of progress in Vietnam. In the late summer and early fall of 1967, he mounted a large-scale, many-faceted public relations campaign to rally support for the war.

Believing that his major problem was a widespread public perception that the war was a stalemate, he designed much of the campaign to persuade a skeptical public that the United States was in fact winning. He ordered the embassy and military command to find evidence of progress. U.S. officials dutifully responded, producing reams of statistics to show a steady rise in enemy body counts and pacified villages. As part of the public relations blitz, Westmoreland was brought home in November, ostensibly for top-level consultations, in fact to reassure a troubled nation.

The president himself assumed the lead in the public relations

[37] Quoted in Herring, *LBJ and Vietnam.*

[38] Quoted in Herring, *LBJ and Vietnam.*

campaign, for the first time taking the offensive against his critics. Emerging from months of isolation and seclusion, he launched in November 1967 a 5,100-mile tour of eight military bases. In a fighting Veterans' Day speech, he made clear that "Viet Nam is no academic question. It is not a topic for cocktail parties, office arguments or debate from some distant sidelines." The lives of men were "tied by flesh and blood to Viet Nam. Talk does not come cheap for them."[39]

Johnson's public relations campaign was a qualified short-term success, an unmitigated long-term disaster. Polls taken late in 1967 indicated a slight upswing in support for the war and even in the president's job approval rating, and it is possible that under different circumstances the campaign might have bought him some time.

In fact, it merely deepened his problems. On January 31, 1968, the North Vietnamese launched a series of massive, coordinated military attacks throughout the cities and towns of South Vietnam. As perhaps nothing else could have, the so-called Tet Offensive put the lie to the administration's year-end claims of progress, eroding still further public support and forcing the internal reassessment of strategy that Johnson so dreaded and had for so long deferred.

The Tet Offensive is generally regarded as a major turning point of the Vietnam War, and in many ways it was. But in terms of Johnson's management of the conflict, there was no real change. Even under the pressure of the tumultuous events of Tet, the president refused to take control of the war. He continued to evade rather than confront the fundamental strategic issues. His dramatic March 31, 1968, speech, often cited as a major change of policy, was designed as much to quiet the home front as anything else. Like most of his earlier decisions, it was driven by a search for consensus, picking and choosing from conflicting approaches rather than developing a coherent strategy to

---

[39] *Time,* November 17, 1967.

achieve a clearly defined objective.[40] In the aftermath of that speech, the ambiguity persisted; the president's advisers more divided than ever, the lame duck Johnson less certain. The war thus dragged on, and LBJ left to his successor a problem even more difficult than he had inherited in 1963.

Much of the criticism of Lyndon Johnson's leadership in Vietnam is misplaced. The strategy of graduated escalation, if indeed it can be called a strategy, was, to be sure, doomed to failure. It is by no means clear, on the other hand, that the all-out approach advocated by some of Johnson's critics would have produced victory at acceptable cost. Such an approach also ran a huge risk of the general war Johnson and his advisers were seeking to prevent by taking a firm stand in Vietnam. Critics on the other side rightly charged that the administration's proposals to negotiate did not include terms that were likely to bring about successful negotiations. Still, given the persisting military stalemate and the positions North Vietnam took then and later, there is little to suggest that short of an immediate and total withdrawal from Vietnam, which might have had fatal repercussions for the administration at home, a negotiated settlement was within reach.

Johnson's leadership is vulnerable to criticism on other grounds. Korea and especially the Truman-MacArthur controversy had stimulated a veritable cult of limited war in the 1950s and 1960s, the major conclusion of which was that in a nuclear age where total war was unthinkable limited war was essential. Robert McNamara, McGeorge and William Bundy, and Dean Rusk, along with Johnson, were deeply imbued with limited war theory, and it determined in many crucial

[40] In his dramatic speech of March 31, 1968, the product of nearly a month of deliberation, LBJ publicly set forth the proposal by Dean Rusk for a partial bombing halt and joined it with a new appeal for negotiations and the appointment of Averill Harriman as his personal representative at the peace talks. To the shock of the nation, he went one step further, announcing that he was withdrawing from the presidential race. See Herring, *LBJ and Vietnam*.

ways their handling of Vietnam. Coming of age in World War II, they were convinced of the essentiality of deterring aggression to avoid a major war. Veterans of the Cuban missile crisis, they lived with the awesome responsibility of preventing nuclear conflagration, and they were thus committed to fighting the war in "cold blood" and maintaining tight operational control over the military.[41] The United States thus went to war in July 1965 in a manner uniquely quiet and underplayed—in "cold blood." They also operated under the mistaken assumption that limited war was more an exercise in crisis management than the application of strategy, and they were persuaded that gradual escalation offered the means to achieve their limited goals without provoking the larger war they so feared. Many of these notions turned out to be badly flawed.

To an even greater extent, Lyndon Johnson's own highly personalized style indelibly marked the conduct of the war and contributed to its peculiar frustrations: the reluctance to provide precise direction and define a mission and explicit limits; the unwillingness to tolerate any form of intergovernmental dissent or to permit a much-needed debate on strategic issues; the highly politicized approach that gave everybody something and nobody what they wanted, that emphasized consensus over results on the battlefield or in the diplomatic councils. All these were products of a thoroughly political and profoundly insecure man, a man especially ill at ease among military issues and military people. The determination to dupe or co-opt advisers and the public rather than confront them candidly and forcefully also was a clear manifestation of the Johnson style, as was the tendency toward

---

[41] Dean Rusk used the term "cold blood" with reference to the administration's belief that "in a nuclear world it is just too dangerous for an entire people to get too angry, and we deliberately . . . tried to do in cold blood what can perhaps only be done in hot blood." Quoted in Michael Charlton and Anthony Moncrief, *Many Reasons Why: The American Involvement in Vietnam,* 2nd ed. (New York: Hill and Wang, 1989).

personalization of the domestic debate and indeed of war. Johnson repeatedly denied that Vietnam was *his* war. It was "America's war," he insisted, and "If I drop dead tomorrow, this war will still be with you."[42] In one sense, of course, he was right. But in terms of the way the war was fought and the agony it caused, Vietnam was far more his than he was prepared to admit or even recognize.

---

[42] Quoted in Berman, *Lyndon Johnson's War*.

BRIGADIER GENERAL DAVID W. WINN, USAF (RET.)

A POW IN VIETNAM: "SMART PEOPLE, DUMB WAR"

Born in Austin, Minnesota, July 20, 1923, David Winn entered the U.S. Army Air Forces during World War II and earned his wings and commission as a 2nd lieutenant pilot in February 1943. He served in North Africa, Sardinia, and Italy during the war. In 1948 he separated from the Air Force.

Recalled to active duty for the Korean War, Winn chose to make the Air Force a career and subsequently served in Germany, Thailand, Canada, and the United Kingdom as an exchange officer with the RAF. U.S. assignments included duty in Texas, Arizona, Michigan, Colorado, Minnesota, and Washington, DC. He saw staff duty at the Pentagon with the Joint Chiefs of Staff. A graduate of the University of Minnesota, he later earned a master's degree in international relations from George Washington University. He also is a graduate of the National War College.

While on a combat mission in a F-105 out of a base in Thailand, Winn was shot down over North Vietnam and captured in August 1968. He was a prisoner of war in Hanoi until his release in 1973. As one of the senior POWs, he played an important role in establishing camp policies and conduct designed to ensure the survival of his fellow comrades in the North Vietnamese prisons.

General Winn retired from the U.S. Air Force in 1978. His last assignment was commander of the NORAD Cheyenne Mountain Complex, which was the underground space and missile warning operations center near Colorado Springs, Colorado. During his Air Force career, he logged over 6,000 hours of flying time, most of which were in fighter aircraft.

There is a story they tell in Santa Barbara about an elderly dowager and her Rolls Royce in a parking lot. She found a parking spot but had to back up to swing wide. As she was about to turn in, a young sport zipped his Volkswagen into the slot. The woman rolled her window down as the young man slammed the door of his Bug. She said, "Young man, I was going to park there." He said, "Too bad, old gal. I'm younger and quicker." The "old gal" put her Rolls into gear, swung in, and proceeded to bash the rear end of the Volkswagen. The man screamed, "What are you doing to my car? It's a wreck!" The reply was, "Too bad, young man. I'm older and richer." It turns out that that quick-thinking young man did a dumb thing.[1]

That poses a question that has troubled me ever since my body and mind came together again after my first six months as a prisoner of war in a Hanoi prison. That was a long time ago, but I still wonder about it. The question is, how is it that smart people sometimes do dumb things?

The notion that smart people sometimes do dumb things can be inferred from many of today's headlines. In presidential, legislative, judicial, and even cultural matters, we seem to be smarter than history. But my comments will be in the context of the SEA [Southeast

[1] Editor's note: General Winn presented this paper to the UNT Military History Seminar on October 9, 1999.

Asian] War. Only in one sense will the POW [prisoner of war] society microcosm be extended to the real world macro.

You did not have to be very smart to see that America's roof was springing a leak by August 1968, when I was shot down over North Vietnam. I was a colonel just out of the National War College after a tour in the Pentagon. With a quick checkout in the F-105, I was off to Takhli, Thailand. I felt like a smart man doing a dumb thing, but what it amounted to was the "duty calls" thing.

There at Takhli, I found a group of real professionals doing what they had been trained for and had been ordered to do by their civilian leaders. At the clubs and in the "hootch" [living quarters], the men were pensive, a little cowed maybe. But on the flight line and in the air, they were magicians, even if the audience expected comedy or tragedy, depending on your seat in the theater of the sixties.

The hippies at home and the growing anti-war sentiment were real by 1968. I had seen [Robert] McNamara's "Whiz Kids" in action in the Pentagon.[2] The war was being managed; combat leadership was held in close rein.[3] To Navy Lieutenant(j.g.) Everett Alvarez, who had

---

[2] Editor's note: Robert McNamara served as secretary of defense under John F. Kennedy and Lyndon B. Johnson. A University of California-Berkeley graduate with a MBA from Harvard, McNamara was one of the famous "whiz kids" who rapidly moved through managements at the Ford Motor Company, where he became president in 1960 at the age of forty-four. McNamara possessed a sharp, analytical mind and had unlimited faith in technology, computers, and systems management, so he thought it impossible for a backward country like North Vietnam to stand up against American power. McNamara assumed both logistical and operational control over the war, establishing strategic goals and objectives, selecting technologies, and he employed a large group of programmers, accountants, and statisticians to measure the Vietnam War's progress. For McNamara, casualties and victory could be reduced to a form of calculus. Thus, he believed it was only a matter of time before the "superior system prevails." See James S. Olson and Randy Roberts, *Where the Domino Fell: America and Vietnam, 1945–1995* (New York: St. Martin's Press, 1996).

[3] Editor's note: For Secretary of Defense Robert McNamara's personal account of his policy decisions, see Robert McNamara, *In Retrospect: The Tragedy and Lessons of Vietnam* (New York: Times Books, 1995).

been shot down in 1964 and already a POW longer than the entire time span of World War II, the news coming to him from Radio Hanoi was all propaganda—had to be—except that he was getting a lot of company with more downed airmen coming in, especially in 1966 and 1967.[4]

Our Vietnam episode introduced a new concept in the war lexicon. It had dire meaning for those fighting Communist forces in the field, in the air, and in Hanoi's prisons. That concept was "graduated response" or, more succinctly, "tit-for-tat." "Tit-for-tat" assumes that some power element has more "tits" than somebody has "tats." "Tits" are supposed to end "tats," if they make any sense at all.[5]

In 1969, Italian journalist Oriana Fallaci told Gen. Vo Nguyen Giap, commander of the North Vietnamese Army, that Americans claimed he had lost a half-million men. Giap replied, "The exact number." Giap faulted the NLF [National Liberation Front, a.k.a. Vietcong] in the South for the failed Tet Offensive and said, "The Americans will be defeated in time, by getting tired. And in order to tire them, we have to go on, to last . . . for a long time. That's what we've always done."[6]

---

[4] Editor's note: Alvarez was the first American airman captured by the North Vietnamese. Thus, he became well known from the day he was taken prisoner. His name and photograph were prominently displayed in both American and North Vietnamese news accounts. Alvarez eventually became known as the "Old man of the North." His capture and captivity became symbolic of the American POW experience in Southeast Asia. See Stewart I. Rochester and Frederick Kiley, *Honor Bound: The History of American Prisoners of War in Southeast Asia, 1961–1973* (Annapolis: Naval Institute Press, 1998).

[5] Editor's note: On August 4, 1964, in the Gulf of Tonkin Resolution, Congress essentially gave Lyndon Johnson *carte blanche* in Indo-China, allowing aerial bombardment, intervention in Cambodia and Laos, or any other "tit-for-tat" response that would bring North Vietnam to the negotiating table. At the time, the president's decision to conduct bombing raids over North Vietnam followed by his stated willingness to go to the negotiating table seemed tough but reasonable to most Americans. See Olson and Roberts, *Where the Domino Fell*.

[6] Quoted in Douglas Pike, "The Other Side," in *Vietnam as History: Ten Years after the Paris Peace Accords,* ed. Peter Braestrup (Latham, MD: University Press

A senior North Vietnamese officer, responding to Col. Harry Summers's reminder that they had never defeated U.S. troops in battle, replied, "That is correct. It is also irrelevant."[7]

Herbert Schandler has written, "The United States did not stumble into Vietnam. Each step was a deliberate choice by a careful president who weighed the alternatives as he saw them, limited each response, and took into account the opinion of the public. . . ."[8]

How did this play out for those on the other side of Washington's world? Politically and socially acceptable target selection became for the first time in U.S. history the dominant policy for conducting the

---

of America, 1984). This anthology focuses on the fundamental question of why the U.S. failed in Vietnam.

[7] Editor's note: In July 1974, Colonel Harry G. Summers returned to Vietnam as chief of the Negotiations Division of the Four Party Joint Military Team (FPJMT). The main task of the U.S. delegation was to resolve the status of those Americans still listed as missing in action. During one of his liaison trips to Hanoi, Summers had his now-famous exchange with his North Vietnamese counterpart. When Summers told him, "You, know, you never beat us on the battlefield," Colonel Tu responded, "That may be so, but it is also irrelevant." In 1982, Summers wrote *On Strategy: A Critical Analysis of the Vietnam War*. Relying on the ideas of General Karl von Clausewitz and using the time-tested *Principles of War*, Summers argued that the cause of America's failure ultimately lay in a confused and incoherent national strategy that had no clear objective. Summers attempted to answer the question: "How could an unbroken string of battlefield successes still add up to a strategic failure?" According to popular opinion, and to some extent even today, the U.S. military lost in Vietnam because it could not adapt to guerrilla warfare. Summers disagreed. He pointed out that the Vietcong insurgents ceased to be a major factor on the battlefield after they were all but annihilated in the Tet offensive of 1968. When Saigon fell in April 1975, it fell to four corps of NVA regular troops. In part because of the publication of *On Strategy*, Summers had a wide impact on military thinking. In the ten years that followed the collapse of the Republic of Vietnam, the U.S. military went through a complete and agonizing reappraisal of its doctrine and philosophy of fighting wars and rediscovered Clausewitz and his classical theories of war. See Harry G. Summers, Jr., *On Strategy: A Critical Analysis of the Vietnam War* (Novato, CA: Presidio Press, 1982).

[8] Herbert Y. Schandler, *The Unmaking of a President: Lyndon Johnson and Vietnam* (Princeton: Princeton University Press, 1977).

war. To F-105 pilots, that meant going in on obscure jungle river fords or a Hanoi bridge, into the most sophisticated air defense hardware the entire communist world was free to provide with impunity. Smart people were making a dumb war for the guy fighting it.

For the prisoner in Hanoi, "graduated response" had a more painful aspect. Hanoi "graduated" prisoner abuse. Reading America well, Hanoi knew where and how its war was to be won, and prisoners were going to play. As early as 1965, American POWs were paraded through the streets of Hanoi. This was a photo opportunity that backfired. The General Political Department of the North Vietnamese Army went back to the drawing board.[9]

The name of the game then became POW participation in the people's war. The propaganda "learning" quizzes that had always been POW fare turned mean. Torture became an element of national policy. *Meet the Press* in Hanoi took a terrible toll to provide prisoners apparently now seeing the error of U.S. involvement in Southeast Asia.

The heat was turned up. By the time I reached Hanoi, Yanks were "reading the news" over the prison public address system and really meeting the press. Six Hanoi prisoners had actually been released, having "seen the light." The years 1968 and 1969 were probably the

[9] Editor's note: The North Vietnamese at first publicly identified the POW fliers as "air pirates, mercenaries, and imperialist agents," occasionally threatened to try them for war crimes, and used them in efforts to extract concessions from the U.S. government and gain the sympathy of the American people and the international community. They paraded the POWs before North Vietnamese civilians to inflame anti-American sentiment, occasionally released a few in response to anti-war demonstrations in the United States, and constantly used them to gain advantages in the Paris peace negotiations. The POWs' resistance to, or cooperation with, their captors and revelations of their conduct and treatment through released photographs and tapes (in which they often sabotaged North Vietnamese intentions), influenced public opinion throughout the world. Near the end of the war, the POW issue was the ultimate issue to be settled in the final political settlement. See Rochester and Kiley, *Honor Bound.*

worst years in Hoa Lo.[10] American prisoners were going to play, or else. POWs were beaten up to tell the world of Hanoi's "lenient and humane treatment." They were even more savagely hammered if caught communicating between cells or attempting leadership and organization.

I was in solitary confinement for my first twenty-two months in Hanoi. During that time I was in covert communication with a small group for less than a month. When our link was discovered, the purge was swift and decisive. The "rule of silence" was law within the prison, but to the world it was "sing like a birdie," or else.[11]

---

[10] Editor's note: Located in Hanoi, Hoa Lo, meaning in Vietnamese "fiery furnace," had been built by the French at the turn of the century and was still being used as the main municipal prison in North Vietnam. Surrounded by thick concrete walls 15 to 20 feet high, it occupied an entire block in the center of the city. The prison complex was divided into four general areas for which the American captives had given nicknames: "Heartbreak Hotel," "New Guy Village," "Little Vegas," and "Camp Unity." "Camp Unity," by far the biggest section, opened in late 1970 when the North Vietnamese concentrated almost all the POWs in Hanoi. The prison's security system was formidable. Guard towers ringed the exterior walls, which were topped by several strands of barbed wire thought to be electrified and jagged glass shards. There was only one entryway into the prison, and it was further divided by a series of heavy iron gates that sealed shut one after the other. No U.S. POW escaped from Hoa Lo, and few considered trying. The first group of American occupants sarcastically renamed the prison the "Hanoi Hilton." See Rochester and Kiley, *Honor Bound.*

[11] Editor's note: Over time the POWs devised numerous systems of communication. The methods included Morse code, tap code, and hand signals. The most effective system, and the one that eventually became the most commonly used by American prisoners in the North, was the tap code. It originated with Air Force Captain Clyde Harris, who devised it in the summer of 1965. The tap code consisted of a five-by-five matrix of the alphabet that was to serve as a covert basis for POW contacts. This form of POW communication boosted and maintained morale by serving as a vital source of news and information.

Communication was an essential asset for the survival of the American POWs. It provided shared observations and experiences, insights about their captors, particularly about the personalities and behavior of individual guards, and information about the policies and procedures of the North Vietnamese in the different camps. The network was most active at Hoa Lo, where the tap code originated and which remained the primary prison camp for most American POWs. For a detailed description of how the tap code operated, see Rochester and Kiley, *Honor Bound.*

In late 1969, Hanoi's prisoner abuse became known. Viewers in the U.S. and Europe were perplexed at an earlier TV viewing of then-Commander Jerry [Jeremiah] Denton's appearance. His hollow eyes blinked strangely—but not to the Office of Naval Intelligence. His eyes were blinking Morse code. The word was "TORTURE." Over three million letters protesting prisoner treatment went unaccepted in Paris during the "peace" meetings there.[12]

I believe that even Moscow and Beijing began telling Hanoi that confirmed prisoner torture was counterproductive. Perhaps as a result, in 1970 the prisoners' lot improved considerably, if they liked cabbage and pumpkin soup throughout their seasons. Even limited outside time was permitted, but still, "No talk." Solitary confinement ended except as punishment for some real or imagined "crime," usually when one group of men was caught communicating with one another.

Even as late as a year before my release, I was pulled from my mates in 1972 for a communication violation, pounded all night, and slammed back in solitary for six weeks, including denial of food and water for three days.

By late 1971, nearly all the POWs were "under one roof" at Hoa Lo. Collectively we were a slick bunch of crooks; the guards were never able again to prevent prison-wide communication for any prolonged

[12] Editor's note: Because they considered Denton as the person who had the most propaganda value, the North Vietnamese intensively drilled him for three days to tell the "truth" about the war and then sat him before the news media. In two separate televised interviews, Denton refused to follow his pre-written script and instead staunchly defended American policy in Vietnam. Speaking to a group of Japanese newsmen, and with the TV cameras operating, he deliberately stared into the glaring floodlights, at first blinking reflexively. Then, despite his extreme fatigue, Denton took advantage of this opportunity, and with calculated eye movements he spelled "TORTURE" in Morse code. After reviewing the tape after buying it from a U.S. television network, Naval Intelligence picked up Denton's message, the first confirmation the U.S. government had that American POWs were being tortured. See Rochester and Kiley, *Honor Bound*.

time. That fact was of critical importance. We could help each other; we could fashion an organized recovery community. We literally rebuilt a civilization. Each cell block became a squadron, with a commanding officer, executive officer, operations officer, communications officer, intelligence officer, and flight commanders. There weren't any "grunts" except by choice in a few cases. We were a kingdom of fools, and nobody knew who was the wisest man in the palace. But everybody had a job. The healing began.

Overall command rested in eight men: the most senior officers plus a few "habitual troublemakers."[13] By segregating us in one corner of the prison, the prison authorities hoped to take us out of the system. They were wrong. But it did not really matter. Lopping off the head of the monster they had created only revealed a new leader of resistance. So long as there was communication, they had problems. We all had bad attitudes.

Date of rank wasn't always the deciding leadership factor, especially in the early years. There were captains who thought like kings and senior officers who could not meet the standards of a corporal. Career success in freedom was no guarantee of leadership greatness in captivity.[14]

---

[13] Editor's note: Although the group of most senior varied from time to time due to new, higher-ranking POWs coming in, for instance, by coincidence four senior officers led the American POW resistance for most of the decade of captivity. They had all been shot down early in the war and almost all at the same time. These four were USN Commander James Stockdale, USN Commander Jeremiah Denton, USAF Colonel Robinson Risner, and USAF Major Lawrence Guarino. In 1970, they recognized a later shootdown, USAF Colonel Vernon Ligon, as outranking them. Still later, they acknowledged USAF Colonels John Flynn, David Winn, and Norman Gaddis, as seniormost. In almost all instances, a spirit of cooperation and solidarity was the rule, reinforced by common interests that overcame personal ego and service rivalry. See Rochester and Kiley, *Honor Bound*.

[14] Editor's note: The role of senior officers was "to provide leadership; to conceive, plan, and coordinate tactics; to create and operate an effective organization; and to sustain morale." Unlike the POW senior officers in South Vietnam, those in North Vietnam had the advantage of working with a fairly homogeneous and

While we were climbing out of oblivion, smart people both in Hanoi and Washington were still in a dumb war. Hanoi clearly was determined to get communist unification of Vietnam. So long as their casualties didn't exceed their birth rate, they could shoot every bullet and rocket half the world was giving them. [15] China, the Soviet Union, the communist world, and even many democratic nations were making their war logistically and politically durable. And Kent State helped a lot.[16]

---

well-trained group of men. The Navy and Air Force aviators, who comprised the overwhelming majority of the POWs in the northern camps, were career servicemen who took discipline and motivation for granted. However, even these professionals were not immune from the debilitation and emaciation of imprisonment. A principal objective of the senior leaders was thus to restore somehow the "fighting" capability of these men by establishing and maintaining a semblance of organization, and to foster hope and a will to resist at a time when they themselves bore the brunt of punishment that tested the limits of their endurance. There were, nevertheless, individuals who could capably handle this responsibility of command, men who cleverly and skillfully devised such a resistance organization. See Rochester and Kiley, *Honor Bound*.

[15] Editor's note: As with the air war, the American strategy of attrition had flaws. It assumed that the U.S. could inflict intolerable losses on the North Vietnamese while keeping its own losses within acceptable bounds, an assumption that was, according to historian George Herring, "contrary to previous experience with land wars in Asia and the realities of Vietnam." Herring maintains that an estimated 200,000 North Vietnamese reached draft age each year, so Hanoi was able to replace its losses and match each American escalation with one of its own. The enemy, moreover, employed a strategy to control losses. The North Vietnamese and Vietcong fought at times and places of their own choosing and on terrain advantageous to them. If they incurred unacceptably high losses, they simply slipped back into the jungle or retreated to sanctuaries in North Vietnam, Cambodia, or Laos. See George Herring, *America's Longest War: The United States and Vietnam, 1950–1975* (New York: John Wiley and Sons, 1979).

[16] On April 30, 1970, President Richard Nixon announced to the nation his decision ordering American troops into Cambodia, using as a pretext the argument that that country was being used as a sanctuary by enemy troops. The invasion exacerbated the anti-war movement in the U.S. and caused one of the worst eruptions of civil disobedience in modern American history. Mass student demonstrations erupted on college campuses. At Kent State University in Ohio, Governor James Rhodes called out National Guard troops to maintain order. While doing so, soldiers fired into a crowd of students, killing four and creating martyrs for the anti-war movement. See Olson and Roberts, *Where the Domino Fell*.

The U.S., whose history included use of atomic bombs and full mobilization to end two wars, denied both logistic and political commitment to win that war. Victory for the U.S. was seen as an unsafe target because such a policy widening might have led to a confrontation with China and the Soviet Union. Victory was for Hanoi the only target.

Life is a matter of choices whether in freedom or under tyranny. The prisoners in Hanoi were totally captive in the early years, totally separated from everything that had made them who they were. In the later years, we created a unique society. It consisted of a corporate collection of individual experiences dealing with tyranny. In that sense, it more resembled a democracy than a military structure. And it had all the warts of a democracy, while at the same time possessing the glue that holds any military unit together.

I said we made laws. There was one law we could not write. It concerned escape. There had been two "slips," as we code-named escapes. The first was during the period when Hanoi was being bombed every day. The two men were recaptured and punished severely. The second "slip" was after President Johnson's decision to stop bombing the North in hopes Hanoi would reciprocate in the South and accept a peace agreement.[17] On recapture these two escapees were separated for punishment. One was beaten to death that night.[18] But in this

[17] On March 31, 1968, as an inducement to get the enemy to the bargaining table, Johnson announced that the bombing of North Vietnam would henceforth be limited to an area just north of the demilitarized zone. He stated that even this limited bombing campaign could come to an early end if Hanoi reciprocated with a level of restraint that would match Washington's. See Herring, *America's Longest War*.

[18] Editor's note: On the night of May 10, 1969, POWs Captain Edwin Atterberry and Captain John Dramesi escaped from the "Zoo" and were captured by sunup just four or five miles from the prison. As retribution, Dramesi was beaten with a fan belt, hit in the face with fists, strapped in unnatural positions with ropes, and forcibly kept awake. He was then placed in heavy irons that soon tore into his flesh. Then he was strung in ropes more than fifteen times, fed only two small

case, all the men in that prison, code-named the "Zoo," suffered terrible retribution.[19] Maybe there is a lesson in that, say, in dealing with hostage-takers. Hanoi went easier on the escapees when the bombing pressure was greatest. When there was no pressure on them, they killed.

Later, when all the men were together and a rule of law established, the memory of what happened at the "Zoo" had a profound effect. POW leadership could not agree on an escape policy.[20] Probably at least half of the men believed that the chances of a successful escape from the middle of Hanoi were too low and the cost for those behind too high, notwithstanding the U.S. Military Code of Conduct. Others lived, dreamed, and devoted their lives to planning and plot-

---

pieces of bread and two cups of water each day, and made to sit in his own filth. Dramesi survived, but Atterberry died on May 18, eight days after the breakout.

Due to the escape attempt, a reign of terror ensued in the camp. For the next two months, at least a couple dozen inmates of the "Zoo" were beaten severely and dozens others dragged off for questioning. One POW was hung from the ceiling by his arms and subjected to electric shocks from an auto battery. In addition, the prison guards plugged all light and air holes, eliminating not only POW communication but also ventilation, which sent summer room temperatures soaring. See Rochester and Kiley, *Honor Bound*.

[19] Editor's note: The "Zoo" was the second POW facility opened in August-September 1965 and was situated on the outskirts of Hanoi a couple miles southwest of Hoa Lo. It had once been a French film studio and recreation center. The "Zoo" became a primary detention center during the early years, holding more that fifty prisoners by February 1966 and about 120 at the start of 1967. The POWs were scattered among a dozen or more one-story structures, making communications difficult. There were no beds for sleeping, so concrete floors had to suffice. The windows were at first barred and then were bricked up later on. The padlocked doors were solid, having an eyehole that enabled the guards to peer in at the prisoners, the feature that led to the nickname "Zoo," which was adopted in 1966. See Rochester and Kiley, *Honor Bound*.

[20] Editor's note: The issue concerned a clause in Article III of the Military Code of Conduct that required POWs to "make every effort to escape." Even the most dedicated senior officers were hesitant to approve escape attempts where the odds seemed hopeless or where failure, or success, could have serious repercussions for those left behind. See Rochester and Kiley, *Honor Bound*.

ting escape, notwithstanding the certain terrible retribution the last abortive escape from the "Zoo" had taught them. Escape was for them the ultimate act of resistance to tyranny.

In May 1972, our indecision on escape policy forced its way to a decision when a long covert communication exchange with the outside world came to fruition. Two SR-71 sonic booms, accurately spaced in time, at noon that day announced that the necessary outside assistance for the long-planned escape was in place. Full support for the planned "slip" was confirmed.

Now what to do? Fish or cut bait? We cut bait. After surprisingly calm (to me) discussion among the "ruling elders," our senior ranking officer, Colonel John Flynn, elected to get out the "no-go" message to the men concerned. As a result, the agents, helicopters, and other support elements went unused. This affected me greatly, since I was one of those who believed that escape was always an open option.

I began to do some wild things. I made a wooden key that successfully unlocked and locked two doors opening to our unlocked courtyard. I drilled holes in enough of our bed boards so that when tied together they would span from our roof to the walls surrounding the prison. I made enough rope to lower the "walkway" gently to the wall.

I had a partner, Jim Stockdale, the senior Navy PW who was ready to try escape. My cellmates, Colonels John Flynn and Norm Gaddis, watched my progress with bitter contempt, but there was no order from either to stop what I was doing. Both were my seniors. Norm Gaddis was a very steady man—the kind of man anyone would like. He was a gentle man but not without steel. Strongly opposed to escape, he fired both barrels at me late one night. He told me that I was an evil man. He said I had to be, to contemplate going over the wall with a cripple. That alone, he said, was crazy.

Jim Stockdale was one of the smartest, toughest men I had ever known. He had been seriously beaten up in ejection from his airplane, and his treatment by the prison guards had added to his disabilities. His left leg was virtually fused at the knee, and that foot was permanently angled in. I often admired his tenacity at doing push-ups and doing his best to get in shape now that the food was better. His wish to go was not in doubt. He never expressed bitterness at the cancellation of a well-planned and organized escape, but he was of the same school that I was on that matter.

To illustrate, one can almost depend on the lights of Hanoi going out during the violent thunderstorms that occurred during the monsoon seasons. A few days after confirming that my key was a success, such a rainstorm hit, probably at midnight and after our lights went out. I awoke at hearing Jim's voice from across the courtyard corner, saying. "Let's go!" I had not yet had enough rope and wire to complete the "bridge" as I had given first priority to the key. I had to tell him to "cool it," that we were not quite ready. But he was ready to go.

A Navy commander, Harry Jenkins, was the one who made all this possible. He had scrounged a piece of heavy gauge wire and showed me how to make it razor-sharp. That was my principal tool. Drilling through teak was slow work, and concealing the key and rope to withstand periodic cell searches were a real challenge. Several months passed, and with the beginning of winter, the compilation of the necessary "hardware" was about finished. Jim, a fine mathematician, had calculated the length of rope we'd need to lower the boards some eighteen feet to the wall. Since there were no thunderstorms yet, there was time to plan. In my mind, weather permitting, I had set the anniversary date of May 17, 1973, as the target.

A failed peace negotiation in November 1972 kept the intention in my mind, but the real thing, a release protocol in Paris, got us over the wall without folly. Linebacker, the B-52s, and a strong-minded president got us out of there beginning in February 1973. We all "slipped," and nobody got hurt.

That split between escape hawks and doves divides the prisoner community to this day. Probably the majority still accepts the low-chance, high-cost position.[21] In any case, the organizational leadership ducked the issue, writing no law on "slips." We chose no choice. We chose safer ground. We addressed issues designed to heal. We avoided decisions that would divide. In a sense, we led by reading the polls. Sound familiar? Today was important, but yesterday seemed more important than tomorrow.

The POWs today, like all free people, live with choices we would rather not make. It is a fair statement that dominant U.S. elements of national power are dedicated to the high-chance, low-cost approach to leadership. I call it the "safe target syndrome." Tobacco is a safe target. The underground economy is not. Religion is a safe target. Homosexuality is not. Bill Gates is a safe target. Environmentalism is not. The Defense Department is a safe target. The IMF, World Bank, and the UN are not. Try taking on the Department of Health and Human Services or the Department of the Interior.

The Vietnam War is a safe target. Maybe because it was a dumb war. But we do not often mention two million dead Cambodians. Unification of Vietnam cost humanity the boat people and reeducation camps. A smart president [Richard M. Nixon] sent B-52s to Hanoi and brought the POWs home, only to be toppled by Watergate.[22]

---

[21] Editor's note: Even after liberation, and despite the euphoria of homecoming, Dramesi had to confront the censure and ostracism of comrades who blamed him for much of their suffering and Atterberry's death. See Rochester and Kiley, *Honor Bound*.

[22] Editor's note: In April 1972, Nixon announced the initiation of Operation Linebacker. He eventually shifted more than 100 B-52s from the Strategic Air Command for tactical strikes over South Vietnam and strategic air raids over North Vietnam, including missions on targets within a few miles of Hanoi and the major port city of Haiphong. Part of Linebacker also included the mining of Haiphong harbor as well as a naval blockade. North Vietnam suffered extensively from this latest round of American bombing, and although it was prepared to continue the war if necessary, it was eager for peace if it could be accomplished

Why is it that smart people do dumb things? I don't know. But my Vietnam experience suggests one answer: it is accountability. When I broke the rule of silence one day in Hanoi, I was tortured and confined for a time in "Calcutta," a tiny, dark cubicle pounded by the summer sun.[23] I was held accountable. I was a very safe target and of no account to my captors. I was accountable only to myself. When the "Whiz Kids" and Ho Chi Minh made dreadful choices, somebody else paid.

I believe history proves over and over again that smart people do dumb things when authority and accountability are not man and wife. That young sport in the Santa Barbara parking lot thought brains and speed had no consequence. Accountability came as a rude surprise. It always does, when choice and consequence say goodbye to each other.

---

without sacrificing its long-range goals. See Herring, *America's Longest War* and Olson and Roberts, *Where the Domino Fell.*

[23] Editor's note: "Calcutta" was a tiny cell near Hoa Lo's kitchen area infested with cobwebs and layered with dust. Others who did time in "Calcutta" included Stockdale, Denton, and John McCain. See Rochester and Kiley, *Honor Bound.*

Section VI
THE LATE COLD WAR

Lt. Gen. Charles Hamm transforms the reader from the broad world of nuclear strategy and limited war to another important element of national security affairs: intelligence gathering. General Hamm was appointed to the demanding position of the defense attaché stationed in Moscow with the primary responsibility for gathering intelligence and serving as the military advisor to the ambassador. A distinguished fighter pilot in the USAF, Hamm was promoted to general and assigned as U.S. defense attaché in Moscow in the early 1980s during the closing years of the Brezhnev regime. Through the period of the Cold War, service in the Soviet Union was considered to be the most sensitive and important for a military attaché.

With self-effacing humor and insight, Hamm describes his duties in the USSR. He and his spouse had to learn the language and the culture and win the respect of the host nation as well as of the other attachés from allied nations. His sensitive assignment required him to learn as much as possible about new Soviet military equipment and policies and provide reports and analysis to various agencies in the United States.

During his stay, the Soviet Union became embroiled in its own war in Afghanistan. Hamm's observations and reports were vital to the development of American foreign policy during these sensitive years. Through General Hamm's service in the Soviet Union, the reader comes to appreciate the critical role of human intelligence in the nation's intelligence gathering business. Ironically, twenty years later, the United States would be involved in its own war in Afghanistan as part of its War on Terrorism. While the Cold War may have ended in the early 1990s, it has been replaced by a new form of conflict.

LIEUTENANT GENERAL CHARLES HAMM, USAF (RET.)

COLD WAR DUTY AS A DEFENSE ATTACHÉ IN MOSCOW

From 1981–1983, General Charles R. Hamm served in Moscow as U.S. defense attaché to the USSR, after completing Russian language training in Washington, DC, as a new brigadier general. A 1956 graduate of the U.S. Military Academy, he opted for an Air Force commission and earned his pilot's wings. Various flying assignments followed, including tours as a member of the Air Force Thunderbird Aerial Demonstration Team and experiences as a flight commander with 103 combat missions during the Vietnam War. Eventually, he commanded two different fighter wings and three times had progressively responsible tours as a staff officer at USAF Headquarters in the Pentagon.

In addition to the staff assignments, General Hamm graduated from the Air Command and Staff College in 1969 and from the National War College in 1972. After his service in the Soviet Union as defense attaché, he became vice-commander of what is now the Air Force Education and Training Command and climaxed his career at the Air Force Academy as its superintendent from 1987 until his retirement in 1991.

I always welcome the opportunity to think back and to reminisce about my experiences in the Soviet Union twenty years ago. In recent years, however, I have not really thought much about the Soviet Union. I spoke a great deal about my experiences there, after I returned from that tour, for a few years, trying to tell people what I had learned. Since that time I have been embroiled in other things, but it has been fun bringing out the memories and looking at some old notes and reading some books that were favorites of mine about Russia in that era.[1]

I am a two-year "expert" on the Soviet Union. I was the commander of an F-15 wing at Eglin Air Force Base, Florida, which is a wonderful location. We had brand-new airplanes right out of the factory in Saint Louis. It was time for me to be a brigadier general, and my four-star superior said, "We don't have anything for you yet assignment-wise, so we think we'll leave you there for a while." I said, "This is great! I'll stay here as long as you'd like."

A couple of weeks later, I got a call from my three-star boss, the 9th Air Force commander, General [Arnold] "Arnie" Braswell, whom some of you in the room might know, a famous West Pointer. He said, "I can't tell you what your assignment is, but it's unique and challenging." So, I got out the roster of Air Force general officer assignments and looked at all the brigadier jobs. I was looking for something unique and challenging, and there were some, but for the life of me, I couldn't pin it down.

Well, finally he told me in another phone call that I was going to be the defense attaché to the Soviet Union. Of course, it was not on the Air Force list because the job was rotated among the military services. I replaced a Navy admiral who, by the way, was an aviator also. He had a sign on the wall behind his desk in Moscow that said, "Tailhook

[1] Editor's note: General Hamm presented this paper at the UNT Military History Seminar on September 15, 2001.

[So-and-So], Most Carrier Landings." That always impressed me. He did a good job, too, and handed me a good outfit to take over.

After that selection, I spent the next year in training. I spent a month or so at the Defense Intelligence School at Bolling Air Force Base in Washington. Both my wife and I studied the Russian language for a year, and it was a wonderful experience. It was one of the highlights of that tour. I really enjoyed the language, and at my age I was taxed to try to learn how to speak Russian. After that experience, I always give a big pitch for language training. I probably worked harder than I have worked at any course in my career because I knew the better I spoke the language, the better I could do my job.

I was a general, so I was the ranking man in the class. That meant that I got the head instructor, who was a wonderful lady named Madame De La Cruz. She had left Russia as a six-year-old child with her father, who was a colonel in the tsar's army. He blew up a bridge as they left the country. Then they moved to Brazil, and then finally they immigrated to the United States. She worked for the Foreign Service as a native Russian instructor. She was an instant interpreter at the UN. She was a wonderful lady, and she taught me a lot of the tsar's Russian, which was not too appropriate when I got there, since the Communists were in charge by that time.

My wife was in a separate class with a separate teacher, the class being one or two students, which kept your attention. They would ask you a question, and you had to answer it. They would ask the other person a question, and you would think, "Oh, boy! I can rest for a minute." Then they'd say, "Now, what did I ask her, and what did she answer?" It was tough! But my wife learned how to curse in Russian, and as it turned out this was much more effective in dealing with the KGB than to talk to them in the tsar's language.

Halfway through my training, they gave me a TDY [temporary duty assignment]. It was a weeklong, all-expenses-paid trip to Moscow to practice my language, which was poor at that time and never better than fair, to be honest. But I worked hard at it. I was to look at the lay of the land. I went and lived with the defense attaché at that time. The admiral showed me around and gave me the Cook's tour of Moscow. I got to watch what they were doing from the office. Every night, I noticed, we went to a party: a dinner party, a cocktail party, a reception. I was trying to remember names because I knew I would be back in six months, and I would be interested in knowing these people because those parties were not frivolous. It was a way to get together and exchange information on what the Soviets were doing.

Finally, about the fifth night, I was at a party at the British defense attaché's house, who was a fellow named Ted Williams. I was talking to a few men, and finally I was talking to one individual. We were having a great political conversation, and he was telling me some pretty bright stuff. I said, "Tell me, now, what's your job?" He said, "Oh, I'm the British ambassador." Well, I was very embarrassed. Here I was, trying to figure out how to handle these cocktail parties, and I had been previously introduced to him, I am sure. Maybe I had not been, but I should have known who he was, and I did not.

Later on that evening, I confessed to my host: "I've made a terrible 'boo-boo' here. Please forgive me." He said, "That's not the worst thing that's ever happened. You're not the first American to have done that. There was a famous American . . ." By the way, his name was Douglas Fairbanks, Jr., and I always thought he was a Brit. He talked like one, but he was born in New York City. Douglas Fairbanks, Jr., was at a party in London and was talking to people. Finally, he found himself talking to a sophisticated woman. They were having a great conversation about the weather and the sights to see and all that. He looked down and noticed she had a ring. He said, "How's your husband?" She said, "Oh, fine." He said, "What's he doing now?" She said, "Oh, he's still king." Ted Williams endeared himself to me, and, indeed, the Brits were our very best and closest compatriots in Russia. They were aggressive intelligence collectors, and we spent a lot of time with them and learned to love the Brits.

The other thing I noticed on my first trip to the Soviet Union was how dull and drab and depressing and oppressive it was. The only color was from the red banners and the red slogans, and pictures of [Vladimir] Lenin and pictures of [Leonid] Brezhnev. Later on, I found that that was true throughout the Soviet Union. Things got to look a lot alike. The government buildings were usually well done and looked sophisticated, but everywhere they had these huge apartment buildings where everyone lived, these gray apartment buildings. I don't know how you found your place after a few drinks, because they all looked alike. Immediately after they built them, they started falling apart. Indeed, all over the Soviet Union, there were signs that said: "Under Repair." One day, the KGB got me for trying to take a picture of a beer hall that had a sign: "Under Repair." I thought that was the last straw—when the beer hall was under repair. That was my first impression, and it was a lasting impression.

As I left that first visit to the Soviet Union, another thing happened. When the plane became airborne, people applauded. The only other time I had seen that was in Vietnam during the war. That told me that I was in for a different kind of life there for the next two years.

The main point of this presentation is to provide a feel for what we did in the Soviet Union. First, I will talk about attachés. They do three things, basically. First, they serve as advisors to the ambassador and his staff on military matters. We got along very well with the ambassador. Art Hartman was his name. He came from Paris, where he had been the ambassador to France. I was fortunate enough to meet him and his wife in Paris when I flew with the crew of our DC-9 to pick them up. The DC-9 was a plushed-up medevac [medical evacuation] airplane based in Frankfurt and was at the disposal of the ambassador. We served Art and his wife eggs Benedict on the way to Moscow. From that point on, he always associated me and my blue suit with this DC-9 trip to freedom. In fact, we got him out of the country as often as he needed to go on business trips, which ended up being pretty often.

We got along well with the civilians, the Foreign Service people. One of the reasons was that many of us had attended the Foreign Service language school together, and we really got to know them. They were a crackerjack bunch of bright people, and many of them were well experienced in things Russian and Soviet. We learned a lot from them, and we helped them out. The defense attachés traveled more than anybody in the embassy, and we would provide the Foreign Service people with information on matters other than military.

The second task of attachés was to serve as representatives to the host nation and to other nations that are represented in the country. It was a responsible job—a very responsible job—and it was a gratifying job because I found myself as a representative of the Free World as the head of the United States of America's military delegation.

We ended up making a lot of friends among a lot of people from a lot of different countries. My wonderful wife was a better representative than I was. She particularly attracted the Third World country people, who were lost in Russia. She would entertain the wives. They would come over at least monthly and have a great time. It was amazing to me. My wife spoke Russian, but most of these people's wives didn't speak Russian or English, and it was amazing to me how they could communicate. Of course, one of the things that they were interested in during that era was *Dallas*, the TV program. We would show them tapes every now and then just to whet their appetites.

The third, and most important, thing we did was that we were overt collectors of military intelligence. It was done in a very hostile environment. We had trained for hostile intelligence collection with the FBI's help in Washington, DC, which was a lot of fun, playing "Cops and Robbers." It was more serious in the Soviet Union. It was not deadly serious, but it was a serious game, and it was a tough game for three main reasons. The first was the secrecy that was attached to things Soviet and Russian. The Marquis de Custine, who went to Russia from France for a five-month visit in 1839, said a lot of telling things about Tsarist Russia. As a matter of fact, his catchphrase was: "If your son is discontented with life in France, take my advice. Send him to Russia, for after he has seen Russia he would be content to live anywhere else." It was a very biting criticism of about almost every phase of Tsarist Russian life, which the Soviets banned after they determined that it was also a great deal like Soviet life. There were many similarities between Tsarist repression and the repression by Stalin and the Communist Party.

One of the things that the Marquis de Custine talked about was the secrecy that the government used to control people and the fear and/or terror that the country used to control people. So, there was this element of secrecy, and there was the element of fear, also. The people were paranoid; they were xenophobic. We would probably be, too, if our country had been invaded by the Mongols, the Tatars, the Turks, the Swedes, the Poles, the French, and the Germans. Indeed, we see the elements of paranoia and xenophobia here in the United States based upon what happened on September 11 [the terrorist attacks on the World Trade Center in New York and the Pentagon on that date]. But that meant that not only was the KGB after us, but that also meant that the average citizen was steeled against us.

Another thing that was used against foreigners was their victory over the Nazis in the Great Patriotic War [World War II], which was indeed a great victory. It was the biggest thing they ever did. Now, space exploration was good; Sputnik was good; Yuri Gagarin, the first man in space, was good. But winning the Great Patriotic War was the greatest thing that they ever did. I certainly give them credit for that, and I empathize with their losses. But the thing that really got to me was that they equated us with the Nazis. The new capitalists-imperialists, led by the United States of America, were the new Nazis. That was an uncomfortable position to be in.

We heard about the Great Patriotic War every day. It was in the newspapers, on the radio, and on television. The name of a program was *Forty Years Ago Today*. They recaptured the events of a battle. Of course, this is the period from 1981 through 1983, so we are talking about Phase One and Phase Two. They were not doing very well, but you would never know that from listening to the radio and hearing the glorious stories. I have been to many of the battlefields and have seen the huge monuments. They are eerie but spectacular, and you cannot help but be sympathetic, especially as a professional soldier, when you see people dressed up on a military day. They celebrated at least one military day each month. They would put on their best clothes, and they'd be covered with medals from World War II. You would be surprised at the number of women who were involved in that.

The big problem we had was with the KGB. Of course, there was no unemployment under communism in the Soviet Union. That meant that they only had about 500,000 people watching us. Here we were, outnumbered 13 to 500,000. Well, it seemed that way. The most action I ever actually saw was on one day in Leningrad. I was traveling with two assistant naval attachés and looking at Soviet shipbuilding, and we noticed throughout the day that we were followed by seven carloads of "goons." Now, those were the ones we spotted. Maybe it was a training day or something for them. They were always there. I have had them in lockstep behind me as we walked by military bases and, of course, were dying to take photographs. They were not going to let you do that, but we could still eyeball the targets.

Dealing with the KGB was tough. They were looking to deter us, of course, or they were looking to embarrass us. We tried not to let that happen. We tried very aggressively to do our job of seeing what was going on over there, but we wanted to toe the line because we did not want to step over it. The penalty was getting kicked out of the country, as my counterpart had been kicked out of the United States about five months after I arrived. General Shitzov was caught red-handed, if you will, handing money to one of our traitors for American secrets. So, I had to dance on those eggs for a while, but I finally decided—I had a great deal of autonomy, which was nice—"I'm going to press on. I'm here to do a job. I'm not going to do covert intelligence, but if they kick me out, they kick me out. What the heck!" They never did, obviously. As a matter of fact, one of my supporters in Washington said, "Charlie, the reason they did not kick you out was because they were afraid that we might replace you with someone competent." There may have been something to that.

I used to brief my attachés on how you handled this strange life in the Soviet Union. I would say, "It's the 'Four Bs.'" I tried to keep it really simple because a third of them were Army guys. The "Four Bs" were: "bugs, booze, blondes, and black market."

Bugs were everywhere in your house or apartment. We lived across from the embassy. There was a huge apartment building, and there were huge amplifiers pointed at us. We were radiated all the time, and I am sure they heard every word we said, so we were cautious about what we said. We thought before we spoke. I have since forgotten how to do that, but it is an interesting thing. You would go to a hotel room in some God-awful place in Kazan or wherever. It would always be the same hotel room in the same hotel that Intourist put you in. Of course, you knew that was because it was bugged. You would go sit in the restaurant in the hotel, and it was always at the same table. They'd say, "Here's your table." We'd say, "Well, can we sit [over there]? There's nobody else there." They'd say, "No, this is the best table. Take it." We'd go along with it. You learned how to use sign language, how to write notes, and how to get along without speaking into the bugs.

Booze was a problem. That is the national sport over there, and, of course, it is a big activity in the diplomatic circle. You learned right away that you could not drink your way through an attaché tour. We had a lot of mineral water. I cautioned my guys because I never met anyone whose judgment got better when they drank. We needed to be sharp all the time because we were right on that fine line, trying to do our jobs as best as we could without stepping over it. Where we got caught there was that we liked to mix with the people. We liked to get a feel for the culture, but it was difficult to do because we were foreigners. We never deceived people about who we were. When they asked, we would say that we were military attachés from the embassy, and that was it. Of course, we also knew that if we were talking to someone, an average citizen, seconds later after we left, the "goons" who were following us would be on them like a dirty shirt. We did not want to bring that wrath on them.

You would go into a restaurant or bar, especially down in Georgia, where they were very fun-loving and drank a lot of vodka, and they would come over to the table and bring their bottle of vodka. You wondered what was in there, because you knew that two years ago the Japanese attachés were poisoned down there. They would say, "Let's drink to peace and friendship." Well, how are you going to diplomatically say, "I don't want to drink to peace and friendship. Are you kidding?" Well, you learned how to do that and tried to do it in a smooth way. But booze was a problem. The idea that the Russians have about having a drink is two guys sitting down and finishing off a bottle of vodka.

The third one is blondes. I had been trying to make myself attractive to the other sex for at least forty-five years, and I finally succeeded in the Soviet Union. We'd be in Siberia, say Novosibirsk. We would be at a table having dinner, and next to us would be two good-looking girls, always blondes. We were always traveling in pairs, so there would be two of them. It was pretty blatant. I was armed with my own guidance here, so I could fend that off. We also warned people when they could expect things like this. We had an annual meeting with the NATO defense attachés. We talked about things that were happening and passed on information. I remember one time the Brits said, "They're using women in Murmansk." A couple of their naval attachés had just been there. They checked into their hotel room, and there was a knock on the door. They opened the door, and there was this good-looking blonde. It was always a blonde. My apologies to the brunettes and redheads. She said, "I'd like to practice my English with you." Of course, their story was: "No, we're not interested." There was a knock about a half-hour later, and there were two blondes: "We'd like to practice our English." So, we were prepared.

Now, the interesting thing about that was that the reason the KBG did it was because it worked. I won't mention the country or their service, but not long before my time, an attaché was caught in a compromising position out in the "boondocks." The door flew open, and the KGB came in, and he was with one of these blondes. They were taking pictures, and a few minutes later, a friend of his from Moscow, a Russian military officer, showed up. He said, "Pal, I can make all this go away, but you'll have to work for us." Fortunately, this individual had the guts to own up to it. The sad thing about that is you wonder: "How many didn't own up to it?" So, it worked.

The fourth "B" was the black market. Thank God for the black market, or the economy wouldn't have provided any goods at all. The official rate when I was there, I believe, was about a dollar-and-a-half to buy a ruble, but you could buy three or four rubles for a buck if you were dealing on the black market. You would walk down the street, and they would stop you. The first thing a citizen would ask was: "What time is it?" You would usually stumble in telling them what time it was in Russian, and then they would say, "Ah! You're a foreigner! Where are you from?" You would say, "America," and then they would start looking at you. Invariably, they would look at my Eddie Bauer boots. They would say, "Do you want to sell your boots?" Often, we wore blue jeans because they were very durable for travel in a dirty country. They'd say, "Do you want to sell your blue jeans?" I always wondered what you did if you did that. What were you going to wear? The black market was a danger because it was illegal. That was another way that you could embarrass yourself or your country, by getting caught in black market activities.

So, what did the attachés do? We were looking for new equipment, by and large. In the Army, we were looking for a new tank, other personnel carriers, and artillery pieces. In the Air Force, we were looking at the Antonov AN-24, the big C-5-like transport airplane; we were searching for the next generation of fighters, which ended up being the MiG-29 and the SU-27. Indeed, we got some early prototype pictures to help predict that next generation. The Navy was looking hard for submarines, which was the strength of their navy, and cruisers. They were building a large aircraft carrier. We were looking for those kinds of things.

We were trying to figure out their state of readiness, and, of course, we would love to have known what their military intentions were. As I have told you, that was difficult. We were trying to record as much as possible on film, but they had very stringent laws against people taking pictures of anything that was of interest. That is the way it boiled down: "If it looks interesting, don't take a picture or make a sketch of it." But we figured how to do that, anyway.

We spent a lot of time traveling. That was our job. My attachés averaged about three trips a month, and I did about half that many. We wanted to keep people out looking around. We had requests, usually from the Defense Intelligence Agency, our parent organization, to look for particular targets. We would then plan it. It was like a fighter mission for me. You'd get the requirement, you'd get the target, and then you'd sit down and plan it; then you briefed it; then you executed it; then you came back and debriefed it with the photos, which we had the capability to develop right away; and then you'd write up your intelligence report, the report that went on to Washington. It was part of a big puzzle. We never saw the "big picture" there. We just provided the information, which went into making up the whole puzzle in Washington, and we hoped that it was something that was worthwhile.

At least on a weekly basis, I went over to the outfit that owned us in the Soviet Union, the Military Liaison Office. I either complained about their harassment of our attachés in the field, or I answered complaints from them about our provocative activities out in the field. It was a negotiation with the Russians that I really did not enjoy. They, by nature, were much nastier than I was, but I learned how to do what I could to protect our guys and our country's rights. Of course, the big hammer that we had was the FBI in the United States in our foreign liaison mission, which could curtail their activities or kick them out, if we saw that as necessary.

I want to describe, first of all, the easiest collection we did. It was when they put on the great parade—it was in early November, but it celebrated the October Revolution—through Red Square. It was a magnificent parade—such precision, such wonderful marching! The troops were spotless; the equipment was spotless. It was usually a chance to see something new because, if they had something new, generally speaking, they wanted the West to know about it.

The bad thing about our situation was that this was two years after [the Russian invasion of] Afghanistan started, and we had interrupted our diplomatic social intercourse with the Russians as a message to them that we were very displeased with that activity. Now, from 1981 to 1983, when I was there, the sanctions were still in effect, and the bad thing about that was that we cut ourselves off from an opportunity to do more with the Russians. We refused to go to their functions when they were celebrating a national day; we would not go to their military headquarters. We were invited. They continued to ask us to this stuff. We were invited to the big parade, but we would not go. What we did—and it was more effective, anyway—was we would split up into groups and go to the feeding points into Red Square. We would catch the equipment while it was slowed down or stationary and take close-up pictures. We traditionally followed that up over at my quarters with a chili party, which was a new dish for most of the attachés from the various countries who came to the party. We also had hot wine or something else warm because it was invariably ten or twenty degrees below zero outside. The problem we had as photographers was trying to change film when your fingers were near-frozen. We practiced that, and, indeed, we could change film in the dark, because that was the thing that we did.

The other thing that was important in Red Square was how the hierarchy of the Communist Party was lined up: "What's the Politburo look like this year?" "Who's standing where?" "How high can [Leonid] Brezhnev wave?" It was getting pretty low; indeed, he died while I was there. I, along with our ambassador, saw him lying in state, which was a highlight of my tour, too. It was a great ceremony, is what I'm saying.

I must now talk about my people. We had thirteen attachés: twelve others and myself. I had an Army colonel, an Air Force colonel, a Navy captain, and then they had three assistants apiece. They were all volunteers. They had studied hard, most of them, to get the honor of being selected to go to the Soviet Union as an attaché. It was a real career step for them. Many of them were intelligence officers, and this was a very important assignment for them. They were all eager, bright, and gutsy. Some were better at the language than others; some were more experienced than others. The Army was head and shoulders above the other services because of its Area Studies Program. All of the services need to do more of that, certainly.

The wives were extra special. Most of them were raising children. A few of them had jobs, a couple in the embassy and a couple working for Western businesses in Moscow. They traveled with us when they could, and they entertained a lot. That was the name of the game: "Bring your friends over, and let's find out what's really going on." We did that about five nights a week. We usually got the weekend off, unless it was somebody's special national day. Often, we would have our own parties together, just to remind ourselves of who we really were. The greatest party we ever had was when each year the Defense Attaché Office went to the embassy's *dacha* out in the country and had a wonderful Thanksgiving party. I'll tell you something: Thanksgiving over there really meant a lot. We had a lot to be thankful for.

We had great NATO friends, of course. There were others. The Indians, the Japanese, and the Chinese come to mind. The Indians, I read, were embarrassed by their close friendship, if you will, with the Soviets. They had a lot of their equipment, and they did a lot of training there, and I think that they were trying to make up for it. We spent a lot of time with them, and we learned a lot from the Indians. The Japanese were small in number, but they were very aggressive and very effective. I will never forget what the Japanese defense attaché told me early on. I think it was astute, and he was probably right. He said, "The Russians are more Oriental than they are Occidental." The Chinese were strange bedfellows, it would seem now. They had a lot of border problems with the Russians, and they were eager to talk to us about the Russians.

We saw a lot of media representatives. We lived in our apartment complexes, and they would come over. They would come over also to Alfredo's, which was a restaurant in the embassy, or more like a snack bar. Alfredo, an Italian who was probably an Italian "commie," ran it, but, anyhow, he did good things. We had cappuccino, caviar, and hamburgers, among other things—at that time, it was the only place in Moscow that could serve hamburgers—so people were eager to come over there as our guests. We talked to the media, recognizing that they were in the same kind of business we were: collecting information. The only thing was that you had to be careful because you knew they'd sell you in a minute for a Pulitzer Prize. Those were some of our friends.

I want to mention briefly our foes, the Soviets. The Canadian ambassador left about the time I got over there and was quoted as having said, "The only regret I have is that, after seventeen years in the Soviet Union, there's not one Russian I can call a friend." It was difficult to get to know a Russian. I got to know my driver pretty well, Viktor, but it took a long time. Early on, I would talk to him and tell him little things about the United States—not in a bragging way, but just trying to educate him. Invariably, he would say, "Ours is better." After about six months, it turned into a question: "Is ours better?" Tanya was our cook and housekeeper. She was a wonderful lady who ended up serving American defense attachés for eighteen years. I think the thing that won her over to our side were the kids that she saw. Kids are just about alike everywhere. Tanya cried when we left. Maybe part of the reason was she knew she was going to go work for the Germans, and she wasn't happy about that.

I must just very briefly mention two trips. I had my wife on both of these, and this is partly for the benefit of the ladies. The first one was a train trip through Georgia. We traveled any way we could—airplanes, trains, and cars. We had three or four cars stashed around the Soviet Union, and we'd use those. We spent a lot of time on foot, because often you can see more on foot. This was a train trip, and we were going to go by the target. It was planned so we could look at an airbase. We knew that the "Frogfoot" [the NATO designation], the SU-25—the equivalent to the A-10, which was being used in Afghanistan at the time—was based there. We were hoping that we would be able to get some long-range shots, so we took a telescopic lens, the kind that any normal tourist would use, of course, and got on the train.

The good news was that Intourist, which controlled all our travel, had not booked us at night, which was what they usually did on trains so you could not see anything. The only thing that was wrong was that they turned the car backwards. We were in a compartment, but we were not on the side where you could look right out the window at the airfield. If you did have a direct view, they would usually put axle grease or something on the window so you wouldn't have a clear shot at it. But this one was turned around, so we opened the door to the compartment. We sent the two women out either to give us a warning or to try to distract the KGB onboard. We were able to get shots, shooting across the aisle and through the window, and they turned out pretty decently, considering. We had a blanket ready to throw on the camera, which was up on the top bunk, if the KGB got to us. We also had an open bottle of vodka and a couple of glasses to offer them a drink if they started in. That was the kind of thing we did.

We had another trip that was interesting. My naval attaché was a great friend—he lived next-door to us in the embassy—and he wanted me to go on a cruise on a real boat that would come in from the West, sometimes from the Netherlands or from one of the Scandinavian cities. The naval attachés would get on board, and the Navy intelligence back in the States loved this. I looked at it as a boondoggle, but for about fifteen minutes, they would get a real good look at the waterside of shipbuilding in Leningrad. He kept saying, "Why don't you and your wife come on this one with me?" I couldn't make myself do it. I said, "I'd love to go on that, and I'd love to take my wife on that, but I think you need trained naval eyes to spot the vessels and figure out what's going on." Finally, he convinced me to go on a boat tour of the Black Sea. It ended up not being on a luxury liner, but more like a garbage scow. One day out, the toilets backed up; two days out, no more hot water in the shower. But we did get to see several ports. It was a worthwhile trip. There were more KGB "goons" on the boat than there were people running it. We wondered: "Where are we going to go, and what are we going to do?" Not much! I guess they were looking at it as a boondoggle, too, so they wanted to get in on a good deal.

I want to mention kind of a "so what." General Bob Dixon of the Air Force was famous for making sure that briefers put at the bottom of a slide something that said "so what [does all this mean?]"[2] Well, this is how I am going to try to throw some of this together as my "so what." First of all, it was a very challenging and unique experience, just as my boss had said, and I would not trade it for anything. I found that knowledge of history and the language is important to understanding another country. I had the privilege of living overseas in France, where I spoke the language somewhat, Germany, Korea,

[2] On October 1, 1973, General Robert J. Dixon took command of the Tactical Air Command, which was the crowning assignment of his career. This was one of the most challenging times in the TAC's history, a low point in public support for the post-Vietnam military, and the Air Force badly needed to rebuild its morale and force structure. He implemented more realistic air combat training and pioneered a form of "system of systems" thinking about airpower and how to integrate the new technologies then becoming available. Dixon thus got the airmen to think about integrated concepts of operations. He was a hard taskmaster and famously impatient. Those who briefed him had to move fast. To an aide during a briefing, he once said, "Cut the striptease and show me the naked lady!" See Rebecca Grant, *Air Force Magazine* 87 (Mar. 2004).

Japan, and Southeast Asia, of course, but I was really able to get more of a feel for the culture and the people because I knew the language and a little of the history of the Soviet Union.

We knew that the Soviet system would not last. We did not believe that it would end so soon. The Marquis de Custine said when he came back from Tsarist Russia in the nineteenth century that if the Russians were opened up to free communication with Western Europe, in twenty years they would be free. Well, it did not take twenty years. It took about three or four years after [Mikhail] Gorbachev introduced *glasnost*, which was a pretty amazing thing. The collapse of the Soviet military was probably starting, and we were seeing some early signs of the decay. There was the drunkenness problem, but that probably had been there all the time. There were drugs, which was exacerbated by the Afghanistan experience.

The Afghanistan experience itself had a big impact upon conscription, which was the way they fielded an army. It was not a professional fighting force, as far as the fighters were concerned, because they were conscripts. What happened was that mothers used to be excited about sending their sons off to fight in the Great Patriotic War. They were sad, but they certainly felt a sense of pride. Now they didn't want their sons to go and die in Afghanistan, which made no sense to them.

Barracks life and discipline was starting to get really bad. The two-year conscripts just could not run the enlisted force. Basically, I think the Soviet army missed out a great deal in not having a professional non-commissioned officer corps. So, a conscript would come in, and if he seemed like a bright guy, they would put a couple of stripes on him. In the barracks, the thing that was starting to happen, which became really rampant, was an upperclass/underclass system. The second-year conscripts would use the first-year conscripts as slaves to do their bidding. There was this decay starting up from the bottom, and at the top there was corruption. Also, the top guys were getting old, and there were a bunch of them. Of 3,000 generals and marshals, 500 were over the retirement age of fifty-five, and they were living "high on the calf," with special restaurants, special stores, special *dachas*, and benefits like that. There was corruption at all levels.

The consensus that we had on the Soviet military was that they were not ten feet tall; they were less than half of that. Their immaculate appearance and performance in the big parades made them look good, but they were not that good as a fighting force. The thing that bothered me most, though—and this was always in the back of my mind—was that if the Soviets could put the priority on the subway system to make such beautiful stations and to have trains run precisely on time, could they do that for the Strategic Rocket Force?

I came back from the Soviet Union with a sense of renewed vigor to do what I could to keep our country good, wise, strong, and free. As a result of this very rewarding experience, in my capacity as the defense attaché, I think I learned a great deal about the strengths and weaknesses of our adversary during these years. Just as important, I came away with an appreciation for the mindset of the Soviets and better understanding of how their history, particularly in the Great Patriotic War, influenced many of their attitudes and conduct toward the United States.

Section VII
TERRORISM

This final section concentrates on what some believe is a new form of military conflict: terrorism. But, is it really new? History books are filled with examples of individuals and organizations dedicated to inflicting violence on an adversary or his/her government, but terrorism may be different. As the West struggles to understand the hatred and the violence of recent events, especially the attack on the World Trade Center on September 11, 2001, one is reminded that something as complex and widespread as terrorism must have historic roots. Yet this new combination of commitment and technology provides the potential for inflicting massive destruction like never before. Both papers in this section emphasize learning from history, not necessarily to find the perfect policy but to understand the complexity of the term and the motivations behind the people who willingly sacrifice their lives to inflict such great violence.

Professor Norman Itzkowitz has spent most of his professional career studying the psychology of terrorism. His expertise is in Near Eastern history with a special focus on Islam and the now defunct Ottoman Empire. Itzkowitz reminds the reader that terrorism is not necessarily new. He uses examples from the Roman Empire, Ghenghiz Khan, and the Conquistadors in Central and South America to demonstrate that terrorism has many forms. All too often, the conquerer uses terrorism in the conquest and administration of any newly acquired empire. Itzkowitz reviews the history of the Middle East to view the long history of brutal and narcissistic behavior by various Moslem sects as they tried to interpret and carry out the creed of Mohammed.

The second paper was delivered by Professor Brian Linn, and it focuses on a conflict in the early twentieth century in the Philippines following the Spanish-American War. The United States had won a relatively speedy victory in the military phase of conflict and then was faced with a difficult period of winning the hearts and minds of a people, many expecting to receive their immediate independence from Spain. The Philippine War proved to be a brutal conflict against a determined adversary. The entire period bears a striking similarity to the current challenge of the United States in Iraq. In both cases, the postwar period of pacification became far more challenging than the conventional phase. The final chapter of the Iraq conflict has yet to be written, but it will surely tell of a challenging time that tested the full array of American military leadership, strategy, and tactics. The first major conflict of the twenty-first century may be one of the most challenging in the history of the United States.

DR. NORMAN ITZKOWITZ

OLD WHINES IN NEW BOTTLES: SOME THOUGHTS ON THE PSYCHOLOGY OF TERRORISTS AND TERRORISM

Born in New York City on May 6, 1931, Dr. Norman Itzkowitz earned his Ph.D. from Princeton University in 1959. He is currently professor of Near Eastern Studies at Princeton and is also a member of the Advisory Board, Center for the Study of Mind and Human Interaction at the Medical School of the University of Virginia.

In addition to his teaching responsibilities and scholarly pursuits, Dr. Itzkowitz has been actively involved in university service at Princeton. He served as Departmental Director of Undergraduate Studies, 1961–66; and Department Director of Graduate Studies, 1971–73. Dr. Itzkowitz also served as Master of Wilson College at Princeton, 1975–89. When he took over the mastership, Wilson College was a four-year college, and the success of Wilson College led to the organization of the Committee for Undergraduate Life (CURL), which devised a residential college scheme whereby all freshmen and sophomores live in five residential colleges in which they have their living space, meals, social life, academic advising, and other support systems.

Dr. Itzkowitz is the author, co-author, editor, or translator of eleven books on Near Eastern or Balkan subjects and the author of eleven articles dealing with the same areas.

I want to share some thoughts on the topic of the psychology of terrorism and terrorists. One of the outcomes of the horrific events of September 11, 2001 [9/11], was to focus the attention of our nation and the world on terrorism and terrorists. Prior to 9/11 terrorism was largely something that happened to other people in far-off places, and terrorists, except for those in the Bader-Meinhoff gang, or the IRA, seldom had faces and stories. We had knowledge about the existence of suicide bombers as well as of Tamils and Algerians, who blew people up as they sat in sidewalk cafes. We knew about the doings of people like David Koresh and Terry Nichols, but that seemed to be the work of psychopaths rather than of terrorists. After 9/11 a new vocabulary implanted itself in our consciousness, such as al-Qaeda and *Jihad.*[1]

Now, more than one year after 9/11, we find ourselves using old and now outmoded terminology—what I call "old whines"—such as "making the world safe for democracy," or "safeguarding our Judeo-Christian heritage," or "we need to consult with our allies and get people on board." Now we are putting those "old whines" in new bottles with such labels as "Nukes: Iraq has weapons of mass destruction," or "Smallpox or Anthrax: Take your Pick," or "America is united, and we will consult the UN but go it alone if necessary."

Indeed, going it alone may be the only course of action available to the United States. Despite the breast-beating around the world by the international community horrified by the events of 9/11, Islamic terrorism has succeeded in the object of its terrorism. As the former CIA psychoanalyst now retired, Jerrold Post, has so eloquently put it, the purpose of terrorism is to terrorize.[2] Only Great Britain appears to

[1] Editor's note: Dr. Itzkowitz presented this paper at the UNT Military History Seminar on September 28, 2002.

[2] Editor's note: Dr. Jerrold Post is Professor of Psychiatry, Political Psychology,

be willing to stand with America against the threat of al-Qaeda's terrorist campaign and Saddam Hussein's projection of himself as sitting on a pile of both biological and nuclear weapons he is ready to unleash upon the West. There are still reasonable doubts whether British Prime Minister Tony Blair can carry his country along with him in his allegiance to the United States. Up until the recent elections in Turkey that brought an Islamic-oriented government to power, we could count on Turkey's support. But now it is not clear whether Turkey will allow the United States to use Turkish air bases in a war against Iraq, and it is equally unclear whether the United States will be willing to allow Turkey to annex some parts of northern Iraq to forestall the creation of a Kurdish state on its eastern border. What is still lacking in all the discussions about terrorism and terrorists is some thoroughgoing, meaningful overview as to the psychology of terrorism and terrorists. Let me try to offer a beginning on such an overview.

Views on terrorism suffer, it seems to me, from a Eurocentric bias. Such a view sees the origins of terrorism in the French Revolution with Robespierre and the Reign of Terror. Even in Europe, terrorism existed long before the last quarter of the eighteenth century. We need to go no farther back than the Roman Empire and the terror visited upon the unfortunates who happened to be in the path of the feared Roman legions, which were let loose upon the people by their leaders as rewards for their steadfastness in battle.[3] What the Eurocen-

and International Affairs and Director of the Political Psychology Program at The George Washington University. Post came to George Washington after a career of twenty-one years with the Central Intelligence Agency where he founded and directed the Center for the Analysis of Personality and Political Behavior, an interdisciplinary behavioral science unit that provided assessments of foreign leadership and decision-making for the president and other senior officials to prepare for summit meetings and other high-level negotiations and for use in crisis situations. See his book *Political Paranoia: The Psycho-politics of Hatred* (New Haven: Yale University Press, 1997).

[3] See Caleb Carr, *The Lessons of Terror* (New York: Random House, 2002).

tric view of terrorism does do, however, is remind us that terroristic violence from the end of the eighteenth century onward was largely a matter of intimidation of civilians by their own governments. This was what has come to be called "terrorism from above." That form of terrorism over two centuries killed, maimed, and caused more psychological damage than all the acts of non-governmental terrorism, or "terrorism from below," including the toll from 9/11.

When we look at terrorism beyond the geographic limits of Europe, we find in the Near East, for example, an early form of terrorism in the group known as the Assassins. What we deal with, in the case of the Assassins, is the fallout from the end of the Fatimid Empire, based in North Africa.[4] The Fatamids were Shi-ites, that is, they saw themselves as the descendants of Ali through his wife Fatima, who was the daughter of Muhammad. They claimed descent through Ismail, who was the seventh Imam or leader after Ali. The Fatimid leaders took the title of Caliph in emulation of the Abbasid caliphs. Being followers of Ismail, the seventh Imam, they were also known as the Seveners. Their rule began to unravel in the last decade of the eleventh century upon the death of Caliph al-Mustansir (1035–1094). A number of Ismailis left Egypt and continued to preach the Sevener Shi-ite doctrine. One such person was Hasan-i Sabbah, who ultimately settled in the Elbruz Mountains of Iran where he took over the castle of Alamut. In 1090, he became known as the "Old Man of the Mountain" since he never left his castle until his death in May 1124.

Hasan-i Sabbah was part of the Ismaili resistance to the power of the Seljuk Turks, who had come into the central Islamic world in the late eleventh century and had taken control of Baghdad and other main cities of the Fertile Crescent. They reestablished Sunni Islam in place of Fatamid Shiism. Unfamiliar with the culture and politics of

[4] See the classic work by M.G.S. Hodgson, *The Order of Assassins* (New York: AMS Press, 1980).

the central Islamic world, they were tutored by the man to whom they gave authority as vezir, a man named Nizam-al-Mulk. Hasan-i Sabbah's response was to organize a group of devout followers who were willing to sacrifice their own lives to carry out his orders. He began a campaign of violence, employing the tool of assassination against the leading figures of Seljuk power. His first victim was Nizam al-Mulk himself, who was assassinated in 1092. Other members of his family followed him as victims of the Assassins.

Many tales have arisen with respect to the Assassins, much of it based on the work of Marco Polo.[5] These stories connect the name of Assassins with the use of hashish, from which the word assassin is then derived. According to the stories, the devoted followers were given hashish and drugged into believing that they had been taken to paradise and would return there after fulfilling their murderous mission. There is much in common between these stories about the Assassins and the present-day suicide bombers and terrorists, but in the final analysis, the tales about the Assassins and hashish are nothing but that—imaginative tales. But, the Assassins did unleash a wave of terror that shook the ruling classes of the Near East until it was dissipated by the restoration of orthodox, Sunni Islam in most of the area except in Iran, which in 1500 became an area dominated by the Shiis of the Twelver (named after the twelve leaders, or imams, of the Shii Muslims) dispensation under Shah Ismail.

More evidence of old terror, if we still need more, is provided by Genghiz Khan and his descendants, who wreaked havoc across Central Asia and down into the central Islamic world. In the thirteenth century, Hulagu, the grandson of Genghiz Khan, destroyed the mountain sanctuaries of the Assassins and sacked Baghdad in 1258. The Mongols had so terrified the populations of Central Asia that there

[5] See Manuel Komroff, ed., *The Travels of Marco Polo the Venetian*, Book I (New York: Horace Liveright, 1926).

began great migrations of peoples, Muslim and non-Muslim alike, westward to avoid the power and wrath of the "Scourge of the East."

One such group, after establishing themselves in western Anatolia, would emerge ultimately as the Ottomans and establish a great empire, which at its zenith would extend from the Balkans and Asia Minor across to Iran, and down the Fertile Crescent and Arabia, then through Egypt all the way across northern Africa to Algeria. Their empire would last until Mustafa Kemal Ataturk would do away with it in the aftermath of World War I. The Ottoman Empire was the antithesis of that of the Mongols. Until violence fueled by the introduction of nationalism into the Near East from the mid-nineteenth century made its appearance in the Ottoman lands, terror was not the state's policy for the maintenance of public order. Rather, in the Ottoman Empire everyone was equal, but the Muslims were more equal. As long as the non-Muslims accepted their status as "second-class citizens," which carried with it the payment of a special tax, the *cizye*, or poll tax, they could go about their daily lives in security, enjoy their own religion, and regulate their own affairs according to the dictates of their own religion. Religion was the source of one's identity. The Ottoman Empire had a place for everyone, and it was one of the functions of the sultan to keep everyone in his place.

Once nationalism took root in Europe, together with the ready availability of weapons, and then spread eastward through the Balkans, violence and terror became a part of daily life that undermined the old Ottoman policy of keeping the populace disarmed, which had played a great role in curtailing violence and terror.[6] Political assassination, reminiscent of the Assassins, spread across Europe and Russia, and then made its way into the Balkans and the Near East, where it is seen these days most prominently in the form of suicide bombers.

---

[6] On the Ottoman Empire, see Norman Itzkowitz, *Ottoman Empire and Islamic Tradition* (Chicago: University of Chicago Press, 1980).

The argument outlined so far is that terror and violence are not strangers to the Near East. Politics, religion, and the amassing of wealth together played roles in the practice of terrorism and violence in the past. When I first learned that there was such a thing as history, I remember being taught that the New World was opened up by men who were interested in the three G's—Gold, Glory, and God—and the strength of each of those three elements varied in each particular case. Needless to say, exploration and conquest of the New World by the Old, or anywhere else, was accomplished with both violence and terror on both sides, mostly government-sponsored, as was the accomplishment of our own Manifest Destiny. That is also why we do and will continue to remember the Alamo, remember the *Maine*, and remember 9/11, and why we and others will remember the Soviet gulags, the Ustashe regime of Ante Pavelic in Croatia, the concentration camps of the Holocaust, Pol Pot's killing fields in Cambodia, genocide in Rwanda, and Slobodan Milosevic's ethnic cleansing areas of the former Yugoslavia.

It goes without saying, of course, that one man's terrorist is another man's freedom fighter. The definition of terrorist and what constitutes terrorism is highly vulnerable to changes over time. For example, when he was a member of the underground terrorist organization Irgun in Palestine, Menachem Begin was considered a terrorist. Once the state of Israel was formed, however, he became a national hero. PLO leader Yasir Arafat's reputation is in danger of changing from Nobel Laureate for peace into either a martyr or a political incompetent.

That brings me back to my theme: the psychology of terrorism and terrorists. Terrorism can be defined as violence designed to bring pressure on governments, through the acts of terrorists themselves, in order to effect change in governmental policies or change in governments. That is, terrorism has a political agenda carried out by an organized group of people who operate in a clandestine way. They are bound together by the hatred of "the other," that is, the common enemy. It is extremely difficult to come up with one definition of terrorism that would encompass all kinds of terrorists for the simple fact that there are too many kinds of terrorists, each kind with its own objectives, interests, and methods. There are ethnic terrorists such as the Basque separatists, also known as the ETA, Euskadi ta Askatasuna; LTTE, also known as the Liberation Tigers of Tamil Eelam, who are once again back to their old policy of impressing adolescent boys and girls into service; and the PKK, or Kurdish Workers Party, in Anatolia.

Ethnic terrorists concentrate on trying to forge a distinct ethnicity and fostering ethnic mobilization. They engage in violence to foster communal identity and to provoke the government or other communities in the country to retaliate against them, which serves to achieve greater communal identity and draws attention to their cause. This is also a means for increasing their numbers and their financial support. What those who are engaged in ethnic terrorism want to achieve is a separate state for their own ethnic community. Perhaps the one ethnic terrorist group most widely known is the PIRA, the Provisional Irish Republican Army, in Northern Ireland. This Catholic terrorist organization is devoted to the attempt to achieve the union of Northern Ireland with the Republic of Ireland by forcing the British army and the Protestants of Northern Ireland to leave the territory through a campaign of violence in Northern Ireland and in the UK proper. In that way they hoped to achieve their objective. What ultimately frustrates their plans is a peace movement led initially by a coalition of Catholic and Protestant women, who fear for their children's lives and the long lasting effects of the violence upon those youngsters. This movement has morphed into a political solution through mediation led by an American, former U.S. Senator George Mitchell. He himself has said that the only thing that enabled him to carry out his assignment in Northern Ireland was the fact that people on both sides were finally fed up with the bloodshed and had had enough. They were then willing to give peace a chance. It remains to be seen whether in an environment in which people have been killing each other for a long time, peace can really have a chance.

Terrorist organizations, while lethal in the extreme, are just like most groups: there is a leader and followers. The leader is usually someone who himself has been traumatized through some sort of abuse, and yet is charismatic and able to exert an almost hypnotic effect on the followers. Largely consisting of young men who are single, sexually inhibited, and like the leader traumatized, the followers are in search of a sense of selfhood and some kind of cohesive identity. The leader, by means of his capacity as a speaker, soft-spoken or a screamer, coupled with daring accomplishments, plays on the infantile desire of his followers for maternal love and acceptance. In addition, the leader is seen as the group's father, who then manipulates aspects of the group's identity.

Dr. Vamik Volkan, the distinguished authority on ethnic conflict studies and the psychology of large-group identities, looks at the issue of large-group identity as a tent held up by a large pole.[7] The pole is the leader, and the tent is the group's identity. Like any canvas, it is woven of many different strands. When the tent, or their identity, is challenged from the outside, the people put on their national costumes, eat their national foods, and sing their national songs, rush to the tent pole/leader and support it and him, thereby holding the canvas, their own identity, taut and strong. When the challenge recedes, they take off their national dress and go about their daily lives

[7] See Volkan's discussion of this phenomenon in his article, "Large Group Identity: Border Psychology and Related Processes," *Mind and Human Interaction* 13 (2002).

with a renewed sense of well-being in their identity. In this process children learn to share in the identity elements of the adults with whom they interact. There are four essential elements of those identities: religion, ethnicity, nationality, and ideology with ideology being the least basic since it is the least durable. As children pass through the psychosexual and psychosocial stages of development, developing a sense of their own personal core identities, a kind of "I"-ness, they also begin to develop a sense of belonging to their large group, forming a large group identity or "we-ness." The child's personal sense of self becomes linked with the experiences of the large group identity, a process that is completed through the second individuation period or adolescence.

Two other essential threads in this group identity or canvas are chosen glories and chosen traumas. These are shared mental representations of historical events and historical figures. Shared glories are passed on from generation to generation through public demonstrations during the anniversary of such a shared glory, such as the Fourth of July, which is one of our shared glories supported by the proto symbol of our flag. Chosen glories serve the purpose of binding the group together. Each group also has its shared trauma equally serving as a bonding mechanism.

Groups have shared moments of chosen glories and chosen traumas. That is, the members share in histories replete with accomplishments and setbacks. The leader, assuming the role of the sought for father, recounts the group's chosen glories, their past victories, and accomplishments in an exaggerated manner. He also reminds them of the trauma they can agree upon as the most dreadful they have experienced, the one that is accepted as the chosen trauma.

To the Serbs, for example, Milosevic harped upon the defeat the Serbs suffered at the Battle of Kosovo in 1389 at the hands of the Ottoman Turks. That chosen trauma had been enshrined in popular Serbian literature, poetry, and folk songs. On the 500th anniversary of the Battle of Kosovo, he vowed to his people that never again would such a disaster be allowed to befall the Serbs. For al-Qaeda under Osama bin Laden, whose history goes back to its foundation in 1988, they have chosen glories already from the first attack on the WTC [World Trade Center] in September 1993, the attacks on the Khobar Towers housing complex in Dhahran, Saudi Arabia, on June 25, 1996, and the attacks on the United States embassies in Kenya and Tanzania on August 20, 1998, all of which pale before the events of 9/11. It is not yet clear what al-Qaeda considers its chosen trauma, but bin Laden is fixated on the presence of United States troops in Saudi Arabia as a deep trauma.

Once the leader has sufficiently browbeaten his followers on the subject of the past injustices they have received at the hands of their enemies, it is easy for him to shift their pent-up aggression toward those outside the group. That step knits the group even more closely together, while at the same time it tightens the leader's hold on the group. As Dr. Salman Akhtar has noted, the leader "comes to exert an hypnotic influence on his followers. He can diminish their shame and guilt, increase their narcissism, and help project their felt inferiority onto others." What is crucial here is that individual members "lose their previous sense of right and wrong, surrendering their personal values on the altar of group approval . . . feeling itself to be a victim, the group begins to victimize others in an act of externalization."[8] The oppressed of yesterday have become the oppressors of today. Individual acts of terrorism such as 9/11 contain unconscious enactments of childhood abuse by the parents, with a reversal of the roles of perpetrators and victim. We need only to recall the words of the father of Muhammad Atta, one of the perpetrators of 9/11, quoted in the *New York Times* shortly after 9/11 to the effect that his son could not have

[8] See Salman Akhtar, "The Psychodynamic Dimension of Terrorism," *Psychiatric Annals* 29 (June 1999).

been involved in the deeds of 9/11 because he was a bit of a sissy, and he had told him in his childhood that he would have to toughen up. Muhammad Atta showed his father how tough he could be.

What is perhaps most paradoxical about the psychology of terrorism is that the terrorist organization, which is established on the principle of externalization of one's own victimhood in search of an exalted and conflict-free identity, cannot afford to succeed in its surface agenda. If the group were to succeed, it would no longer be needed. Because the terrorist leader cannot tolerate such a depressive crisis, he unconsciously aims for the impossible. What we see in the relationship between the terrorist organization and its victims is a stark example of the psychological defense mechanism of splitting. This is something that starts early in infancy where the mother who gives the child the breast is perceived as all good and the mother who takes away the breast is seen as all bad. We all engage in that infantile splitting, but with good enough mothering we learn that Mother is not all good or all bad, but somewhere in between—we merge toward the center and recognize that everything is not all white or all black, and we come to appreciate the gray areas. As we grow older, it is that hard-won ability to merge toward the center that enables politics to function in a democracy, for we call that merging the capacity to compromise.

Enough said about terrorism. Let us shift now to terrorists. Soon after 9/11, many of those who look at violence through a psychological lens were quick to attempt to dispel the public notion that terrorists were monomaniacal psychopaths. While it is true that when one begins to examine what is known about leaders of terroristic groups or organizations, they do not appear to have trouble with reality and reality testing. They are not psychopaths, but rather malignant or destructive narcissists. Narcissists, those people with inflated self-images, and who use their charisma and the historical situations in which they find themselves to become recognized leaders, usually come in two stripes—malignant narcissists and reparative or constructive narcissists. Unfortunately, the destructive narcissists appear to outnumber the reparative ones. Saddam Hussein and Osama bin Laden are only the latest examples of malignant narcissistic leaders. Mustafa Kemal Ataturk, the founder of the modern Republic of Turkey, is the prime modern example of a reparative narcissist.[9]

September 11, however, did bring about a major change in our thinking and response to terrorists. It became clear that we were no longer dealing with terrorists in one county; terrorism is a global problem. Cells of al-Qaeda are everywhere, and they have even appeared in the United States in such places as Lackawanna, New York, a suburb of Buffalo. The borders of the United States are porous. Our attention is riveted on our border with Mexico, but our long border with Canada is more porous with respect to terrorists than is that with Mexico. We are attempting to close the barn door after the horse has been stolen. The challenge to America is more serious than we ever thought, and in the end it will probably mean that we will have to discuss in a democratic fashion our government becoming less democratic with respect to rights we have grown complacent about, such as habeas corpus, the pursuit and protection of information in the information age, that is, dealing both with human beings and with technology, to mention just a few areas.

What has also altered the political landscape is the serious fact of the emigration of huge numbers of people from their original homes in places east and south of Europe and the United States to areas in the heart of Europe and the United States. I was in Amsterdam last summer, and from the taxi driver who drove me to the hotel, its management, including the cleaning staff and the kitchen staff, everyone was

[9] On Mustafa Kemal Ataturk's personality, see Vamik Volkan and Norman Itzkowitz, *The Immortal Ataturk, A Psychobiography* (Chicago: University of Chicago Press, 1984).

Moroccan. It took some searching before you found a Dutch person on the street. There are 5,000,000 Arabs in France, millions of Turks and Kurds in Germany, Belgium, and Holland, and untold thousands of Near Easterners in Afghanistan and Pakistan. Not all of them are al-Qaeda agents, but there are enough of them to give one pause. Not that many Mongols were chasing the vast numbers of people they had set into motion westward, and after some time the Mongols withdrew to their original homeland. That does not appear to be what will happen now. While the terrorist organizations deplore the materialism of the West, if our national borders were even more porous than they are now, the shift of population would be even greater.

I want now to take a look at terrorists and try to formulate a way of thinking about them psychologically that is broad enough to cover a variety, and hopefully helpful in thinking about what we can do about them. What I have to say relies heavily upon the work of Dr. Vamik Volkan, who is newly retired from the Medical School of the University of Virginia [UVA], and Dr. John Mack of the Harvard Medical School, both of whom are psychoanalysts, the work of Matti Steinberg of the Hebrew University, Dr. Jerrold Post, and some of my own work inspired by my association with Dr. Volkan in the Center for the Study of Mind and Human Interaction at the Medical School of UVA, a center devoted to the study of ethnic conflict, and the only such center in this country housed in a medical school. For starters, when we look at a number of ethnic conflicts around the globe, we can do no better than follow Dr. Mack's presentation of Dr. Volkan's ideas on the conflict in Cyprus under seven categories[10]:

1) The Identity of Self and Nation:

Before 9/11 we used to talk about the identity of self and nation.

[10] See Vamik Volkan, *Cyprus—War and Adaptation* (Charlottesville: University of Virginia Press, 1979). The presenter also wishes to thank Dr. Matti Steinberg of the Hebrew University of Jerusalem for the information taken from one of his oral presentations at Princeton University in the fall semester 2002.

There is a deep emotional attachment here to one's nation or to the idea of one's nation if it does not yet exist, or no longer exists. We derive much of our sense of self and self worth through our identification with a nation, with its language, customs, and boundaries. Those people who have not yet been able to give geographic expression to their nation live in a constant state of injured self worth and inner rage. We need only to look at the Arab-Israeli conflict or Northern Ireland to understand this phenomenon. We also need only to recall the use of the terms "motherland" or "fatherland" to realize the depths of emotions associated with the nation. The attacks of 9/11, however, have taught us that religion acts in much the same way as a nation. Osama bin Laden and the members of al-Qaeda, as well as those who share its outlook, its religion, specifically the religion of Islam, have taken the place of the nation. The theology of al-Qaeda, as much as there is of it, can be learned from a few books published by leading al-Qaeda theorists and from a number of websites where al-Qaeda partisan sheikhs post their writings. The essence of al-Qaeda starts with the *shahadah*, the profession of faith: *la ilaha illa Llah*. ("There is no God but Allah.") That means you cannot associate anything with God, including the nation, democracy, constitutions, elections, or idols. That is why the "path of Ibrahim," Abraham being the first monotheist, is revered in the Koran. He gave up everything, including idols, to follow the path of God.

As a result, al-Qaeda is anti-everything that is not Islamic, including being anti-Muslim when Muslims are only nominally Muslims through birth and not Muslims through commitment. For a long time, since the foundation in 1929 in Egypt of the Society of the Muslim Brotherhood by Hasan al-Banna,[11] fundamentalist Muslims, people who wanted a return to the original form and spirit of Islam, had

[11] On the Muslim Brothers of Egypt, see the classic work by Richard P. Mitchell, *The Society of the Muslim Brothers* (Oxford, UK: Oxford University Press, 1969).

taken as their central enemy not Israel, but their own modernizing and westernizing governments. It was, after all, their own Egyptian government who put members of the Muslim Brotherhood and other radical fundamentalists in jail, tortured, and even killed them. Those murdered by the government included Hasan al-Banna in 1949 and Sayyid Qutb in 1966. That violence was reciprocated by political assassinations, including that of Anwar Sadat in 1981.

Al-Qaeda made a distinction between the close and distant enemies of Islam and at first went after the near enemies. Then in 1998 al-Qaeda shifted its concentration to the distant enemy, the United States and United States interests, which meant Jews and Israel. At the same time, al-Qaeda pressed for a worldwide *jihad* against the enemies of Islam. Agents were recruited especially in Egypt, Yemen, and Saudi Arabia. The fruits of that activity were seen in the attack on the USS *Cole* (October 5, 2000) while in a Yemeni port. Previously not particularly interested in the Palestinian struggle since it represented a nationalist struggle which earlier had been anathema to al-Qaeda, Osama bin Laden joined forces with the Palestinians in January 2001. Al-Qaeda is interested not in nations, but in the entire Islamic world, and also perhaps in turning the entire world Muslim, and resurrecting the glory that was Arab Islam's in its heyday from the seventh to the thirteenth centuries. It was then that Islam shone and was an economic leader in world trade, and a great Arab Muslim civilization rich in the arts, humanities, and sciences flourished. This type of thinking, which harkens back to a golden age, is often accompanied by what I call "historical amnesia." After the influx of the Seljuks and other Turks into the central Islamic world in the late twelfth and early thirteenth centuries, there occurred a shift in power accompanied by a relocation of creative energies to the Ottoman Turks, centered eventually in Istanbul, and the Persian Safavids in Iran. The Ottomans conquered the Arab world in 1517, and the ruling Turks did little to include their Arab subjects in the ruling apparatus of the empire except for making use of the Barbary Coast seamanship. This situation lasted until near the end of World War I when Emir Faisal threw in his lot with the British against the Ottomans, and the Arab Revolt, so well depicted in the film *Lawrence of Arabia*, put the Arabs into Britain's debt.

Why is it important for the Arabs to look back to their Golden Age? For one thing, the truth of Islam as a religion is intimately associated with its success. The Arab cause was looked upon with favor and made to flourish because it was the true religion. Islam needs to demonstrate once again that it is the true religion by becoming successful again in and over the world.

2) Historical Grievances:

Dr. John Mack[12] astutely states that prolonged conflict between two adversarial nations, whether they are neighbors or not, must be seen in the context of accumulated memories and historical hurts that each group has experienced at the hands of the other. The real hurts have also mingled with fantasies of hurts. These losses and hurts are memorialized in statues and other art forms such as paintings. When these hurts and tragedies are profound, the "other" becomes the object of blame even when the "other" is not solely or entirely responsible for them. Histories relating the so-called facts of encounters between the two groups when written by members or partisans of one group or the other often involve unconscious mechanisms that tend to blame the "other" and portray one's own group as morally and ethically superior. This has clearly been the case in the Cyprus situation[13], and

[12] Dr. John Mack is a psychiatrist at the Harvard University Medical School and a member of the Center for Psychology and Social Change at that institution.

[13] This is in reference to the struggle between Greece and Turkey for control of Cyprus. Cyprus became an independent republic in 1960 under the protection of Greece, Turkey, and the United Kingdom. Fearing that the military junta in Greece planned to overthrow the government of Cyprus and allegedly wanting to protect the Turkish minority on the island, Turkey invaded the northern part and now controls approximately 40 percent of the land.

it is actively at work in the Arab-Israeli case. In the confrontation between Islam and modernity as played out in such places as Egypt, Saudi Arabia, and Lebanon, the West and the host governments of those countries are seen as corrupt, immoral, and irreligious. Most recently it is the United States that is seen as the responsible party. One of bin Laden's earliest grievances toward both Saudi Arabia and the United States was the stationing of American troops on Saudi soil, which he saw as jeopardizing the sanctity of the holy mosques of Mecca and Medina. He also harbors grievances against Saudi Arabia for exiling him from his country in 1991.

3) The Intergenerational Transmission of Attitudes Toward the "Other":

In the musical *South Pacific*[14] there is a song entitled "You Have to be Carefully Taught," sung by Lieutenant Cable in Act Two, Scene Four, where Nellie tells Emile she cannot marry him because of his Polynesian children and the fact that their mother was Polynesian. Nellie says she does not know why she feels that way. It is emotional. She says, "This is something that is born in me." Emile says, "It is not. I do not believe that it is born in you." Emile then turns to Joe Cable and says, "What makes her talk like that? Why do you have this feeling, you and she? I do not believe it is born in you. I do not believe it." Cable then says, "It's not born in you! It happens after you're born..." and he sings:

You've got to be taught to hate and fear,
You've got to be taught from year to year,
It's got to be drummed in your dear little ear
We are not born prejudiced or hating others.

Thus, prejudice and hate have to be transmitted to the young, and that process of transmission is begun at a very young age, even sooner

---

[14] See *South Pacific,* Music by Richard Rogers, Lyrics by Oscar Hammerstein, 2nd ed. (New York: Random House, 1949).

than the song maintains. Mothers, fathers, other relatives, and siblings transmit to children through their conversations, gestures, facial expressions, incorporation of amulets into the clothing of babies, and other ways their attitudes toward members of the other group.

My mother came from eastern Poland, the part of the Austro-Hungarian Empire known as Galicia, a rather anti-Semitic part of the world aptly depicted in the stories by Isaac Bashevis Singer.[15] My mother, somewhat traumatized by early experiences with deep-rooted anti-Semitism, taught me and my siblings to spit three times before passing a church. That was any church because in Galicia my mother had never encountered a Protestant church, so in America they were all the same to her. I suppose a sign of the Americanization of her children, which was not accomplished without fear for the well-being of her children, was when we stopped doing that. The point is that children are consciously and unconsciously drawn into the processes of ethnic conflict by the adults and siblings around them. As children grow up, teachers, the media, including movies, newspapers, television, and politicians and others contribute to this process of the transmission of attitudes toward the "other." Just as the mother externalizes the unconscious unwanted parts of her and her internalized world populated by the externalization and fears to which she herself had been exposed, the child will pass all that on to his or her children.

It is not surprising that one of the leading Arab Palestinian newspapers has a weekly supplement for children that extols the virtues of young suicide bombers. It is unfortunate, but true, that children

[15] Isaac Bashevis Singer (1904-91) was a Polish-born American journalist, novelist, short-story writer, and essayist, who won the Nobel Prize for Literature in 1978. Singer's chief subject is traditional Polish life in various periods of history, largely before the Holocaust. He especially examined the role of the Jewish faith in the lives of his characters, who are haunted by passions, magic, asceticism, and religious devotion.

are the primary resource of nations for their future wars. Therefore, governments begin to contribute to the process of this transmission when the children are still at an early age, and we have even seen and experienced the images of children soldiers in many war-torn areas. It is important to know that children have difficulty understanding such concepts as nationalism and patriotism prior to the onset of puberty at about the age of twelve. It is not surprising then that even the Boy Scouts do not accept boys until they have attained the age of twelve. The Boy Scout motto is "Be Prepared," but what is it we are being prepared for?

4) The Demonization of the "Other":

Dr. Mack writes, "There is a human tendency to displace onto others, to split away and externalize the negative aspects of oneself, the dimensions one wishes not to acknowledge, or for which one will not or cannot take responsibility. Disacknowledged aspects of the self may be reflected or mirrored by the 'other' . . . Virtue is the possession of oneself or one's group. Evil resides in the 'other.'"

But, when the "other" is another group, it is difficult for someone to be comfortable with any ambiguity about where the good and the evil reside. There can be no apportionment of blame. The matter is black or white, right or wrong. The group's leaders, who assign blame and foster the devaluation of the other group, further the process. If the leader is a demagogue and such devaluation is a matter of national policy, the situation may easily degenerate into bloodshed, murder, and even genocide. This is especially true when the groups have had little first-hand experience of each other, making it difficult for real experience of the other to moderate the group's view of the other as the demon. With continuing disputes over land and boundaries, or the perception that threats to national security as represented by actions of the "other" do exist and are seen to exist by both sides, then the primitive psychological processes of externalization, splitting, and demonization emerge.

We have seen this many times, but for Americans perhaps this has been most clearly seen in American-Iranian relations at the time the Iranians took the United States Embassy in Teheran toward the end of Jimmy Carter's presidency. There were demonstrations in the streets of Teheran in which young Iranians marched around with *papier-mâché* likenesses of Jimmy Carter made to look like a devil. They put signs on him depicting him as *shaytan*, a word in several Near Eastern languages, including Farsi and Turkish, that means "the devil." Cartoonists on both sides of the Israeli-Palestinian conflict have a field day in demonizing leaders on the other side.

The demonizer of the United States *par excellence* is Osama bin Laden. Starting with his protest in 1989 about the presence of American military in Saudi Arabia, he has consistently portrayed the United States as the arch villain in the world. He struck at America and American interests abroad in many places, ending up with the World Trade Center attack on 9/11. That raised his profile and his status around the world as the leader of the anti-American establishment. He has demonstrated that he is flexible, astute, possessed of great managerial skills, and committed to his projects of the destruction of the United States and the reestablishment of the Islamic empire. Practically overnight Osama bin Laden and al-Qaeda became household terms. He and al-Qaeda must be taken seriously in the context of a world that has been terrorized, and yet is largely unwilling to make the effort and the sacrifices necessary to uproot and destroy the al-Qaeda organization. Once again, as has happened so often in the past, it is a matter of whose ox has been gored.

5) The Egoism of Victimization:

That brings us to the discussion of empathy. On the one hand, it is shocking to realize how little empathy one group feels for the suffering of their traditional enemy. This lack of empathy, which is another way of saying the inability of one group to identify with the suffering experienced by members of another group who are the object of one's own hostility, is in the long run one of the necessary steps for the outbreak of war. Having themselves suffered traumatization, the members of that group experience something we can call the "egoism of victimization." Only one's own suffering, that is, the suffering experienced personally and/or by one's group, is all that matters. One's own suffering is always greater, whether in fact or not, than the suffering of the hated other. As Dr. Mack says, "The value of one's own group is thus enhanced; the value of the other is reduced. The egoism of victimization thus has two fundamental interrelated aspects: the justification of continuing hostility on the grounds of having been victimized by the other, and the narcissistic focusing of empathy upon one's own people with the consequent inability to identify with the suffering of the other group."

We see this phenomenon in the recent upsurge of suicide bombers in the Middle East. Many of the Palestinians feel humiliated and reduced to a position of feeling that they have nothing to lose; and inflicting death and pain upon Israelis is done without any sense of remorse or conscience. Personal suicide continues to be illegal and anathema. A religious construction is placed on suicide that makes it lawful since it is being done in the interests of Islam. It will result in raising the status of the suicide bomber and his or her family, guaranteeing the bomber a place in heaven among the Hurris. The strength of the egoism of victimization was made more obvious through the instrument of television as we saw in our living rooms. Al-Qaeda supporters were actually rejoicing in the streets in Cairo and elsewhere at the news of 9/11.

6) War as Therapy:

War has the capacity to make the passive aggressive, and those who feel victimized may experience mastery. War focuses group purpose and helps the nation achieve a sense of cohesiveness. War turns the leader into a national hero, and war raises national self-esteem. It does so even if war proves to be a disaster, as it did in the 1973 Egyptian attack on Israel, which was turned into a costly defeat for Egypt. Yet, it was not experienced as a narcissistic injury, but rather as a victory, if only a political one, as the Egyptians could hold their heads up after experiencing nothing but humiliating defeat in previous rounds with the Israelis. The trouble with war today is that it has been inconclusive. Much wealth is expended; much suffering is endured, for little gain. The Gulf War provides such an example. True, Kuwait was freed from the grasp of Saddam Hussein, but a recent poll taken in Kuwait shows that over 80 percent of the Kuwaitis support al-Qaeda. So much for war as therapy.

7) Aggression and the Inability to Mourn:

War means losses. Those losses have to be mourned. We expect to mourn our own dead, but those are not the only casualties in war. There are dead on the other side, but we find it difficult to mourn those losses. They are not ours; they belong to the hated, devalued and despised others. Mourning is a process, something that has to be gone though, as D.W. Winnicott, the famous British psychoanalyst, said about analysis. Failure to mourn often carries with it dire consequences in the form of unfinished psychological business with the dead. Failure to mourn the dead and the losses on the other side may also carry with it dire consequences, such as a perpetuation of distrust and a need to be in a constant state of preparedness. When the aggression that has been committed by the other is so barbaric that the inability to mourn is heightened, mourning would be a completely shattering experience, a blow to the group's self-esteem. Such is the case with 9/11.

Mourning involves an act of forgetting. Can we forget? Perhaps the best we can hope for is to forget, but to remember that we forgot. Thus, in that way we may be able to remember the *Cole*, and remember 9/11, and we will always be able to remember the Alamo. What I am proposing, then, is to abandon the "old whines" with their outmoded Euro-centric mindset and develop new vintages to deal with modern terrorists and terrorism.

PHILIPPINE ISLANDS, 1898-1902

DR. BRIAN LINN (TEXAS A&M UNIVERSITY)

FORESHADOWING THE WAR IN IRAQ: THE U.S. WAR IN THE PHILIPPINES, 1899–1902

Dr. Brian Linn is currently professor of history at Texas A&M University. He is perhaps the foremost authority in the United States concerning the American military experience in the Pacific in the aftermath of the Spanish-American War.

Dr. Linn received his Ph.D at The Ohio State University in 1985 and has been a member of the Department of History at Texas A&M since 1989. In 2000 he published *The Philippine War, 1899–1902* (University Press of Kansas), which was a selection of the History Book Club in 2000 and winner of the Society of Military History's Distinguished Book Prize in 2001. In 1997, he published *Guardians of Empire: The U.S. Army in the Pacific, 1902–1940* (University of North Carolina Press). This book also was a History Book Club selection in 1997 and winner of both the Society of Military History's Distinguished Book Prize in 1998 and the Army Historical Foundation's Distinguished Book Award in 1997. In 1989 he published *The U.S. Army and Counterinsurgency in the Philippine War* (University of North Carolina Press). In addition to the monographs, he has published sixteen articles and book chapters as well as numerous essays, encyclopedia entries, and book reviews. His current project is a study of war in American military thought.

Watching the operations in the Balkans, Afghanistan, and now currently in Iraq, one can quote the great American philosopher Yogi Berra: "It's like *déjà vu* all over again."[1] A number of distinguished authors have identified the connections between the Philippine War of 1899–1902 and the current conflicts. Robert Kaplan, for example, wrote a recent *Atlantic Monthly* article entitled "Ten Rules For Managing The World." Rule Number Seven was to remember the Philippines. Kaplan argues that the American occupation of the Philippines a century ago might offer the best case study for how to deal successfully with the problem of establishing stability in the world's troubled regions.[2] Similarly, Max Boot, a journalist for the *Wall Street Journal*, and a strong supporter of U.S. intervention in Iraq, argues that the Philippine War was not only America's most successful counterinsurgency campaign, but it is *the* case study we should employ as a guide for imposing order on the world today.[3] Indeed, some writers are suggesting that we are in a situation much like that we faced in 1898 and that America may be embarking on a new imperial drive.

I am first going to discuss some of the parallels between the conflict in the Philippines a century ago and what is currently occurring in Iraq. Then I am going to address briefly some of the lessons that I think the Philippines might teach us. Historians are very leery about lessons learned, as if we can use history as a great database from which to pick and choose selective examples. I do not necessarily think that

---

[1] Editor's note: Dr. Linn presented this paper at the UNT Military History Seminar on October 4, 2003.

[2] See Robert Kaplan, "Supremacy by Stealth: Ten Rules for Managing the World," *Atlantic Monthly* 292 (July/August 2003).

[3] See Max Boot, *The Savage Wars of Peace: Small Wars and the Rise of American Power* (New York: Basic Books, 2002).

we can apply the template of the past on the present or the future, but I do think that if we study the past, we can better appreciate some of the complexities and problems that we are facing today.[4]

One of the most interesting parallels to me is the altruistic rhetoric of both administrations. In the Philippines, the United States intervened—some would say invaded—for the noblest purposes. President William McKinley claimed that the United States did not annex the Philippines for control of Asian trade or to exploit Philippine resources or to seize a naval base or to impose U.S. hegemony in the Far East. These were factors, certainly, and McKinley acknowledged that people had advocated them, but the president claimed that his primary motive in occupying the Philippines was "to improve the condition of the inhabitants, securing them peace, liberty, and the pursuit of their highest good." Now, such altruistic rhetoric, if followed through, would have implied a virtually unlimited commitment of American military, social, economic, and political resources for perhaps infinity, and, in fact, we did wind up there for forty years.

In an even more interesting parallel with Iraq, the McKinley Administration appears to have convinced itself that the liberated peoples would not only welcome U.S. rule, but that military occupation would very soon be replaced by a civilian government. Then, as now, the

---

[4] Editor's note: See Brian Linn, *The Philippine War, 1898-1902* (Lawrence, KS: University Press of Kansas, 2000); *Guardians of Empire: The U.S. Army and the Pacific, 1902-1940* (Chapel Hill, NC: University of North Carolina Press, 1997); and *The U.S. Army and Counterinsurgency in the Philippine War* (Chapel Hill, NC: University of North Carolina Press, 1989). For other pertinent works about the American military experience in the Philippines, see: Andrew J. Birtle, *U.S. Army Counterinsurgency and Contingency Operations Doctrine, 1860–1941* (Washington: Center of Military History, 1998); Karl I. Faust, *Campaigning in the Philippines* (1899: Reprint, Arno Press, 1970); John M. Gates, *Schoolbooks and Krags: The United States Army in the Philippines, 1899-1902* (Westport, CT: Greenwood Press, 1975); Glenn A. May, *Battle for Batangas: A Philippine Province at War* (New Haven: Yale University Press, 1991); and Marion Wilcox, ed., *Harper's History of the War in the Philippines* (New York: Harper Brothers, 1900).

administration maintained that the enemy was not the people of the occupied country; it was an evil dictator—in 1898 Emilio Aguinaldo played the role of Saddam Hussein—and the dictator's tribe, assorted bandits, and former soldiers.[5] American soldiers, under this rhetoric, were not conquerors; they were liberators. Their mission—and this mission was in the form of an order—was "to win the confidence, respect, and affection of the inhabitants." McKinley defined this mission as "benevolent assimilation." According to the president and his top military and civilian advisors, once the Filipino people learned of the benefits of American rule, and once they were protected from this tiny minority of would-be dictators, revolutionaries, and terrorists, they would welcome occupation and become dutiful colonial wards.

As many noted then and later, there was a profound contradiction in the administration's reasoning. On one hand, the United States Government was declaring that the Filipino people were too ignorant, lawless, or fanatical to govern themselves; and on the other hand, the administration was claiming that these same ignorant, lawless, and fanatical people would somehow immediately shed these negative

[5] Editor's note: Emilio Aguinaldo was born into the local elite of Cavite on the island of Luzon. He joined the secret nationalist brotherhood *Katipunan* founded by Andres Bonifacio. After the Philippines erupted in revolt against the Spaniards in 1896, Aguinaldo emerged as the dominant political figure. In December 1897 he signed an armistice with the Spanish and went into exile.

After the U.S. declared war on Spain, Aguinaldo saw the possibility that the Philippines might achieve its independence; the U.S. hoped instead that Aguinaldo would lend his troops in the effort against Spain. On June 12, 1898, Aguinaldo declared Philippine independence. When it became clear that the United States had no interest in the independence of the islands, Aguinaldo's forces remained apart from American troops.

On January 1, 1899, following meetings of a constitutional convention, Aguinaldo was proclaimed president of the Philippine Republic. Not surprisingly, the United States refused to recognize Aguinaldo's authority, and on February 4, 1899, fighting broke out between his forces and American troops. After his capture on March 23, 1901, Aguinaldo agreed to swear allegiance to the U.S. and then left public life. He died in Manila in 1964.

traits, recognize that their interests were well-served by American occupation, and collaborate willingly. This logical conundrum was never quite resolved.

A further contradiction was that soldiers in the field, exposed as they were to guerrilla attacks, ambushes, and terrorist activities, very soon came to view "benevolent assimilation" as not only idealistic and naïve, but positively suicidal. As a result, there was often great discrepancy between the administration's rhetoric about what Americans were doing in the Philippines and the conduct of the troops in the field.

This leads to another parallel between the Philippines and Iraq. McKinley committed American troops without really appreciating either the situation he was sending them into or the possible consequences of his orders. For his information, McKinley relied on people who were either misinformed or had an agenda. He may have been unduly influenced by the 1898 version of the neo-conservative, which in those days was called an imperialist, which I think is a far more direct and accurate title.

McKinley's "man on the ground" was Army commander Elwell S. Otis, who reported that this evil dictator [Aguinaldo] was victimizing the Filipinos and that all that the Americans faced were a collection of revolutionaries, brigands, and lawless elements. He claimed that the Filipino people themselves were willing to be occupied, and essentially the problem was a military one. If we could just smash this dictator and his army, peace would immediately follow. This view reflected, I think, General Otis's sources of information, which were a small group of rich, powerful, Westernized Filipino elites who no more represented the typical Filipino than Ahmed Chalabi represents the typical Iraqi.[6] Now, I do not think that McKinley exaggerated or

[6] Editor's note: Dr. Ahmed Chalabi is one of the best-known Iraqi opposition leaders in the West. Some analysts have suggested this former businessman, as leader of the Iraqi National Congress, could be a possible successor to Saddam

deliberately suppressed intelligence reports—I have read the message traffic—but he was certainly guilty of giving too much credence to reports that confirmed his preexisting views.

This American misunderstanding of the situation translated into over-optimism, or, if one prefers, arrogance. This is more than just historical finger-pointing; it had very serious consequences. For one thing, the McKinley Administration and its military advisors grossly underestimated the number of troops that would be needed in the Philippines. The initial estimate for the occupation of the archipelago was 5,000 troops. After the urgent pleading of the officers who were being sent on this expedition, it was raised to 13,000, then to 20,000. Ultimately, over 125,000 American soldiers would be committed to the Philippines between 1898 and 1902. This was an excellent case of "mission creep," to use current terminology.[7]

A second consequence of this over-optimism was that the United States attempted to impose a civil government at the same time it was

---

Hussein. A Shia Muslim born in 1945 to a wealthy banking family, Chalabi left Iraq in 1956 and has lived mainly in the U.S. and London ever since, except for a period in the mid-1990s when he tried to organize an uprising of Kurd-controlled northern Iraq. The venture ended in failure with hundreds of deaths. Chalabi then fled the country.

In May 2004, U.S. intelligence briefed top Bush administration officials that Chalabi and some of his top aides had supplied Iran with sensitive information on the American occupation of Iraq. Chalabi had allegedly told Iranian contacts about American political plans for Iraq as well as details about U.S. security operations. According to U.S. intelligence officers, Chalabi had disclosed to an Iranian official that the U.S. had broken the secret communications code of Iran's intelligence service, betraying one of Washington's most valuable sources of information about Iran. The Bush administration then cut off financial aid to Chalabi's organization, the Iraqi National Congress, and American and Iraqi security forces raided his Baghdad headquarters.

[7] According to historian John Morgan Gates, almost every unit in the U.S. Army served in the Philippines during the conflict, as well as a number of state and federal volunteers. Of some 125,000 Americans who fought in the islands at one time or another, almost 4,000 died there. The U.S. Army's death rate in the Philippine War (32/1,000) was the equivalent of the nation having lost over 86,000 during the Vietnam War. See John M. Gates, *Schoolbooks and Krags.*

fighting a war. A civilian commission headed by William Howard Taft was sent out after General Otis declared that major combat operations were over. The commissioners arrived in April 1900 to find the United States Army engaged in a vicious and increasingly serious guerrilla war. Not surprisingly, the new American commander, General Arthur MacArthur, argued that civil government could not be established until the military had dealt with armed resistance. Taft and the commissioners, on the other hand, concluded that MacArthur was obsessed with hanging onto power, that the military was using military means for what was essentially a political problem, and that MacArthur was incapable of imposing the methods necessary to ensure peace. Taft and MacArthur soon embarked on a very vicious power struggle that ultimately caused MacArthur's relief and the transition of most of the archipelago to civilian rule in 1910.[8]

A third consequence of this over-optimistic appraisal was serious political consequences at home. I do not think that McKinley or his advisors deliberately lied to the American public or to Congress. However, they certainly over-simplified the problems that the United States would encounter, and they badly underestimated Filipino resistance to American occupation. They maintained this misperception long after it was clear to virtually everyone else that it was no longer correct, and they failed to convey to the American public and Congress why the occupation of the Philippines was absolutely necessary to the security of the United States. Not surprisingly, as the war continued and the cost in blood and treasure rose, American popular opposition rose as well. The war was the fundamental issue in the presidential election of 1900, and had the Democrats nominated anyone but the absolutely unelectable William Jennings Bryan, it might have been a much closer race than it was.[9]

[8] For a fuller account, see Linn, *The Philippine War*.

[9] Editor's note: In the presidential election of 1900, the Democratic Party included an anti-imperialist plank in its platform, but the nomination of Bryan alienated

It is important to remember that in 1902 the Senate opened up an investigation into the conduct of American troops, which revealed that American soldiers had burned thousands of farms and villages and had murdered and tortured Filipino civilians. The United States won the war, but the reputation of the United States Army was permanently tainted; and if one does not believe me, pick up any university-level textbook, and in this section one will read: kill and burn, howling wilderness, concentration of civilians, and so forth. The military came out of the war permanently angry at what it viewed as betrayal by the American people. People think this is unique to Vietnam, but they really need to read the letters from people fighting in the Philippines. Also, the Army leadership was convinced that imperial adventures were such a nasty, dirty, unpopular mission that they should give it to the Marines.

Five years after the declaration of peace on July 4, 1902, the Philippines still cost the American taxpayers millions of dollars. The islands still tied up 20 percent of the entire U.S. Army in occupation duties, and they were held largely by the threat of military force. The Filipino people, for whom McKinley had said that we were sacrificing so much blood and treasure, were clamoring for independence and demanding immediate U.S. withdrawal. Moreover, the military officers were convinced that the Philippines actually weakened our strategic position in the Far East. They provided an easy target for anyone who

---

many anti-imperialists. Bryan had supported ratification of the Treaty of Paris in which Spain had ceded Puerto Rico, Guam, and the Philippine Islands to the U.S. The Anti-Imperialist League ultimately supported Bryan, however, as the most effective means of defeating McKinley. For many of the League's officers, though, Bryan himself became the "paramount issue," and the anti-imperialist vote was ultimately divided. The presidential election of 1900 was the last time the anti-imperialist movement tried to make anti-imperialism the "paramount issue" of a political campaign. By the time of the next election, the U.S. had established firm control over most of the Philippines, and the issue was receding into the background of public consciousness.

wanted to strike at Americans with relatively little risk. One of the leading spokesmen for Philippine annexation, President Theodore Roosevelt, in 1907 concluded that, as far as American economic, political, and strategic interests were concerned, the Philippines were simply not worth the cost. He termed them "our heel of Achilles."[10] He was correct. From a strategic standpoint, the American presence in the Philippines was not to our benefit because we were put in a position of having to make concessions in the Far East in return for guaranteeing the security of the islands.

There are other parallels as well. One of them is the way the war was fought. Like the current war in Iraq, the Philippine War had a conventional phase in which the United States Army did remarkably well. But the destruction of the enemy's army, the flight and disappearance of Emilio Aguinaldo, and the occupation of the entire country did not end resistance. For two years after "major combat operations" were over, Filipino insurgents continued to ambush patrols, attack supply lines and communications, assassinate individual American soldiers, and then disappear into the population, where they became "*amigos*." I do not think one can even call these battles. Rather, these were what contemporaries termed engagements: thirty or forty a week, leaving over the course of a month maybe ten or twenty Americans dead and thirty or forty wounded. As a point of comparison, the statistics for

[10] Editor's note: American acquisition of Guam and the Philippines from Spain was followed within a few years by the emergence of Japan as a world power after defeating Russia in the Russo-Japanese War of 1904-05. The question then arose whether the Philippines, at the end of a long, vulnerable line of communications, could be defended against the modern armed forces of Japan. Since both the U.S. Army and Navy would take part in defending these islands, the Joint Board, an agency created to develop plans and policies which would most effectively use the available forces of both services, turned its attention to developing a coordinated plan for possible war in the Pacific. Defending the Philippines, however, seemed so difficult a task that President Theodore Roosevelt, writing in 1907, termed the islands "our heel of Achilles." See Linn, *Guardians of Empire* and Henry F. Pringle, *Theodore Roosevelt: A Biography* (New York: Harcourt and Brace, 1931).

Iraq average around fifteen to twenty attacks a week, twelve to twenty-four American soldiers and Marines killed, and eighty wounded. Like those in the Philippines, the engagements in Iraq are brief and fought between very small groups of individuals on both sides.

Moreover, Aguinaldo's supporters were not the only ones who resisted American authority. As American troops spread out throughout the archipelago, they encountered enemies who had no connection at all with the Philippine independence movement; in fact, some of them actively opposed Aguinaldo. These were people like the Moors (Muslims) and religious cults like the *Dios Dios* or the *Pulahanes*, who believed that the apocalypse was coming and that anyone who was an unbeliever needed to be killed immediately.[11] American troops ran into bandits and warlords, who commanded gangs numbering in the hundreds and controlled entire provinces in some cases.

In occupying the Philippines, the United States placed its military into a society that was in the process of breaking apart, and it fell to the Americans to put it back together again, village by village. This was more frustrating and far more costly than had been the conventional operations against Aguinaldo's army. The following numbers need to be taken with some qualification, but during the last four months of major combat operations, from September 1 to December 31, 1899, there were 229 engagements in which the Americans had sixty-nine officers and men killed. After major combat operations were over, in the next four months, from January 1 to April 31, 1900, there were 442 engagements in which 130 Americans died.

Another parallel, which should be of much more concern, is that the resistance movement did not simply attack Americans. It attacked those who collaborated with the Americans, the very people who were going to be responsible for creating a native-based civil-

[11] See Brian Linn, "The Pulahan Campaign: A Study in U.S. Pacification," *War in History* 6 (January 1999); and Linn, *Guardians of Empire.*

ian government. Thousands of suspected *Americanistas*, as they were called, had their houses burned, their crops destroyed, and their livestock slaughtered. Thousands were kidnapped, tortured, mutilated, and killed. Often they were killed in public executions that would let everybody in the village know, American and Filipino, that the guerrillas could strike anywhere.

William Howard Taft bluntly declared that the primary reason that resistance to Americans continued was due to what he called the guerrillas' "system of terrorism, assassination, and murder." The same problem is emerging in Iraq. Arabic stations now broadcast hit lists of suspected collaborators and urge that killing those people has an even higher priority than killing Americans. Iraqis suspected of aiding Americans have had their houses burned out, their property destroyed, and have been assassinated. In some cases, they have been killed by their own relatives in front of the village in a sort of ceremonial execution to let everybody in the village know the consequences of assisting the Americans. There are no statistics on this war so far, but anecdotal evidence at least suggests that these are high numbers.

One could continue with these parallels, and there surely are others. But it is important to note two crucial differences. One of them is the international situation. The United States' war in Iraq has had very little support from other governments and a great deal of popular opposition. McKinley's occupation of the Philippines had widespread international support, at least from the great powers that mattered, and very little popular opposition. Indeed, Rudyard Kipling wrote his infamous poem "White Man's Burden" to urge the United States to annex the Philippines.[12] One of the reasons that the international

[12] Editor's note: Published in *McClure's Magazine* in February 1899, Rudyard Kipling's poem, "The White Man's Burden," appeared at a critical moment in the debate about imperialism within the United States. The Philippine-American War began on February 4, and two days later the U.S. Senate ratified the Treaty of Paris, which officially ended the Spanish-American War. Although Kipling's

community was so eager for the United States to intervene was a real concern about China at that time. The Boxer Rebellion had already broken out, and the Germans had just taken the Shantung Peninsula, and it appeared that China was about to be divided. The Great Powers were beginning to prepare for a world war, and had the United States not taken the Philippines, then Germany or Japan may have invaded them. Would the British or the French have tolerated this action?

A second difference is that, in contrast to today's Army, which narrowly defines its mission as fighting and winning the nation's wars, the United States Army in 1900 had a very much more broad interpretation of its duties. Basically, it existed to serve the national interest, whether as war makers or as peacekeepers. Although our armed forces today are obviously the best in the world and have an extremely high level of professionalism, the Army of 1900, I think, was far better designed for peacekeeping and occupation than today's military.[13]

Again, one could continue this assessment for some time, but at this point I would like to shift and say: "So what? What are the lessons we can learn from this? What are some of the things that we can take from this that might be useful?"

I think the first lesson is that the Philippine War provides crucial insight into the problem of fighting what might be called "stateless wars" or "regional insurgencies." Americans were dismissive of Filipino military capabilities, and they have been dismissive of Iraqi and Afghan (or Taliban) military power, largely because of the poor showing of both military leaders and the conventional forces on the battlefield.

---

poem mixed exhortation to empire with sober warnings of the costs involved, imperialists within the U.S. latched onto the phrase "white man's burden" as a euphemism for imperialism that seemed to justify the policy as a noble enterprise.

[13] See Linn, *U.S. Army and Counterinsurgency in the Philippine War, 1899-1901.*

But Afghanistan, Iraq, Somalia, the Balkans, and maybe even Haiti are in some ways much like the Philippines were in 1900 in that on one level they are nation-states, and on another level they are really federations of tribes, families, regional warlords, and religious factions. Not surprisingly, officers and soldiers fight poorly on behalf of a government for which they have neither loyalty nor trust, particularly when asked to fight in a manner that is in conflict with their culture and traditions and with weapons and technology that are unfamiliar to them. But when those same rather inept conventional warriors go back to their home areas, they can become very effective fighters, not only because they know the terrain and the local dialects, but also because they have longstanding personal contacts with the inhabitants. In many cases, they already have control of the infrastructure and government. They know where to raise recruits; they have access to a tax base; and they have access to information provided by relatives and friends. And in many cases, these same people, who are very inept conventional warriors, prove to be very, very good guerrilla warriors.

Now, this certainly happened in 1900. The Philippine army was not destroyed; it simply melted away, much like the Iraqi army did. But the officers and men took their weapons and went home, and a few months later, they reconstituted themselves as guerrilla bands and began to attack the U.S. occupiers. The war became a local war. Once it became a war for each village, each province, and each island, fought by local forces largely for local and not national issues, then it became a war that Philippine society was very well equipped to wage, because the issues were local, as far as they were concerned.

Six months after General Otis had declared that major combat operations were over, his successor, MacArthur, was claiming that the war might go on for years. The Philippine War is a very important precedent for these stateless wars or regional conflicts that are what we are encountering today. We know that Lieutenant General Ricardo Sanchez, who is the coalition's military commander in Iraq, claims that the war is being fought on a local and, in some cases, provincial level. It is not being fought by a nationally controlled resistance; it is being fought by a locally controlled resistance. If one wants a case study of local resistance, I do not think that one can do better than to look at the Philippines.

Another reason why it is worth studying the Philippine War is because the Americans won, and they won in a relatively short time and at relatively small cost. The Philippines are an important counterargument to the Vietnam myth that Americans cannot fight insurgencies, that we should not get involved in them, and that they are not the type of thing we do well. I do not claim that this is something that we can do anytime we want, but if one wants a case study of a successful counterinsurgency campaign, the Philippines offer an outstanding example. The reasons for the American success are lessons that can be taken and applied to the present and foreseeable future.

The first reason involves the importance of local commanders. For Robert Kaplan, when he wrote "Ten Rules For Managing The World," Rule Number One is that the United States military had to produce more Victor Joppolos, the hero of John Hersey's book, *A Bell For Adano*.[14] It has to produce officers who have the character, intel-

[14] Editor's note: In John Hersey's novel, *A Bell for Adano,* Army Major Victor Joppolo represents a victory for common sense over abstract rules and regulations. What Hersey is showing is that no matter what rules someone draws up, ultimately the man in the field is going to interpret them based on his instinct and common sense. Joppolo loves to talk to people, he speaks Italian, and he is not interested in being rewarded for his successes. He really does not care who gets credit as long as something gets done. He also realizes that for each little problem there is a different solution because each problem he encounters in this town of Adano means a problem with a specific citizen in that town. They all have different personalities, so he has to approach each in a different way. There almost is no rulebook. The rulebook boils down to what one has in the field.

ligence, flexibility, and creativity to deal with local populations. In the Philippines, the high command promulgated policies, but their implementation was usually by company officers. These men were scattered into hundreds of garrisons, and they were isolated and surrounded by a hostile or apathetic or traumatized population while their mission was to reestablish order in their neighborhoods. They led patrols and performed other military functions, but they also had to innovate and adapt to the civil level. They had to, in essence, reestablish a working society in a country that was ravaged by war, disease, and banditry, where law and order had broken down.

This leads to my second point: the integration of civil and military duties. Until July 1901, the commanding general in the Philippines was also the governor of the islands. That dual authority went down to the lowest second lieutenant. Regimental colonels were in charge of their regiments, but they were also the governors of provinces; captains and lieutenants ran companies as well as tactical operations, but they also served as town mayors, sanitation engineers, police chiefs, and readers of town accounts, which is an ideal way to break guerrilla bands. If you tell a typical American officer, "You really ought to be more of an accountant and less of a war fighter," you will get a very strange look, but "following the money trail" is essential in counterinsurgency or counterterror operations. In the Philippines, officers served as judges; they were the ones who built the roads; they were the ones who eradicated malaria; they were the ones who inoculated children against smallpox. This close interaction between civil and military duties ensured that there could be no division between war fighters and peacekeepers. The same officers were responsible for both duties, and that allowed the United States military to deal with the insurgency at a political level. Almost all studies of insurgencies conclude that they are essentially a political problem and not a military one. In passing, this is one lesson of the Philippine War that I do not think either the Bush administration or the military understands or is capable of making adjustments.

The third point—and this is not going to be welcome news—is the importance of garrisoning. In the Balkans, Americans have been criticized for building vast cantonments in which thousands of troops hunker down behind rows and rows of barbed wire and obstacles. They eat McDonald's burgers and go to movies and work out in the gym, but they never go out in the countryside except in large armed caravans. Europeans refer to them as "ninja turtles" because of their Kevlar protective gear and their heavy weaponry. This emphasis on comfort would have been an absolute anathema to troops in the Philippines. They lived in garrisons of a hundred people if they were lucky; sometimes there were only five or six in a village. Their job was local security, and they knew that they were going to stay there until the job was over. There was no thought of rotating home after an eleven-month or six-month tour of duty. They had a long-timer's view of the situation, rather than the short-timer's view that a lot of troops have nowadays. They had every incentive to develop local government—to build the roads, to build the schools, to work with the locals—because the sooner they did this, the sooner their own lives would be safer and the sooner, perhaps, they could go home. The implications for the present are clear and perhaps not what people want to hear. Pacification campaigns take a long time, even very successful ones. In some areas in the Philippines, it took twelve years. The troops who go to Iraq will have to remain, because in a local insurgency, only local contacts matter. If you keep rotating people out every six months, they will never establish the language skills, the personal contacts, and the informant structure that is necessary to break up a guerrilla war.[15]

[15] See Linn, "Provincial Pacification in the Philippines, 1900-1901," *Military Affairs.*

This leads to the fourth thing that the Americans in the Philippines did right. From the beginning, they were very good at using Filipino auxiliaries. The American troops in the Philippines were incredibly undermanned. At the peak, the number given is usually 70,000, and the average was about 45,000 troops. But those numbers are simply military bookkeeping. They count troops in the United States recovering from disease; they include troops in transit; and they identify troops who were assigned to civil duties. On the other hand, average rifle strength in the Philippines numbered about 26,000 troops. Now, that is an infinitesimal number to pacify an archipelago of between 7 and 8 million people.

Very early on, and to his credit—even before the war broke out—McKinley realized that the Americans were going to have to rely on the Filipinos for almost everything, beginning with logistic support. The American Army employed over 100,000 Filipinos in the first year of the war as scouts, police, and eventually as armed troops. By the end of the war, there were 15,000 Philippine troops fighting for the Americans, not to mention two to three times that many informal paramilitary forces and militias and local defense forces. The Americans, by the end of the war, had far more Filipinos fighting for them than the guerrillas did, by a magnitude of perhaps 10:1 or 20:1. These troops were so successful that by 1905, the American Army essentially withdrew from combat operations in the Philippines, except for the Moro areas, and turned them over to Filipinos. So, the importance of getting auxiliaries and getting the locals to work for us was not only crucial to winning the war, but for securing the peace. After the last of the Moro uprising, the United States governed the Philippines for about thirty years without a serious popular rebellion.

Turning to the so-called "Moro Wars," a study of the resistance that the Americans encountered in 1902 indicates that it never came from a united Moro movement. Moro resistance mainly came from individual chieftains or warlords of various tribes. Also, the Americans defused the one thing that would have united the Moros, and that was a religious *jihad* against Christians who tried to oppress them. The Americans stayed out of religious issues. I have read the personal accounts of officers in the field, such as those of [John J.] Pershing and [Robert L.] Bullard, and one is struck by how many of these men had read the *Qu'ran.* American officers on Mindanao in particular had read the *Qu'ran*, and they spent hours with the imams, talking to these people trying to understand them and defusing the perception that the Americans were Christians attacking Muslims.

Pershing even became an honorary Moro chieftain, which undercuts the canard that he executed Muslims and buried them with pigs. That story is a complete fabrication. Pershing would not have done that; and, moreover, it would have been completely antithetical to what he was trying to do, which was to persuade Muslims that Americans did not pose a threat to their religion or culture.[16]

I will close with two somewhat contradictory observations. The first of these is that if a reader looks at the Army Chief of Staff's read-

[16] Editor's note: John J. ("Black Jack") Pershing served with the U.S. Army during the Philippine-American War and later held the position of governor of Moro Province from 1909-1913. According to the myth, in 1911, on Pershing's orders, fifty Moro prisoners were forced to dig their own graves and were then tied to posts to be executed by firing squad. American soldiers then brought in pigs and slaughtered them, rubbing their bullets in the blood and fat. The Moro prisoners allegedly were terrorized, for they would then be contaminated and could not enter Heaven even if they died as martyrs. All but one was supposedly shot, and their bodies were thrown into a grave, and hog entrails were then dumped atop the bodies. The lone survivor was allowed to return to the terrorist camp and tell his brethren what had happened to the others. This episode purportedly stopped Moro terrorism in the Philippines for the next fifty years.

According to Frank E. Vandiver, professor of history at Texas A&M University and Pershing biographer, the above tale is apocryphal. He commented to a query on the matter: "From extensive research on Pershing's Moro experiences, I never found any indication that it was true. This kind of thing would have run completely against his character." See also Frank E. Vandiver, *"Black Jack": The Life and Times of John J. Pershing* (College Station, TX: Texas A&M Press, 1977).

ing list as it was, at least, until a year ago, they will find a number of works on the Civil War and on World War II. But one will find virtually nothing on guerrilla warfare, on nation-building, on peacekeeping, on counterinsurgency—really, on anything like what our troops have faced in the last ten years. The bias toward big wars is found at West Point, at Leavenworth, where the Command and General Staff College is located, and at the Army War College. I know that the Air War College is perhaps even worse, and the Navy is very much still focused on big wars. A recent course that I have been asked to vet for Army ROTC has something like two weeks on Gettysburg and two weeks on D-Day and not a single lesson on guerrilla warfare. So, "big wars" are what our young officers are learning now, and our old officers, too.

My second observation is that over the last ten years, I have been asked to speak before a number of military audiences about the guerrilla resistance and American counterinsurgency. When I start describing this combination of patriots and bandits and warlords and religious sects and how American counterinsurgency became so localized that it got down to the company level, where lieutenants were running towns as well as fighting guerrillas, I will inevitably have some veteran of Somalia or the Balkans or Haiti or Afghanistan or Iraq tell me just how closely that resembles his or her own experience. At West Point on one occasion, I had a lieutenant colonel who had just come back from Iraq stop the talk, pound on the table, and say: "This is exactly what I was running into. We had gangsters; we had local religious authorities we had to deal with; we had the police we had to try to create; we had to rebuild the town and restore electricity and water." Inevitably, they ask me the same question: "Why wasn't I told about this when I was going through my professional education? Why did I learn all about big wars but not about the wars I'm actually fighting?" I think this is a systemic problem throughout the American armed forces, and one they ignore at their peril.

In 1909, Maj. Robert Lee Bullard, after ten years of pretty well constant imperial service—he had been overseas for eight of those ten years—wrote to his fellow officers in a journal article:

> We cannot fail to be impressed with the fact that if Army officers and the Army have had something to know about the art of war, they have had to know and use far more of the art of pacification. Our work was four-fifths peace and one-fifth war making. Our present duties and future prospects all point to the idea that if we are going to study how to make war alone, we shall be but little prepared for the far greater burdens of duty which will fall to us, which are the making of peace.[17]

[17] Editor's note: Robert Lee Bullard (1861–1947) established his reputation while serving with distinction in the Spanish-American War and later in the Philippines. In April 1917, Bullard received command of the 1st Infantry Division. Bullard led his forces in what was the U.S. army's first major offensive at Cantigny in April 1918. In July 1918, while commanding III Corps, Bullard played a role in the Aisne-Marne and Meuse-Argonne offensives, earning the nickname "Counter-Attack Bullard."

INDEX